AMERICAN HISTORY

Library of Congress Cataloging-in-Publication Data is available.

ISBN 978-0-7611-6083-0

Writer Lily Rothman   Illustrator Tim Hall
Series Designer Tim Hall   Designer Tim Hall
Editors Nathalie Le Du, Justin Krasner   Production Editor Jessica Rozler
Production Manager Julie Primavera
Concept by Raquel Jaramillo

Workman books are available at special discounts when purchased in bulk for
premiums and sales promotions as well as for fund-raising or educational use.
Special editions or book excerpts also can be created to specification.
For details, contact the Special Sales Director at the address below,
or send an email to specialmarkets@workman.com.

Workman Publishing Co., Inc.
225 Varick Street
New York, NY 10014-4381
workman.com

Big Fat Notebook is a trademark of Workman Publishing Co., Inc.
WORKMAN and BRAIN QUEST are registered trademarks of
Workman Publishing Co., Inc.

Printed in Malaysia

First printing August 2016
10 9 8 7 6 5 4 3

EVERYTHING YOU NEED TO ACE
AMERICAN HISTORY
IN ONE BIG FAT NOTEBOOK™

Borrowed from the smartest kid in class
Double-checked by Philip Bigler

WORKMAN PUBLISHING
NEW YORK

EVERYTHING YOU NEED TO KNOW TO ACE

AMERICAN HISTORY

HI!

These are the notes from my American history class. Oh, who am I? Well, some people said I was the smartest kid in class.

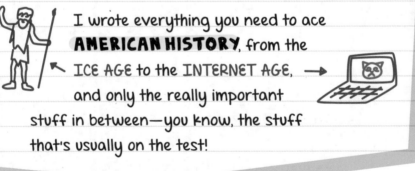

I wrote everything you need to ace **AMERICAN HISTORY**, from the ICE AGE to the INTERNET AGE, and only the really important stuff in between—you know, the stuff that's usually on the test!

I tried to keep everything organized, so I almost always:

- Highlight vocabulary words in **YELLOW**.
- Color in definitions in green highlighter.
- Use BLUE PEN for important people, places, dates, and terms.
- Doodle a pretty sweet Eleanor Roosevelt and whatnot to visually show the big ideas.

AGREED!

If you're not loving your textbook and you're not so great at taking notes in class, this notebook will help. It hits all the major points. (But if your teacher spends a whole class talking about something that's not covered, go ahead and write that down for yourself.)

zzz...WHAT?

Now that I've aced American history, this notebook is **YOURS**. I'm done with it, so this notebook's purpose in life is to help **YOU** learn and remember just what you need to ace **YOUR** American history class.

CONTENTS

THIS ONE IS A DOOZIE!

Unit 1

Prehistory— Early 1600s

So much happened in America before it was called America. The first people crossing into North America; the first major civilizations in Central and South America; the first European exploration; the first interactions between the Europeans and the native people; and the establishment of European colonies.

The very beginning is a very good place to start.

☆ Chapter 1 ☆

The FIRST PEOPLE IN
★ ★ ★ ★ ★ ★ ★ ★ ★ ★
AMERICA EVER!

MIGRATION

People have been living in the Americas much longer than scientists used to think. The first people started arriving around 38,000 BCE (BEFORE the COMMON ERA—this marks when the year was 0!), 40,000 years ago.

They were **NOMADIC HUNTER-GATHERERS**. They followed herds of the animals they hunted and ate the plants they found. Like the rest of early humankind, they started out in Africa, but after thousands of years they made their way east and north across Asia. When a group moves from one place to another, it's called a **MIGRATION**.

> **NOMADIC HUNTER-GATHERERS**
> communities of people who move from place to place, relying on plants and animals found in the wild for food

> **MIGRATION**
> the movement of a number of people (or animals), usually to establish a new homeland

The ICE AGE and the BERING LAND BRIDGE

The nomadic hunter-gatherers
lived during the ICE AGE,
when much of the earth was
covered in ice and snow and
entire oceans were frozen
over. When seawater is frozen
solid, the ocean level gets lower, exposing entire
stretches of land that are underwater during
warmer climates. The land connecting the northeast
tip of Asia and present-day Alaska, now called
the BERING LAND BRIDGE (or BERINGIA), emerged.
According to the LAND BRIDGE THEORY, nomadic
hunter-gatherers crossed on this land bridge from Asia
into North America, most likely in search of food. The Americas
were filled with woolly mammoths, mastodons, and other
huge creatures. Just one could feed an entire
nomad group for months.

TOOK PLACE DURING THE MOST RECENT GLACIAL PERIOD

WOO-HOO!!!

ASIA

BERING LAND BRIDGE

NORTH AMERICA

SOUTH AMERICA

EAT THIS GUY!

HEY!

People kept crossing until around
10,500 BCE, when the glacial period,
which had lasted about 100,000 years, finally ended. The
oceans rose and covered the Bering Land Bridge, cutting
off further migrations from Asia. Ice Age animals died off
or were hunted into extinction. These animals were replaced
by smaller animals that could thrive in warmer weather,
changing people's diets and lifestyles.

3

ANCIENT AMERICAN CULTURES

MESOAMERICA
the area now called Central America

NORTH AMERICA

SOUTH AMERICA

Gulf of Mexico

Mexico

TENOCHTITLÁN ⋆

Caribbean Sea

Belize

Honduras

Guatemala

El Salvador

Nicaragua

Costa Rica

Panama

Pacific Ocean

Colombia

Equador

Peru

Brazil

CUZCO ⋆

Bolivia

Chile

OLMEC
Mesoamerica, 1200–400 BCE

MAYA
Mesoamerica, 300 BCE–900 CE

AZTEC
Mexico, 1110–1521 CE, capital: Tenochtitlán

INCA
Peru, 1100–1533 CE, capital: Cuzco

MAYA PYRAMID

Some nomad tribes stayed in Alaska, while others continued south through Central and South America. As they spread they became very different from one another. They developed individual **CULTURES**, traditions, and sometimes different physical traits.

> **CULTURE**
> the way a society behaves and its system of beliefs, laws, and customs

SETTLING DOWN

Some tribes eventually stopped hunting and gathering. They realized they could plant seeds in the soil and farm foods like MAIZE (an early form of corn), beans, and squash. Tribes settled down, built permanent homes, formed villages, invented technologies to help them in their daily lives, and formed **SOCIETIES** that would, in some cases, lead to the creation of empires.

> **SOCIETY**
> a group of people living together as a group
>
> **CIVILIZATION**
> an advanced and complicated society

One of the first great **CIVILIZATIONS** was the OLMEC society, which flourished around 1200 BCE on the coast of MESOAMERICA when small groups began to band together. The Olmecs grew enough food to feed thousands of people and are known for the giant stone sculptures and pyramids they built with that large population. Around 400 BCE, the Olmecs disappeared. No one knows why—famine, war, and natural disaster are all possibilities.

Around this same time, the MAYA civilization developed in the Mesoamerican rain forest. As the Olmecs disappeared, Maya

5

cities grew. The Maya also raised crops and built pyramids and temples. They had a **THEOCRACY**; worshipped the sun, stars, and moon; and developed a 365-day calendar. They built a large trade network and canals. Around 900 CE, after more than 1,000 years, they disappeared too.

> **THEOCRACY**
> rule by god(s); government where the priests are in charge

The AZTECS, who began as warriors and hunters, conquered what is now Central Mexico around 1100 CE. In 1325, they founded their capital, TENOCHTITLÁN, on an island in the middle of Lake Texcoco. They built bridges to connect their capital to the mainland, and Tenochtitlán became one of the largest cities in the world. The Aztecs continued to conquer, using some of their prisoners as human sacrifices. By 1500, they were a powerful empire.

The INCAS started as small groups in the Andes Mountains. Around 1100 CE, they founded their capital, CUZCO, in what is now Peru. A powerful government united them into a population of about 12 million people, all speaking the common language of QUECHUA (which is still spoken today in the Andes). The Incas' innovations included terraced farming, a network of roads, and the use of knotted strings (QUIPU) instead of written words for record-keeping. They built cities such as MACHU PICCHU for their religious ceremonies.

> Remember the order in which these first empires rose and fell with this mnemonic device:
> **OH** OLMEC
> **MY!** MAYA
> **AMERICA'S** AZTEC
> **INTERESTING!** INCA

6

CHECK YOUR KNOWLEDGE

1. What was Beringia? Where was it located?

2. Why did people first come to the Americas?
   Why did they stop?

3. How do cultures become different from one another?

4. What is a nomadic hunter-gatherer society?

5. How did innovations in farming affect societies?

6. What is one invention of the Maya people?

7. What is a theocracy?

8. What was the capital of the Aztec Empire?
   When was it founded?

9. What was the language of the Inca Empire?

ANSWERS

CHECK YOUR ANSWERS

1. Beringia was the land bridge between Asia and North America.

2. People were following animal migrations, but they stopped when Beringia was covered by water when the glacial period ended.

3. It happens over time, as they are separated from their roots and develop new traditions.

4. People who move regularly, and hunt and gather for food

5. With food produced in one place, sedentary living increased.

6. A calendar, canals

7. A government controlled by priests

8. Tenochtitlán, founded 1325 CE

9. Quechua

☆ Chapter 2 ☆

NATIVE AMERICANS
★ ★ ★ ★ ★ IN ★ ★ ★ ★ ★
NORTH AMERICA

The millions of people who settled in what is now the U. S. and Canada are called NATIVE AMERICANS.

EARLY NATIVE AMERICANS

> **ANASAZI**
> means "ancient ones"

Around 1200 BCE, the **ANASAZI** people settled in the FOUR CORNERS area. Their first homes were "pit houses," dwellings dug partly into the ground. By about 750 CE they were building PUEBLOS: multistoried, apartment-like buildings made from **ADOBE** and other local materials. The Anasazi were also known for CLIFF DWELLINGS built along cliff walls and mountainsides. For religious rites, they created cavelike underground ceremonial chambers called KIVAS. The Anasazi were astute farmers. Since the Four Corners area was relatively dry, they devised irrigation techniques to grow crops, especially

THE MAP IS ON THE NEXT PAGE.

> **ADOBE**
> a kind of clay still used for building in the Southwest

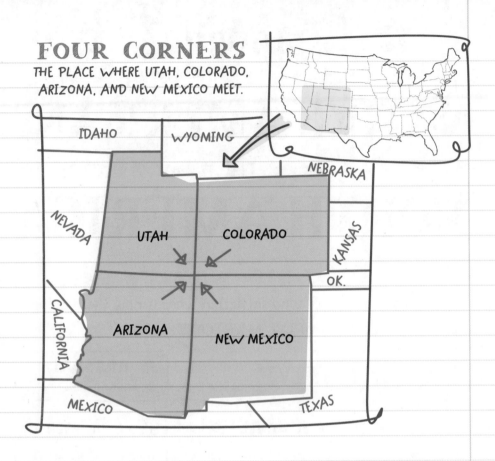

FOUR CORNERS
THE PLACE WHERE UTAH, COLORADO, ARIZONA, AND NEW MEXICO MEET.

IDAHO

WYOMING

NEBRASKA

NEVADA

UTAH

COLORADO

KANSAS

OK.

CALIFORNIA

ARIZONA

NEW MEXICO

MEXICO

TEXAS

maize. The Anasazi inhabited the area until around 1300 CE, when they split into smaller groups. There are many theories as to why they split up, including drought, war, and used-up resources. It's another case of nobody-knows-why.

The HOHOKAM lived in present-day Arizona. They arrived from Mexico around the year 300 CE and stayed for about a millennium. The Hohokam are known for their irrigation channels and pottery.

The MOUND BUILDER societies created huge earthen mounds as temples and burial markers that can still be seen in the central United States. The first were built around 1000 BCE and echo the look of Mesoamerican pyramids. It's a clue that Mound Builders may have come from Mesoamerica.

The Mound Builders were the ADENA, HOPEWELL, and MISSISSIPPIAN peoples. The Adena hunter-gatherers thrived around 800 BCE. The HOPEWELL were farmers and traders at their height around 200–500 BCE. When the Hopewell population declined around the year 700 BCE, the MISSISSIPPIAN people became more widespread. Around 900 CE, they formed their largest settlement, CAHOKIA. Located in present-day Illinois, Cahokia was home to tens of thousands of people and was the site of the Mississippian people's largest mound, **MONKS MOUND**.

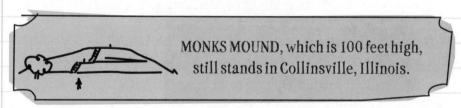

MONKS MOUND, which is 100 feet high, still stands in Collinsville, Illinois.

The Mound Builders created more than 10,000 mounds in the Ohio River Valley area alone. By the time Europeans arrived around 1700 CE, their people had disappeared.

DIFFERENT SOCIETIES FROM

THE NORTH, in present-day Alaska, was so cold that the INUITS and ALEUTS who settled there built **IGLOOS** to protect themselves from the harsh weather. They relied on hunting and fishing. They were likely originally from Siberia and may have been the last migrants to cross the Bering Land Bridge.

THE NORTHWEST had so many forests and such easy access to the ocean that the TLINGIT, HAIDA, and CHINOOK who settled there used wood to build their houses and make **TOTEM POLES** with religious significance. Fish, especially salmon, was their major food source.

THE WEST had such fertile land that the UTE and SHOSHONE tribes could live off abundant crops. These tribes formed small clans rather than large villages.

THE SOUTHWEST was home to descendents of the Anasazi (the HOPI, the ACOMA, and the ZUNI), who continued to work with adobe and grow maize. Around the 1500s, nomadic groups of hunter-gatherers (the APACHE and the NAVAJO) arrived, but within a century they had built villages, too.

THE GREAT PLAINS were filled with herds of buffalo, or **BISON**, so the peoples there became nomads and hunters. The BLACKFEET and the APACHES lived in **TEPEES** (conical tents) that were easy to pack up to follow the bison. Starting in the 1500s, some tribes, like the COMANCHE and DAKOTA, used horses that had escaped from Spanish explorers, and became famous for their equestrian skills.

THE SOUTHEAST had rich soil from its rivers and mountains, and the CREEK, CHICKASAW, SEMINOLE, and CHEROKEE farmed and built permanent villages around their fields.

INDIGENOUS
native to an area

Some early **INDIGENOUS** cultures continue today.

DIFFERENT ENVIRONMENTS

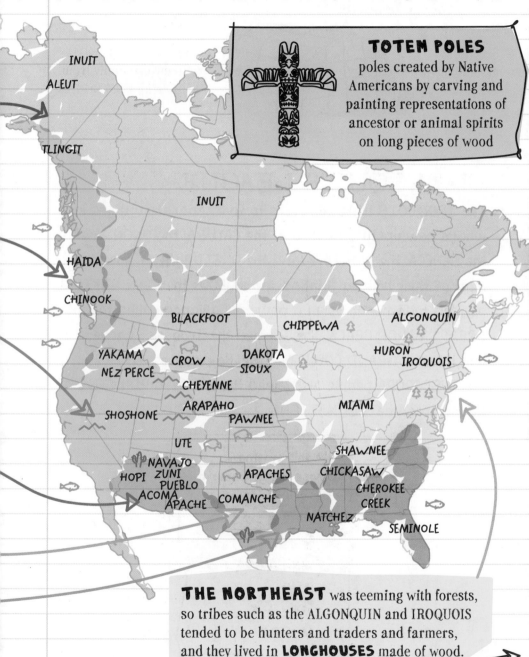

TOTEM POLES
poles created by Native Americans by carving and painting representations of ancestor or animal spirits on long pieces of wood

INUIT
ALEUT
TLINGIT
INUIT
HAIDA
CHINOOK
BLACKFOOT
CHIPPEWA
ALGONQUIN
YAKAMA
CROW
DAKOTA
SIOUX
HURON
IROQUOIS
NEZ PERCÉ
CHEYENNE
ARAPAHO
PAWNEE
MIAMI
SHOSHONE
UTE
NAVAJO
HOPI ZUNI
PUEBLO
ACOMA
APACHE
APACHES
COMANCHE
SHAWNEE
CHICKASAW
CHEROKEE
CREEK
NATCHEZ
SEMINOLE

THE NORTHEAST was teeming with forests, so tribes such as the ALGONQUIN and IROQUOIS tended to be hunters and traders and farmers, and they lived in **LONGHOUSES** made of wood.

NEXT PAGE

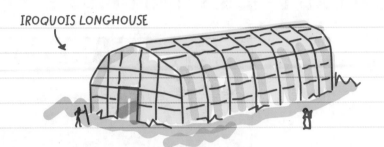
IROQUOIS LONGHOUSE

The IROQUOIS LEAGUE

The IROQUOIS LEAGUE refers to five separate nations in what's now upstate New York: the CAYUGA, the ONONDAGA, the SENECA, the MOHAWK, and the ONEIDA. After spending most of their history fighting, in the 1500s the FIVE NATIONS banded together to form a powerful alliance called the GREAT LAW OF PEACE. This formed the Iroquois League, which had a GRAND COUNCIL to settle disputes. In 1722, the TUSCARORA people also joined the league, and the Five Nations became SIX NATIONS.

Use this mnemonic device to remember the five original tribes of the Iroquois League:

CAYUGA

ONONDAGA

SENECA

MOHAWK

ONEIDA

CHECK YOUR KNOWLEDGE

1. Name three types of homes that the Anasazi created.

2. Why did the Mound Builders build mounds?

3. What was Cahokia?

4. What was a major factor in the differences between the cultures of Native American tribes?

5. What is an example of a nomadic Native American tribe?

6. What was the Iroquois League?

7. Which tribes were members of the League and when did it form?

ANSWERS

CHECK YOUR ANSWERS

1. Pit houses, pueblos, and cliff dwellings
2. To be used as temples and tombs
3. The largest settlement of the Mississippian people
4. Where they lived: climate, geography, and resources
5. Blackfoot/Apache/Comanche/Dakota
6. An alliance of northeastern tribes
7. Cayuga, Onondaga, Seneca, Mohawk, and Oneida created the League in the 1500s; Tuscarora joined in 1722.

☆ Chapter 3 ☆

THEY CAME, THEY SAW, THEY
CONQUERED

The AGE of EXPLORATION

Europeans paid high prices for goods like silk and spices.
The only way to get them was from Arabs and Berbers, who
trekked through Africa, or from other traders who could
travel overland to India and China. Traders used caravan
routes and the SILK ROAD, which united China and the West.

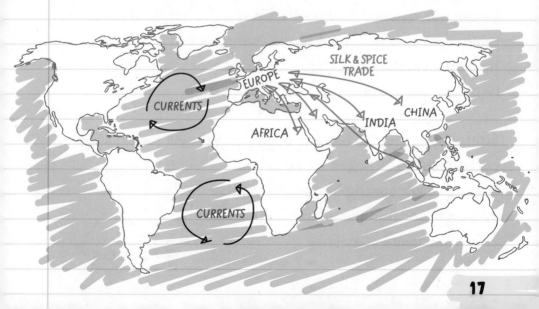

EXPLORATION TECHNOLOGY

Luckily for the Europeans, better maps and new technology changed navigation. These inventions came out of the RENAISSANCE—a period characterized by growing knowledge and innovations in technology.

MAGNETIC COMPASSES improved the safety and efficiency of ocean travel. Invented in China, compasses made determining direction simpler.

ASTROLABES allowed sailors to figure out their location in the ocean by measuring the distance of the sun and stars, like an ancient GPS.

Sailors figured out that the NORTH ATLANTIC CURRENT moves clockwise between Europe and the Caribbean and that the SOUTH ATLANTIC CURRENT travels counterclockwise between Africa and South America. This saved them from being randomly swept out to sea (sometimes that's how they discovered new places; sometimes that's how they disappeared forever).

NICE RIDE!

By the 1400s, the Portuguese began using small sailing ships called CARAVELS. Based on Arab boats, caravels were speedy and maneuverable, and could sail into the wind, so it was easier to explore coastlines.

TRADE in EUROPE

THE CRUSADES in the eleventh through thirteenth centuries and MARCO POLO's travels to China in the thirteenth century introduced Europeans to the four **S**'s (**S**pices, **S**ilk, **S**cents, and precious **S**tones) from Asia and the Middle East. As prosperity grew in Europe, so did appetites for **S**tuff.

HENRY the NAVIGATOR

The Portuguese became the leaders in world exploration. PRINCE HENRY THE NAVIGATOR built a school of navigation in the 1400s (but he didn't do any exploring himself). The school developed the caravel and enabled Portuguese sailors to explore the coast of ⟶ *CALLED THE GOLD COAST* West Africa and trade for gold, ivory, and slaves. What they wanted most was a way around Africa so they could sail to India and trade directly with its merchants.

PORTUGAL

ATLANTIC

AFRICA

THE GOLD COAST

The WEST AFRICAN SLAVE TRADE

West Africa in the 1400s was no longer ruled by the major kingdoms of its past. It was broken up into many small kingdoms warring over land and trade.

Enslaving captured enemies was already an established practice—Arab Muslim traders added slaves to their shipments of salt and gold as early as the 600s CE. In the last half of the 1400s, two kingdoms, the KONGO (on the Zaire River) and the NDONGO (to its south), dominated their neighbors. By the time the Europeans arrived in the 1480s, the African slave trade was big (terrible) business.

PORTUGUESE EXPEDITIONS

1453: CONSTANTINOPLE fell to the Muslims, who cut off overland routes to the east. The Portuguese were determined to find an all-water route.

1487: Explorer BARTOLOMEU DIAS set out. A storm and winds accidentally took his ship to his exact goal: the southern tip of Africa. Dias named the land the CAPE OF GOOD HOPE, in the hope it would lead to a route to India.

1497: VASCO DA GAMA sailed around the Cape of Good Hope and, after nearly one hundred days out of sight of land, reached India in May of 1498. The Portuguese began making more trips and traded for spices, porcelain, silk, etc.

As a result, LISBON (capital of Portugal) became a major trade city, and Portugal became VERY RICH. $$$

WHAT ABOUT THE VIKINGS?

The Vikings, seafaring people from Scandinavia, were the first Europeans to explore North America. ERIK THE RED discovered Greenland, and his son, LEIF ERIKSSON, reached present-day Canada in the year 1000 CE. Eriksson named the land "Vinland," but since the Vikings didn't stay, future explorers were credited with being the first ones there.

Christopher Columbus

IN 1492...

Born in Italy and trained in Portugal, CHRISTOPHER COLUMBUS thought he could reach India faster if he sailed west. Educated people knew that the world was round, but they didn't know how big it was. If the world was bigger than Columbus thought, he would certainly fail, so it was difficult to find someone to give him money to even try his plan. By appealing to their desire to spread Christianity and by promising incredible riches, Columbus convinced KING FERDINAND and QUEEN ISABELLA OF SPAIN to sponsor him.

EXPLORER / HAT ENTHUSIAST

(SPOILER ALERT: COLUMBUS GROSSLY UNDERESTIMATED THE SIZE OF THE NEW WORLD.)

... COLUMBUS SAILED THE OCEAN BLUE

(IT RHYMES.) ←

On August 3, 1492, Columbus set out with three ships (the NIÑA and the PINTA—both caravels—and the flagship SANTA MARIA) and supplies for six months. His crew urged him to turn around after a few months. He kept two sets of logs, a secret one with the real distances traveled, and another with shorter distances (to convince the crew they were just ... moving ... very ... slowly). Finally, in October, they saw land.

They went ashore in the Bahamas, on an island they named San Salvador, or "Holy Savior." Columbus made three more voyages in search of gold and tobacco, and explored Hispaniola (the island of present-day Haiti and the Dominican Republic), Cuba, Jamaica, and the coasts of Central and South America. Though many of the people who already lived in those areas were friendly to Columbus and his men when they arrived, the European settlers were more interested in gold and tobacco than in friendship. In general, they enslaved and cruelly treated the native people.

Columbus and his crew thought they were in the Indies in Asia, and this is why the Caribbean islands are called the WEST Indies, and why Native Americans were called Indians.

DRAWING the LINE

Spain and Portugal disagreed over who owned some of the newly found lands. In 1493, they asked Pope Alexander VI

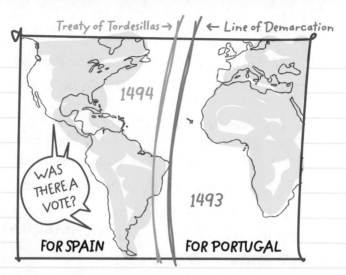

to decide. On a map of the world, the Pope drew a
LINE OF DEMARCATION from the top to the bottom,
giving everything to the west of it to Spain, and everything
to the east to Portugal. Portugal argued that most lands to
the east had already been claimed. The next year the two
countries agreed to move the line about 1,175 miles west in the
TREATY OF TORDESILLAS. Everything left to be discovered
was now pre-divided. Spain got almost all of it except Brazil
(which is why Portuguese, not Spanish, is spoken in Brazil now)
and some islands in the Atlantic.

MORE EXPLORATION

1502: AMERIGO VESPUCCI sailed along the coast of
South America. He was one of the first guys to realize
he wasn't in Asia, and he recounted exotic and grand
descriptions. A German mapmaker labeled the new land
"America" in his honor.

1513: VASCO NÚÑEZ DE BALBOA hiked across Panama and was the first European to see the Pacific Ocean by heading west.

COINED THE NAME PACIFIC OCEAN FROM "PEACEFUL SEA"

1519: FERDINAND MAGELLAN, a Portuguese man sailing on behalf of Spain, reached the tip of South America. He was killed in battle in the Philippines, but his ships returned in 1522 as the first crew to **CIRCUMNAVIGATE** the earth.

CIRCUMNAVIGATE
sail around; "circum-," like a circle

THE COLUMBIAN EXCHANGE

There had been no mixing of plants and animals between the Americas and the rest of the world for over ten thousand years. Things like corn, tobacco, cocoa, and potatoes didn't exist elsewhere until they were brought back from the Americas. In return, Europeans brought wheat, barley, grapes, and onions, as well as cattle, pigs, and horses, to the Americas. The plants changed the diets of people all over the world, and the animals changed the way land was used in the Americas.

The humans hadn't been exposed to any of each other's germs either. Diseases such as smallpox, measles, and the flu were common in Europe, but Native Americans didn't have **IMMUNITY**. About 20 million people died from disease in a 100-year span in Central America alone. This mixing of plants, animals, viruses, and bacteria is known as the COLUMBIAN EXCHANGE or the GREAT BIOLOGICAL EXCHANGE.

IMMUNITY
resistance to a disease or sickness, particularly due to previous exposure to the germs

The CONQUISTADORES

The CONQUISTADORES, a new kind of Spanish explorer and conqueror, were given the thumbs-up from the king and queen to settle in the Americas in return for twenty percent of any treasure found. The conquistadores wanted to:

convert people to Christianity

trade for goods

FIND LOTS OF GOLD

In 1519, HERNÁN CORTÉS came to Mexico with about 500 soldiers, along with horses and cannons. With the help of a native woman called MALINTZIN, Cortés convinced the people whom the Aztecs had conquered to ally with him—they resented paying tribute to the emperor, MONTEZUMA, with human sacrifices. Seeing their shiny metal weapons and horses, Montezuma was worried that maybe Cortés was the god Quetzalcoatl or that the gods had sent Cortés and his men. After welcoming them to Tenochtitlán, he offered them treasures and hoped they'd leave.

That backfired, since Cortés now realized that the Aztecs had a whole lot of gold. With the help of the Aztecs' angry subjects, Cortés and his crew captured Montezuma.

On June 30, 1520, LA NOCHE TRISTE ("the sad night"), the people of Tenochtitlán drove the Spanish and their allies from the city; Montezuma was killed in the fighting, along with numerous Spanish soldiers. But, in May of 1521, Cortés returned with more Spanish troops, and this time, the Aztec Empire fell. Tenochtitlán was destroyed and the Spanish built Mexico City on top of the rubble.

In 1532, FRANCISCO PIZARRO sailed down the coast of South America. He had fewer than 200 men with him and was welcomed by ATAHUALPA, the Inca ruler. Pizarro took Atahualpa prisoner. Although Atahualpa offered the Spaniards gold in exchange for his freedom, they executed him. Pizarro and his troops marched into the capital at Cuzco. By 1534, they had conquered the entire 2,000-mile-long territory in what is now Peru.

How did Cortés and Pizarro conquer powerful empires?

Their weapons, armor, and horses made them seem godlike and gave them the advantage.

They took their enemies by surprise.

They got the support of oppressed locals.

BIG REASON: European diseases like smallpox wiped out a large percentage of the Aztec and Inca populations.

OTHER FAMOUS EXPLORERS/CONQUISTADORES

JUAN PONCE DE LÉON landed in the place he named Florida in 1513. Although he was looking for the Fountain of Youth (he didn't find it), he explored Florida, which, in 1565, became the first Spanish settlement in what would be the U.S.

ÁLVAR NÚÑEZ CABEZA DE VACA led an expedition to Florida in 1528 and was stranded on an island off what is now Texas. He lived as a prisoner among the locals for six years and then escaped to Mexico. His experience led him to call for better treatment of Native Americans.

In 1540, FRANCISCO VÁSQUEZ DE CORONADO arrived in what is now New Mexico. He was in search of seven mythical cities of gold (he didn't find them).

HERNANDO DE SOTO crossed the Mississippi River in 1541. In 1598, Juan de Oñate established the Province of New Mexico. He brought cows and horses.

SPANISH SOCIETY in the AMERICAS

VICEROY
person appointed by a king or queen to rule an area on his or her behalf

Through the COUNCIL OF THE INDIES (formed in 1524), the Spanish monarchs appointed two **VICEROYS**. Each was in charge of a VICEROYALTY, one in

"New Spain" (Central America and its surroundings) and one in Peru. **ENCOMIENDAS** gave settlers the go-ahead to tax local natives or force them to work.

> **ENCOMIENDA**
> a royal grant of land, including all the people on it

The social hierarchy depended on race and birthplace:

Land and positions of influence belonged to the PENINSULARES from the peninsula of Spain. Although they were the smallest population, they held almost all the power.

CREOLES (the first generation born to Spanish parents) ranked below the peninsulares.

MESTIZOS (of mixed European and American race) were next.

Native Americans.

African slaves, at the bottom.

There were three main kinds of settlements:

→ **PUEBLOS**, WHICH WERE TOWNS AND TRADING CENTERS

→ **MISSIONS**, WHICH FOCUSED ON CONVERTING PEOPLE TO CHRISTIANITY

→ **PRESIDIOS**, WHICH WERE FORTS

El Camino Real, the royal road from Mexico City to Santa Fe, connected many of these settlements. In and around the towns, **HACIENDAS** (large estates) and **PLANTATIONS** (large farms raising **CASH CROPS**) grew coffee, cotton, tobacco, and sugar. These huge operations needed a lot of workers. The labor was so intense that many died.

CASH CROP
a plant that farmers grow to make money

BARTOLOMÉ DE LAS CASAS AND THE NEW LAWS

BARTOLOMÉ DE LAS CASAS was a priest who spoke and wrote about the mistreatment of the Native American population. He came to the Caribbean in 1502. His work contributed to the government of Spain passing the NEW LAWS of 1542, making it illegal to enslave Native Americans. But that didn't end slavery: Because the Spanish could no longer enslave Native Americans, they instead enslaved more Africans.

The NORTHWEST PASSAGE and EXPLORATION of NORTH AMERICA

Explorers searched for the NORTHWEST PASSAGE, a water route through North America, so ships could sail from the Atlantic to the Pacific for trade.

LOOK, MOUNT FUJI!

THAT'S AN ICEBERG.

In 1497 and 1498, JOHN CABOT (an Italian sailing on behalf of England) landed in Newfoundland, Canada. Cabot thought he was in Asia, so he set sail for Japan and was never heard from again.

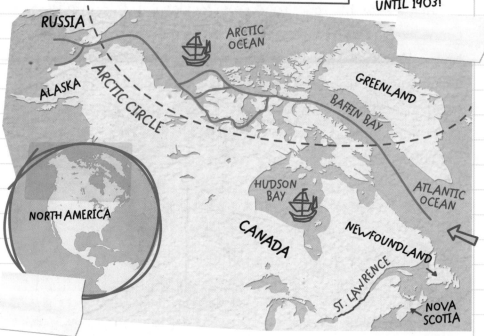

THE NORTHWEST PASSAGE

← WASN'T NAVIGATED UNTIL 1903!

RUSSIA

ARCTIC OCEAN

ALASKA

ARCTIC CIRCLE

GREENLAND

BAFFIN BAY

NORTH AMERICA

HUDSON BAY

ATLANTIC OCEAN

CANADA

NEWFOUNDLAND

ST. LAWRENCE

NOVA SCOTIA

In 1524, GIOVANNI DA VERRAZZANO (an Italian sent by the French) explored Nova Scotia, Canada.

In 1535, JACQUES CARTIER (a Frenchman) explored the St. Lawrence River and claimed what is now Canada for France.

In 1609, HENRY HUDSON (an Englishman sent by the Dutch) explored a river (now the Hudson River) in present-day New York. The next year, he returned on behalf of the British and discovered a bay (Hudson Bay). He planned to go on, but his crew **MUTINIED**, and he was either lost at sea or, more likely, killed.

> **MUTINY**
> to revolt or rebel against authority, especially by sailors against their officers

The SPANISH ARMADA

There were lots of reasons for European countries to be competitive around that time:

The **TREATY OF TORDESILLAS** between Spain and Portugal split the world so Spain owned the western half and Portugal owned the eastern half. Other European countries didn't recognize the treaty because they saw how much profit they could make from exploration.

The economic theory of **MERCANTILISM** said that a nation's power was in its wealth. European countries competed more than ever to establish colonies to get raw materials and gain new markets for exports.

The **PROTESTANT REFORMATION** also created rivalry. When **ELIZABETH I**, a Protestant, became Queen of England in 1558, she ordered sailors to attack Spanish ships (Spain was a Catholic nation) as they transported gold and silver back from America. She wanted to gain the wealth from the New World without incurring the expense of having colonies. One of the most successful and daring of these English sailors was **SIR FRANCIS DRAKE**.

TO THE ENGLISH, HE WAS AN ADVENTURER. TO THE SPANISH, HE WAS A PIRATE.

In response, in 1588, King Philip sent the mighty **SPANISH ARMADA**, a fleet of 130 ships, to conquer the English. The two navies met in the English Channel, and England was the winner. Spain never regained its previous power, and other nations saw they could challenge Spanish claims in the New World.

MORE EUROPEAN COLONIES

The FIRST BRITISH COLONIES

In the late 1500s, explorer SIR WALTER RALEIGH received a **CHARTER**. He sent an expedition in 1584 to settle a land they'd call "Virginia." The next year, the expedition founded a colony on ROANOKE ISLAND in present-day North Carolina. Lack of food forced the settlers to sail back to England after a year.

> **CHARTER**
> permission from the monarch to start a colony

after Queen Elizabeth I, "The Virgin Queen"

In 1587, a group of about 150 English settlers tried again in the same place. One of the leaders, JOHN WHITE, returned to England for supplies but couldn't come back for three years. (War between England and Spain made travel difficult.) When he returned to Roanoke, the people had vanished.

The first person born in the Americas to British parents, **VIRGINIA DARE**, was John White's granddaughter. What happened to her and the other settlers is still a mystery. Her colony is now called the LOST COLONY.

VIRGINIA

NORTH CAROLINA

ATLANTIC OCEAN

ROANOKE

IN THE AMERICAS

FRENCH COLONIES

In 1608, French explorer SAMUEL DE CHAMPLAIN founded a trading post in Quebec, where an active fur and metal trade developed. (The local Native Americans did much of the work trapping beavers and other animals.) A number of Catholic priests also lived in NEW FRANCE, as the colony was named, on a mission to convert the locals.

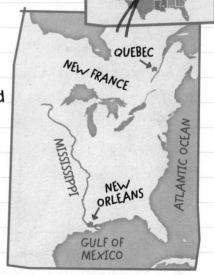

In 1682, RENÉ-ROBERT CAVELIER, SIEUR DE LA SALLE sailed the length of the Mississippi River and claimed the area of what is now Louisiana for the French when he reached the southern end. The French later founded a trading post there in what is now New Orleans. In the 1700s, the French established trading posts in present-day Detroit, Michigan, and St. Louis, Missouri.

QUEBEC

NEW FRANCE

MISSISSIPPI

NEW ORLEANS

ATLANTIC OCEAN

GULF OF MEXICO

Because of these French explorers, French culture in North America is still concentrated in the province of Quebec and the Southern state of Louisiana.

DUTCH COLONIES

The Dutch staked their claim in the Hudson River Valley. In 1614, they set up Fort Nassau (near modern-day Albany). THE DUTCH WEST INDIA COMPANY established the colony of New Netherland in 1621 along the river. In 1626, Peter Minuit purchased the island of Manhattan from the local people (the MANHATES) for what has been described as $24 worth of goods but is a bit more than that in modern dollars—though still not very much. The city of New Amsterdam (today's New York City) became a prosperous center of the fur trade.

FORT NASSAU

NORTH RIVER (HUDSON RIVER)

NEW AMSTERDAM

ATLANTIC OCEAN

The Manhates probably considered the "sale" to be more of a lease for hunting and use rights.

The Dutch West India Company was a **CHARTERED COMPANY**. In that kind of business, investors joined to explore and trade together, with the support of the government of their home country. The government also gave permission to negotiate with foreign leaders and own colonial land. **THE DUTCH EAST INDIA COMPANY** (which did business in India and Asia) was another chartered company.

CHECK YOUR KNOWLEDGE

1. Why did the Portuguese want to sail directly to India?

2. Why did Christopher Columbus have trouble getting funding?

3. Why is Portuguese spoken in Brazil?

4. What does it mean to "circumnavigate" something?

5. What was the Columbian Exchange?

6. How did the conquistadores conquer entire empires with only a few hundred soldiers?

7. Although the Northwest Passage wasn't found by early explorers, what were two resulting explorations?

8. How did the defeat of the Spanish Armada affect colonization of the Americas?

ANSWERS ▶

CHECK YOUR ANSWERS

1. They wanted to cut out the middleman in their trade.
2. Nobody knew how far it was if you sailed west from Europe.
3. Spain and Portugal agreed in the Treaty of Tordesillas that that land would belong to Portugal.
4. To sail around it
5. The exchange of plants, animals, and germs between the two hemispheres
6. They had surprise, the support of oppressed locals, technology, and immunities.
7. John Cabot landed in Newfoundland, Canada, and Henry Hudson explored the Hudson River.
8. Spain could no longer enforce the Treaty of Tordesillas and its monopoly on colonization.

#7 has more than one correct answer.

LOOK, A SAMURAI!

THAT'S... A POLAR BEAR.

Unit 2

Colonial America 1607–1780s

The 1600s and 1700s were a time of transition: Colonies and the institution of slavery were established, along with trade networks, regional identities, and, in the end, states. The goals of the first English settlers in Virginia were very different from the goals of those who followed. Thomas Jefferson, Patrick Henry, and George Washington, who were all born in Virginia, viewed themselves as British living in the New World. They wouldn't stand being denied their rights as Englishmen....

Chapter 4

SLAVERY IN THE AMERICAS

PLANTATIONS
⬇
WANTED
CHEAP LABOR
⬇
SLAVES

Sugar became a major export to Europe, but harvesting sugarcane involved tough conditions. Initially, Native Americans were forced to work on Spanish and Portuguese plantations. Diseases from the Columbian Exchange and constant labor killed much of this population. The Spanish and Portuguese decided they needed another source of labor: **SLAVES**.

BECAME KNOWN AS "WHITE GOLD"

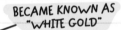
SUGAR

MOST SUGAR PLANTATIONS WERE IN THE

WEST INDIES.

> **SLAVERY**
> the practice of one person legally owning another; involuntary servitude for life passed down to future generations

When the British began to set up TOBACCO PLANTATIONS in North America, they needed more laborers. By the 1700s, sadly, every colony in the Americas imported slaves from Africa.

Plantation owners thought that Africans were ideal workers for plantations because:

They were far from home, so they didn't have a free place to run away to.

UNLIKE MANY NATIVE AMERICANS, WHO RAN FROM THE TERRIBLE WORK CONDITIONS.

Plantation owners could enslave the slaves' children.

Many of the slaves had been farmers, so they had experience.

They already had immunity to the diseases that killed Native Americans.

The TRIANGULAR TRADE

The slave trade was part of THE TRIANGULAR TRADE, a trade route with three stops: Africa, the West Indies, and the Americas.

AMERICAN COLONIES

SUGAR & MOLASSES

RUM & IRON

AFRICA

WEST INDIES

SLAVES & GOLD

The Triangular Trade was just one part of a larger exchange of goods and slaves that included Europe.

FOR EXAMPLE:

Europe had manufactured goods (like textiles) but needed raw materials (like furs or tobacco).

Africa had slaves but needed manufactured goods.

The West Indies had raw materials (like sugar and molasses) but needed slaves, and New England had rum (made from molasses) and iron but needed more goods.

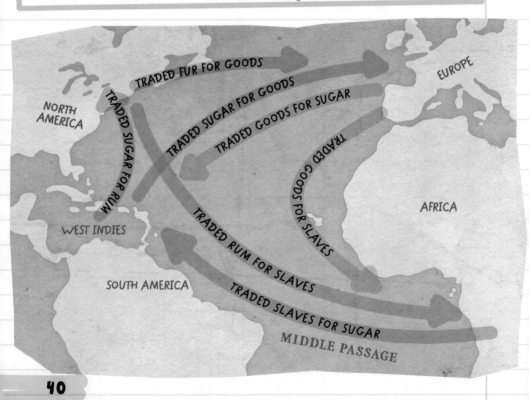

The MIDDLE PASSAGE

The middle leg of the triangular trade, when ships left Africa with a cargo of slaves, was the MIDDLE PASSAGE. Because slaves were considered mere property, they were crammed together, given little food, exposed to disease, and otherwise abused and mistreated. About fifteen percent died during the middle passage en route to the colonies.

> **OLAUDAH EQUIANO** was a slave brought to Virginia from Africa in the 1700s as a child. After buying his freedom, he wrote an autobiography depicting the horrors of slavery, which helped influence British lawmakers to abolish the slave trade.

LAWS ABOUT SLAVERY

Many colonies enacted SLAVE CODES. Slave codes varied from colony to colony, but they all considered slaves property and granted them almost no rights. Although slave codes were meant to define the status of slaves as well as the owner's responsibilities so that fewer slaves ran away, those who did try to escape were severely punished.

NOT THE COLOR—MORE LIKE BEING MAROONED ON AN ISLAND!

> Runaway slaves in Latin America were known as **MAROONS**. Maroons formed communities in forests or swamps, sometimes joining with Native Americans. Slaves also rebelled. The Stono Rebellion of 1739, the New York City Conspiracy of 1741, and Gabriel's Conspiracy of 1800 are just a few examples.

The BEGINNINGS of AFRICAN AMERICAN CULTURE

DIASPORA
a MIGRATION (moving from one place to another) that involves a spreading out of people from the same homeland or culture

Slaves came from all over western Africa and were spread out once they arrived. Because of this **DIASPORA**, African slaves in the Americas formed new cultures built from their differing backgrounds and their common experiences.

Some characteristics of the new slave cultures:

RELIGION: Most slaves were converted to Christianity but still retained their African beliefs. Religion was important in daily life, and **SPIRITUALS** became a major element of it.

SPIRITUAL
a religious folk song created by enslaved African people in the Americas

SONG, DANCE, AND STORYTELLING: Influenced by African traditions, song, dance, and storytelling were also used to teach.

FAMILY: Families were the central unit of society, even though the slave trade often split families apart.

CHICKEN OR EGG? RACISM, CAUSE AND EFFECT

As Africans became associated with slavery (it had previously been a social distinction rather than a racial one), racism took hold in the Americas. Racism, the belief that some races are inferior, also justified using anyone of African descent as a slave, which was convenient for the slave owners who relied on the system of slavery. Racism and slavery were not part of a cause and effect chain—they were the parts of a vicious cycle.

CHECK YOUR KNOWLEDGE

1. Name a crop cultivated by slave labor in the Americas.

2. Why didn't plantation owners continue to use Native American labor?

3. Why were African slaves seen by plantation owners as the best source of labor?

4. What were the three "points" of the triangular trade?

5. To what does the term "middle passage" refer?

6. What is a maroon?

7. Did slavery or racism come first in the Americas?

ANSWERS ➤

CHECK YOUR ANSWERS

1. Sugar, tobacco
2. Native Americans were killed off by European disease and the constant and terrible labor conditions. They were also more likely to run away.
3. They had immunity to European diseases, they had farm experience, and they had no homes to run to.
4. The American colonies, West Indies, and Africa
5. The part of the trianglular trade between Africa and the Americas
6. An escaped slave in Latin America
7. Trick question—they encouraged each other to grow.

⭐ Chapter 5 ⭐

JAMESTOWN:
★ ★ ★ ★ ★ ★ ★ ★ ★ ★ ★ ★ ★
VIRGINIA DO-OVER

If at FIRST YOU DON'T SUCCEED...

Although the Roanoke Colony failed, the English were determined. A group of merchants formed the VIRGINIA COMPANY OF LONDON to make money from the colonies. On April 26, 1607, approximately 125 settlers reached the Chesapeake Bay and founded the first permanent English settlement in North America, JAMESTOWN, on the banks of the JAMES RIVER.

WHAT'S WITH ALL THE JAMESES?

After Queen Elizabeth I died in 1603, James I became king of England. The settlers named Jamestown and the James River in his honor.

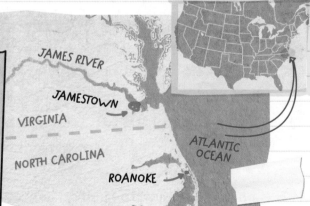

JAMES RIVER

JAMESTOWN

VIRGINIA

NORTH CAROLINA

ROANOKE

ATLANTIC OCEAN

The JAMESTOWN SETTLERS

Although Jamestown eventually survived, most of its first settlers were, let's say, misguided:

> They settled on an island near the river because it could be a defensive position against the Spanish, Native Americans, and others (should they approach by water), but the **WATER WAS DIRTY AND UNDRINKABLE** for most of the year.

> It was bitterly cold in winter, humid in summer, and full of **DISEASE-CARRYING MOSQUITOES** because of the marshy conditions.

> Most of the settlers were rich adventurers or explorers, not craftsmen or laborers, so they **FOCUSED ON SEARCHING FOR GOLD** (of which there was little) instead of building houses or planting food.

It is no surprise that fewer than half of the settlers survived past their first winter.

JOHN SMITH

Jamestown was in trouble, so in 1608, CAPTAIN JOHN SMITH took charge. Smith forced people to plant and build ("Work or starve"), and Jamestown prospered. Smith developed relations with CHIEF POWHATAN, leader of the powerful local Native American group called the **POWHATAN CONFEDERACY**, who taught the English settlers how to grow maize and have something to eat. But...

> **CONFEDERACY**
> an alliance between
> sovereign states

The STARVING TIME

In 1609, about 400 more settlers arrived, including women and children. When John Smith returned to England because of an injury, disease and famine began to take over. Only about 60 people survived the winter of 1609-1610 (THE STARVING TIME). People were so hungry they ate anything in reach (maybe even each other). Relations with the Native Americans fell apart. Concerned about the fate of Jamestown, in 1610 the Virginia Company of London sent them a new governor, LORD DE LA WARR ("Delaware" was named for him later), to set things right again.

> Jamestown was the first permanent **ENGLISH** settlement in North America. The Spanish town of St. Augustine, Florida (remember: explorer Ponce de Léon), was the first permanent **SPANISH** settlement in North America.

JOHN ROLFE

JOHN ROLFE, one of the successful settlers at Jamestown, was the first colonist to cultivate tobacco for export. A cash crop initially grown

mainly in the West Indies, tobacco was hugely profitable for the Virginia Company, and therefore made the settlement profitable for the first time. In 1614, John Rolfe married POCAHONTAS, the daughter of Chief Powhatan, improving the relationship between the English and the Native Americans.

↖ BUT ONLY TEMPORARILY

TOBACCO EXPANDS

Tobacco became a popular cash crop. People knew how valuable it was in England and demanded that the Virginia Company give them a cut of the profit. Instead, the company gave them land: Under the HEADRIGHT SYSTEM (your RIGHT per HEAD), any man who paid his way across the ocean was granted 50 acres of land in Virginia and 50 more acres for each person (head) he brought with him, including women and servants. It was a major incentive to growing tobacco.

The English needed more labor for their tobacco plantations. A primary source was **INDENTURED SERVITUDE**. Indentured servants, often from

INDENTURED SERVITUDE
the condition of being a contracted laborer

Britain or Germany, signed a contract for four to seven years of service in exchange for passage across the Atlantic. After the time was up, they were free to make a new life.

Indentured servitude was outpaced by the growth of the slave trade, which was legalized in Virginia in the 1660s. With more and more tobacco being grown, lifelong slaves began to replace temporary servants.

The HOUSE of BURGESSES

In 1619, the **HOUSE OF BURGESSES**, a **LEGISLATIVE** body, held its first annual assembly. Under the overall governance of the Virginia Company, the people had their own **REPRESENTATIVE GOVERNMENT**.

> **BURGESS**
> a citizen representative in local government

> **LEGISLATIVE**
> having the function of making laws and, in reference to the House of Burgesses, imposing taxes

> **REPRESENTATIVE GOVERNMENT**
> government with elected representatives for the citizens

A ROYAL MESS

In 1622, the Powhatan people became increasingly concerned about the tobacco farms taking up all the land along the James River. When an Englishman murdered a member of the tribe, the Powhatan launched a military campaign. On March 22, they attacked and killed a quarter of the English population. Vicious fighting continued for 20 years.

Since the Virginia Company could neither protect the settlers nor make enough money to justify all the fighting, in 1624 King James revoked their charter. Jamestown became a ROYAL COLONY, meaning the king was in charge. He chose a governor to rule the colony in his place and abolished the House of Burgesses.

After King James I's death, however, KING CHARLES I reinstated the House of Burgesses in 1629. Jamestown had become:

→ THE FIRST PERMANENT ENGLISH SETTLEMENT IN NORTH AMERICA

→ THE FIRST ENGLISH ROYAL COLONY IN NORTH AMERICA

→ AND THE BIRTHPLACE OF REPRESENTATIVE GOVERNMENT IN THE UNITED-STATES-TO-BE

But Jamestown had its share of conflict too. In 1676, a group of frontiersmen led by Nathaniel Bacon led attacks on the Pamunkey people and the governor of Jamestown. Although BACON'S REBELLION quickly ended after Bacon's untimely death from dysentery, it was one of the first acts of rebellion by colonists over land, high taxes, and the colony's failure to deal with the colonists' demands.

CHECK YOUR KNOWLEDGE

1. What was the first permanent English settlement in the Americas? The first Spanish one?

2. What happened in Jamestown in the winter of 1609–1610?

3. What crop was introduced to settler farmers by John Rolfe? Why was it important?

4. Why did people sign contracts to become indentured servants?

5. What were the powers of the Virginia House of Burgesses?

6. What happened when the Virginia Company lost its charter? Why did that happen?

7. What was Nathaniel Bacon angry about?

ANSWERS

CHECK YOUR ANSWERS

1. Jamestown was the first permanent English settlement in North America. St. Augustine, Florida, was the first permanent Spanish settlement.

2. The winter of 1609-1610 was considered the Starving Time, when only about 60 people survived. Some may have resorted to cannibalism.

3. Tobacco. It made the American settlement profitable for the first time.

4. To get free passage to America

5. Taxation and creating local law

6. Virginia became a royal colony. The charter couldn't protect the settlers and wasn't making much money.

7. He was mad about land, high taxes, and the colony not listening to the colonists.

I'M FREE!

NO YER NOT!

Chapter 6

The THIRTEEN COLONIES

New settlements joined Jamestown on the eastern coast:

1) CHARTERED COLONIES

under the control of a joint-stock company with a <u>charter</u>

Examples: Connecticut, Rhode Island

2) PROPRIETARY COLONIES

under the control of the person whose <u>property</u> the land was

Examples: Delaware, Maryland, Pennsylvania

3) ROYAL COLONIES

under the control, via an appointed governor, of English <u>royalty</u>

Examples: North Carolina, South Carolina, and Georgia, which started as proprietary colonies and later became royal colonies

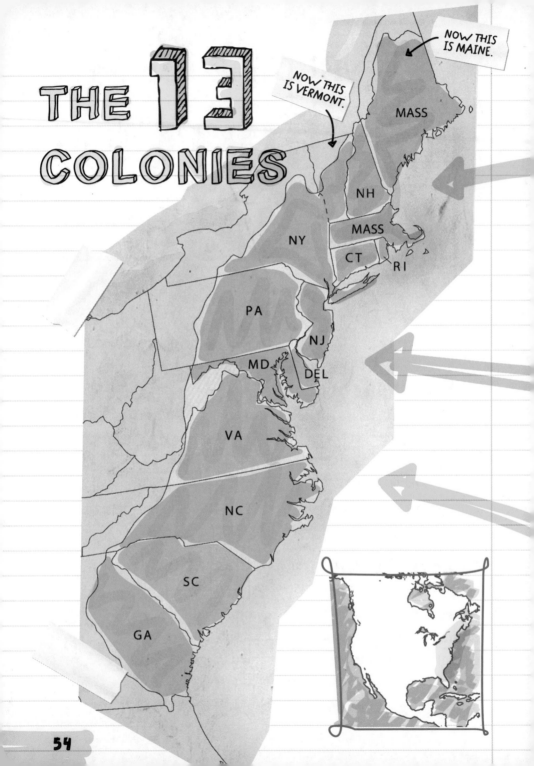

THE 13 COLONIES

NOW THIS IS VERMONT.

NOW THIS IS MAINE.

MASS

NH

MASS

NY

CT

RI

PA

NJ

MD

DEL

VA

NC

SC

GA

NEW ENGLAND COLONIES

Plymouth/Massachusetts Bay (1620)
New Hampshire (1629)
Rhode Island (1636)
Connecticut (1662)

MIDDLE COLONIES

New York (1624)
New Jersey (1664)
Pennsylvania (1681)
Delaware (1634)

SOUTHERN COLONIES

Maryland (1633)
Virginia (1607)
North Carolina (1663)
South Carolina (1663)
Georgia (1733)

THE SOUTHERN COLONIES ESTABLISHED AFTER VIRGINIA:

MARYLAND

George Calvert, Lord Baltimore, wanted to set up a place for fellow Catholics. He requested a charter from King Charles I in 1632. His son, Cecilius, inherited the PROPRIETARY COLONY and named it MARYLAND. Although it was meant to be a safe place for Catholics, Protestants moved in too, causing conflicts. In 1649, Lord Baltimore issued the ACT OF TOLERATION, which made it illegal to **PERSECUTE** any Christian for his religion. However, in 1654, the Protestants gained control of the local government and revoked the act.

> **PERSECUTION**
> punish/harass, usually
> because of one's identity

The CAROLINAS

> "Carolina" comes from "Carolus," the Latin form of "Charles."

After a civil war, CHARLES II became king of England in 1660. To reward the aristocrats who had supported him, he gave them a proprietary colony south of Virginia, which they named "CAROLINA." Most people in the northern half were originally Virginians. Most in the southern half came directly from England, with slaves, attracted by farmland, religious tolerance, and self-government. It became difficult to rule both sides as one unit. The people of the more prosperous South Carolina split from the colony's rule. In 1729, North and South Carolina became royal colonies.

DEBTOR
someone in debt

GEORGIA

Georgia was the last British colony founded in North America. In 1732, JAMES OGLETHORPE received a charter from King George II to establish a colony for **DEBTORS** (being in debt was a crime at the time) and poor people to make a new start. The king saw Georgia as a buffer between the colonies and SPANISH FLORIDA. Because it was an alternative to jail, Oglethorpe had strict rules: no large plantations, no rum, few slaves, and no Catholics. Few settlers were actually debtors, however. Oglethorpe gave up on his plan, and in 1752, Georgia also became a royal colony.

PURITANS and PILGRIMS

Some people settled in North America for religious freedom. Catholics in England had been persecuted since the establishment of the CHURCH OF ENGLAND (Anglicanism) and there was constant fighting between Catholic and Protestant nations.

Catholics weren't the only persecuted Christians.

PURITANS:
wanted to <u>reform</u> the Church of England so that it would be more pure (or closer, they believed, to the text of the Bible)

SEPARATISTS:
wanted to start their <u>own</u> church from scratch

In 1608, many Separatists fled England for Holland. Later, they formed a joint-stock company and were given permission from the Virginia Company to settle in North America. They thought of themselves as **PILGRIMS**.

> **PILGRIM**
> one who travels to a sacred place as an act of religious devotion

The *MAYFLOWER* and the MAYFLOWER COMPACT

On SEPTEMBER 16, 1620, a ship called the *MAYFLOWER* left England. Not everyone on board was a Pilgrim. They were bound for Virginia, but

LAND HO!

PULL OVER!!!

after two months of sailing, they spotted land farther north, in NEW ENGLAND. They decided to settle there instead, where they could make their own rules.

On NOVEMBER 21, 1620, before they went ashore, the men, led by WILLIAM BRADFORD, signed the MAYFLOWER COMPACT, a **COVENANT** agreeing to obey "just and equal laws" created for the "general good of the colony" in order to benefit "the glory of God" and the "honor of our King" (of England). The Pilgrims landed at Cape Cod and later chose to settle at PLYMOUTH ROCK in Massachusetts.

COVENANT
an agreement or promise, with religious overtones

THANKSGIVING in PLYMOUTH

That first winter in Plymouth, about half the Pilgrims died from cold and starvation. The rest were saved when two Native Americans, SAMOSET and SQUANTO, helped them make peace with the local WAMPANOAG tribe, whose leader was MASSASOIT, and taught them to grow maize and other crops. That's where we get the creation myth for the first Thanksgiving, with the idea that the Pilgrims celebrated by inviting Massasoit and his people to a harvest feast.

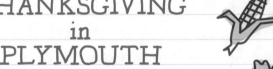

NEW ENGLAND COLONIES:
MASSACHUSETTS, CONNECTICUT, RHODE ISLAND, NEW HAMPSHIRE

MASSACHUSETTS

In 1630, led by JOHN WINTHROP, about 900 people settled in BOSTON. Their goal was to start a perfect Christian society, a concept known as a "city on a hill." A GENERAL COURT was established to create local laws. It was made up of representatives—but only male members of the church (those who were **ELECT**, or thought to be chosen by God) could vote. Meanwhile, the Puritans in England were feeling more and more threatened

> **ELECT**
> not "elected," but thought to be chosen by God

by religious persecution. Tens of thousands left between 1629 and 1640 in what is known as the GREAT MIGRATION. King Charles I granted the MASSACHUSETTS BAY COMPANY, a Puritan joint-stock company, a charter to establish a colony near Plymouth.

> ### THE SALEM WITCH TRIALS
> In 1692, in Salem, Massachusetts, some young girls accused people of casting spells on them. A special court was formed to judge witchcraft cases. The court often forced confessions from the accused. Although people eventually admitted that they had made false accusations, by the time the witch scare ended, nineteen people had been executed for witchcraft.

CONNECTICUT

THOMAS HOOKER, a minister, disagreed with John Winthrop's leadership. He led his **CONGREGATION** to found Hartford, Connecticut, in 1636. Hartford and two other towns joined together to become their own colony, and Hooker drafted the

> **CONGREGATION**
> a group of people brought together for religious worship

FUNDAMENTAL ORDERS OF CONNECTICUT, the first written constitution in North America. Under the orders, male citizens who were not thought to be ELECT could still vote.

RHODE ISLAND

ROGER WILLIAMS, another Massachusetts minister, believed that people shouldn't be forced to go to church, that settlers should pay Native Americans for land, and that church and state should be separate. This was so controversial that he was **BANISHED** from Massachusetts in 1636. His congregation followed him and founded PROVIDENCE.

> **BANISHED**
> forced to leave or no longer welcome

In 1638, ANNE HUTCHINSON was **BANISHED** from Massachusetts because she believed in personal revelation and that ministers didn't need to be members of the elect. (Another reason for her banishment was probably that she was a woman who spoke out.) Hutchinson and her sympathizers founded Portsmouth, near Providence. In 1644, the area became the colony of RHODE ISLAND and PROVIDENCE PLANTATIONS.

NEW HAMPSHIRE

In 1638, Anne Hutchinson's brother-in-law, JOHN WHEELWRIGHT, fled Massachusetts for similar reasons. He led people who agreed with him north and founded the town of Exeter. The area became the independent colony of NEW HAMPSHIRE in 1679.

KING PHILIP'S WAR

In 1675, three members of the Wampanoag tribe were tried and executed by the English for a murder. The Wampanoag chief, METACOMET (known as King Philip to the settlers), son of Massasoit, felt that the British had no right to execute his people. Also, the Wampanoag were losing land in spite of efforts to compromise with the British.

War broke out, and hundreds of settlers and many Wampanoag were killed, including Metacomet. The English claimed victory, with help from their trading partners, the Pequot and Mohegan tribes. Afterward, the English expanded into Native American lands faster than ever.

THE MIDDLE COLONIES:
NEW YORK, NEW JERSEY, PENNSYLVANIA, DELAWARE

NEW YORK

New Netherland was a thriving Dutch colony. Seeing the large number of prosperous Dutch people between New England and Virginia, England wanted this land for itself. In 1664, England sent a fleet and, unprepared for a battle, the Dutch surrendered. The colony was renamed NEW YORK, after the Duke of York, who got it as a proprietary colony.

NEW JERSEY

The Duke of York gave some of his land to LORD JOHN BERKELEY and SIR GEORGE CARTERET, who named it NEW JERSEY. They attracted settlers by starting a representative assembly and offering large amounts of land. But because New Jersey had no harbor, it was hard to make a profit. They sold their shares and the colony reverted to the king's control in 1702.

PENNSYLVANIA

New Jersey had a large population of QUAKERS, a religious group called the SOCIETY OF FRIENDS who were said to tremble (or quake) before God and who had been banished from New England. The Quaker beliefs of equality of the sexes, nonviolence, and tolerance felt like a threat to Puritans.

King Charles II handed over land to Quaker WILLIAM PENN in 1681 to pay off a debt Charles owed his family. Penn established PENNSYLVANIA, where Quakers would have religious freedom, and founded Philadelphia. It attracted thousands of people and became one of the largest cities in North America.

The MASON-DIXON LINE was originally a line of rocks laid down by two people named Mason and Dixon to mark the border between Pennsylvania and Maryland.

UGH, CAN'T WE JUST DRAW THIS ON A MAP?

DELAWARE

Penn also got land from the Duke of York. DELAWARE was south of his other holdings and occupied by a large Swedish population. It was still officially part of Pennsylvania, but Penn let them govern themselves.

CHECK YOUR KNOWLEDGE

1. What were the three types of British colonies in North America?

2. Why did North and South Carolina split?

3. What is the difference between a Puritan and a Separatist?

4. What did the Mayflower Compact promise?

5. Why did Roger Williams leave Massachusetts to found Rhode Island?

6. What did the loss in King Philip's War mean for Native Americans?

7. How did the Quakers get their name?

ANSWERS

CHECK YOUR ANSWERS

1. Royal, proprietary, and chartered
2. South Carolina was wealthier, and the sides were too different to rule at the same time. Eventually, South Carolina split from colonial rule.
3. Puritans wanted to purify the existing English Church; Separatists wanted to start their own church.
4. The Mayflower Compact was a promise to obey "just and equal laws" created for the "general good of the colony" in order to benefit "the glory of God" and the "honor of our King" (of England).
5. He disagreed with the church in Massachusetts (for example, he believed in the separation of church and state, that settlers should pay Native Americans for land, and people shouldn't be obligated to go to church).
6. Expansion of English settlers into their lands accelerated.
7. They were said to tremble before God.

Chapter 7
REGIONAL

DIFFERENCES

As the populations of the thirteen colonies increased from immigration and high birth rates, the differences between them became more prominent. Vast distances and poor communication also led to differences. They developed individual cultures as well as a shared American culture.

The main differences between the colonies hung on **PEGS**:

POPULATION

ECONOMY

GOVERNMENT

SLAVERY

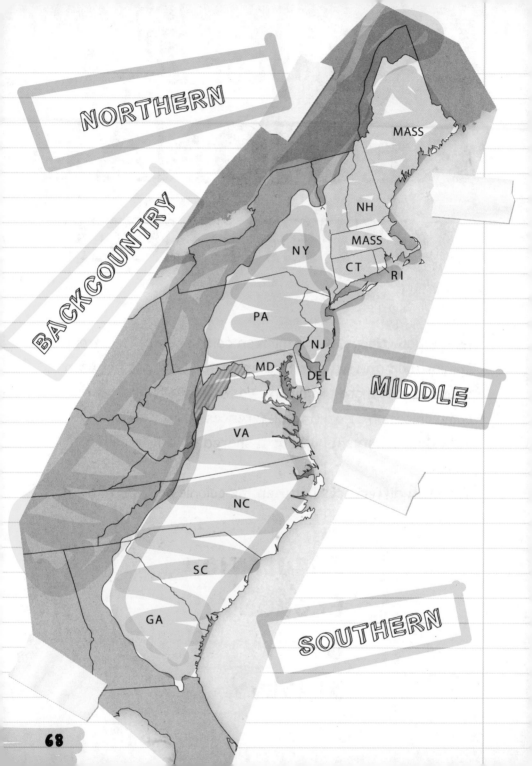

NORTHERN

BACKCOUNTRY

MIDDLE

SOUTHERN

MASS

NH

MASS

NY

CT

RI

PA

NJ

MD

DEL

VA

NC

SC

GA

SOUTHERN IDENTITY

Plantations: The South was filled with plantations that grew cash crops, including tobacco, indigo, and rice. Each plantation was like its own town, and people lived far apart. There was almost no manufacturing or other business.

Tidewater Aristocracy: Because the plantations were large and few, a smaller number of wealthy people lived in the South. A very small percentage of the population controlled almost all the money and power. The wealthiest planters lived along the Tidewater section, which had good soil and navigable rivers and shipped tobacco and other crops to England.

Dependence on Slavery: Even though only a small percentage of the citizens owned slaves, the agricultural economy depended on slavery.

Population Imbalance: There were many more slaves than slave owners. Slaveholders lived in fear of rebellion. This fear caused local governments to make slave codes even stricter.

Elected Representative Assemblies: Starting with the House of Burgesses, most local government was in the form of assemblies. Often these assemblies were **BICAMERAL**, with one house elected by the people and the other appointed by the royal governor.

> **BICAMERAL**
> a legislature having two houses

NORTHERN IDENTITY

Town Life: Life for New Englanders revolved around the MEETINGHOUSE and church, which were usually the same building. The meetinghouse (where churchgoing men worked together to make laws) usually faced a town GREEN, which was shared land that belonged to the town. New Englanders owned small farms (for **SUBSISTENCE FARMING**) and lived close to their neighbors.

> **SUBSISTENCE FARMING**
> producing just enough crops to survive

Trade and Industry: Unable to raise cash crops (due to long winters and poor soil), New England depended on trade, mills, lumber, shipbuilding, fishing, fur trading, whaling, and craftsmanship. New Englanders were, on average, better off than Southerners.

Limited Use of Slavery: With no large plantations, there were few slaves. However, Northern merchants did engage in the slave trade and profited from it.

Puritan Values: New Englanders adopted the Puritan values of hard work, modesty, and education. Massachusetts **MANDATED** schools in any town of more than 50 households. Puritan values did not include tolerance of religious differences.

> **MANDATE**
> to require, usually by law

MIDDLE-COLONY IDENTITY

The Middle Colonies linked the **NORTH** and SOUTH cultures:

Mixed Agriculture and Industry: The Middle Colonies grew some cash crops, especially grain, as well as fruits and vegetables. They developed industries such as ironworking and forestry. Trade was made easier by access to Philadelphia and New York City, the largest ports in the colonies and the centers of shipping.

Mixed Use of Slavery: Slaves were forced to work in both cities and on farms. Some were able to make money when their slaveholders allowed them to work as longshoremen or shipbuilders in exchange for a portion of the slaves' wages. A rare few slaves were able to save enough to buy their freedom.

Mixed Populations: With large immigrant populations and a tradition of tolerance, the Middle Colonies were home to the most diverse populations.

Mixed Government: The Middle Colonies used a combination of assemblies, town meetings, and royal government.

England expected to profit from its colonies. So England passed the **NAVIGATION ACT OF 1651**, making it illegal for the colonies to sell to countries other than England, use ships other than English ships, or go through ports other than English ports. The colonists soon saw that the Acts limited their wealth by cutting back free trade. Many resorted to **SMUGGLING** (conducting illegal/secret trade).

BACKCOUNTRY IDENTITY

The BACKCOUNTRY, or the western frontier, stretched along the APPALACHIAN MOUNTAINS, from the far north to the far south, and was populated by recent immigrants and former indentured servants. Although it wasn't very far west, it had a Wild West atmosphere. Few people had large farms or owned slaves.

NEW and UNIQUE AMERICAN IDENTITY

Even though regional identities became stronger, a culture was evolving, with:

COMMON HISTORY, from a shared English background

Perception of **CHEAP** and **AVAILABLE LAND**

NOT THE CASE IN EUROPE!

AN EMERGING MIDDLE CLASS, from wealth and social mobility because of the lack of aristocrats and use of slaves instead of lower-class white workers

POWER FOR LAND OWNERS, because of the connection between land ownership and the right to vote

SOCIAL MOBILITY (among white males) from lack of hereditary titles or classes

TOLERANCE (mostly) **OF RELIGIOUS DIFFERENCES**, due to diversity

SHARED ENEMIES, from conflicts with Native Americans and French and Spanish settlers

Women mostly worked in the home (cooking, cleaning, raising children, gardening, making soap and candles, etc.) or running stores or inns in cities. Farming was mainly the job of men. Boys were often sent to **APPRENTICE** with a master craftsman, while girls learned their crafts at home.

APPRENTICE
to work for another in order to learn a trade

The ENGLISH BILL of RIGHTS

Changes in England meant changes in the colonies. In 1685, JAMES II became king. He wanted more control. He made the northern colonies the DOMINION OF NEW ENGLAND, a royal colony with very limited self-government. People on both sides of the Atlantic were unhappy with him. After three years, **PARLIAMENT** ousted him. His daughter and son-in-law, MARY AND WILLIAM OF ORANGE, invaded and took over in the GLORIOUS REVOLUTION (called that because it took place without bloodshed).

> **PARLIAMENT**
> the legislative body of Great Britain

In 1689, William and Mary approved an ENGLISH BILL OF RIGHTS, which limited the powers of the monarchy and asserted parliamentary power. The British government continued to make laws governing trade with the colonies, but there was little enforcement in the colonies—a hands-off approach called **SALUTARY NEGLECT**. Still, colonists believed they were full citizens of England and entitled to all of the same rights as someone living in England.

> **SALUTARY**
> good; healthy

> Considered one of the most important legal documents in history, the **MAGNA CARTA** of 1215 forced the king (then King John) to obey the laws of the land. Ever since, British citizens have been determined to limit royal power and protect their rights.

The GREAT AWAKENING and the ENLIGHTENMENT

The GREAT AWAKENING was a religious movement led by traveling ministers in the 1730s and 1740s. Through fiery sermons at outdoor REVIVAL meetings, Americans were encouraged to seek a personal relationship with God.

MOST FAMOUS MINISTERS:
Jonathan Edwards of Massachusetts
George Whitefield of England

The ENLIGHTENMENT was a philosophical movement that emphasized human reason, scientific analysis, and individualism, and applied the laws of nature to politics and society. Led in England by such philosophers as JOHN LOCKE, it held that a SOCIAL CONTRACT ensured citizens' rights, in exchange for obedience to the government. The Enlightenment influenced BENJAMIN FRANKLIN, THOMAS JEFFERSON, and most of the Founding Fathers.

The Great Awakening and the Enlightenment prompted Americans to debate political, societal, and religious questions. Both put forth the idea that there was equality—whether in the eyes of God or the eyes of justice—among all individuals.

THE

New-York Weekly JOURNAL

Containing the freſheſt Advices, Foreign, and Domeſtick.

FREEDOM of the PRESS

JOHN PETER ZENGER, publisher of the *NEW-YORK WEEKLY JOURNAL*, was charged with **LIBEL** in 1735 after printing negative statements about the governor. Since the governor was an appointee of the king and it was illegal to speak negatively about the king, Zenger was put on trial. His lawyer, Andrew Hamilton, urged the jury to determine whether or not Zenger spoke the truth and convinced them that people had the right to do so. It was the beginning of FREEDOM OF THE PRESS.

> **LIBEL**
> a printed statement that defames or misrepresents

CHECK YOUR KNOWLEDGE

1. Did most people in the South own slaves?

2. Where was the center of town life in New England?

3. What values are emblematic of the Puritans?

4. Why was there a successful middle class in North America?

5. Why were the colonists guaranteed the rights promised by the English Bill of Rights?

6. What is salutary neglect?

7. What did the Great Awakening and the Enlightenment have in common?

ANSWERS

CHECK YOUR ANSWERS

1. No
2. The meetinghouse and church, near the green
3. Hard work, modesty, and education
4. There were no aristocrats, wealth was easier to acquire, and slaves did the work of lower-class white workers.
5. They were (they thought) citizens of England.
6. A hands-off approach to government that benefits the people
7. They both advocated equality and encouraged debate.

Chapter 8

PRE-REVOLUTIONARY WAR

TESTING the BOUNDARIES

As British colonists expanded westward, frontiersmen infringed on Native American territory and challenged French claims to the land.

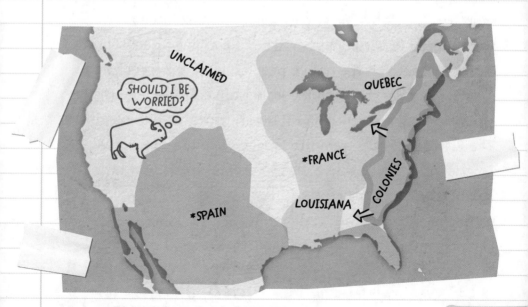

FUR, PORTS, and FIGHTING

French colonists depended on the rivers that provided access to the sea and French markets. They built forts along the rivers to guard against the English. Although some were JESUITS (priests who aimed to convert native people to Catholicism), many were in the fur trade.

British traders had the same idea, and they built the settlement of PICKAWILLANY in present-day Ohio in 1748. The French responded by attacking Pickawillany. The British captured the French settlement of Louisbourg in Canada. France built more forts, such as FORT DUQUESNE in Pennsylvania.

ALLIANCES

Seeing that full-on fighting was coming, the British and French searched for Native American allies. Perhaps because the French were fewer in number, traded European goods, and didn't encroach on the native peoples' land, the French had a better relationship with the local Native Americans. They had allies in the Algonquin and Huron tribes, as well as others. The British got help from the Iroquois League. The Native Americans' main objective was to protect trade and their own land, so they joined whichever side seemed least harmful.

A POLITICAL CARTOON BY BENJAMIN FRANKLIN

BUT I REALLY DO LIKE SNAKES!

JOIN, or DIE.

ALBANY PLAN

The British colonies sent representatives to Albany, New York, to discuss defense. In June 1754, Benjamin Franklin presented the ALBANY PLAN OF UNION (the ALBANY PLAN), the first formal attempt to unite the colonies. The plan was to join to raise money, train **MILITIA**, and organize the government—but not a single local legislature was willing to give up its own power. So the colonies continued fighting on their own, often losing.

GEORGE WASHINGTON

In 1753, a young surveyor was sent by the Virginia governor to find French settlers in the Ohio River Valley and convince them to leave. His name was GEORGE WASHINGTON, and he was twenty-one years old. The French refused, so in 1754 the governor made Washington an officer in the colonial militia and sent him back with troops. Washington attacked a French scouting party, which the French claimed were on a diplomatic mission. The French also claimed that among the ten people killed was a French diplomat. Afterward, Washington built a smaller fort, FORT NECESSITY, near Fort Duquesne. Even though he had little experience and few men, Washington attacked Fort Duquesne. He was defeated, but the attack was the beginning of a war, and Washington's bravery made him a hero in Virginia.

The FRENCH and INDIAN WAR: 1754–1763
(Part of the SEVEN YEARS' WAR: 1756–1763)

The FRENCH AND INDIAN WAR between Britain and France also became known as the SEVEN YEARS' WAR when it turned into a larger European conflict.

> The **FRENCH AND INDIAN WAR** was the first war that started in the colonies and spread to Europe.

Europe split into two factions—countries that sided with England and countries that sided with France—and war broke out across Europe. Meanwhile, the British didn't have a strong army in America. In 1755, King George II sent GENERAL EDWARD BRADDOCK to command the colonial forces. George Washington advised Braddock to fight "Indian style," and that the European style of combat—his army's bright red coats and method of lining up in columns—was a disadvantage. But Braddock ignored the advice. He was soon killed in a surprise attack. The **REDCOATS** took huge losses.

> **REDCOATS**
> British soldiers, so called because of their official uniform of a bright red jacket

British secretary of state (later the prime minister) WILLIAM PITT was determined to drive the French out of British territory. The fighting was costly. The debt would have to be paid. He sent more troops.

The TIDE TURNS

With additional troops, the British army and colonial militia began to capture French forts. Fort Duquesne became **FORT PITT**. Quebec, the capital of New France, seemed impossible to attack, but the British successfully ambushed the city by cover of night. The BATTLE OF QUEBEC was a turning point in the war. When Montreal fell the next year, all of Canada was in British hands.

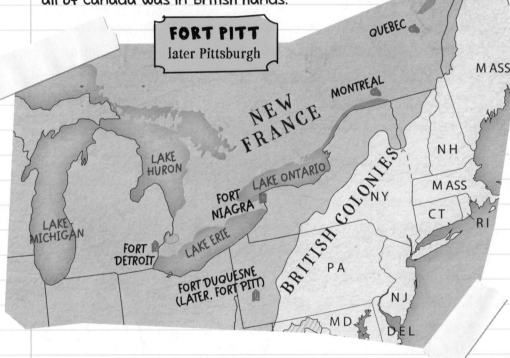

FORT PITT
later Pittsburgh

QUEBEC

MASS

MONTREAL

NEW FRANCE

LAKE HURON

LAKE ONTARIO

NH

MASS

NY

CT

RI

LAKE MICHIGAN

FORT NIAGRA

LAKE ERIE

FORT DETROIT

FORT DUQUESNE
(LATER, FORT PITT)

BRITISH COLONIES

PA

NJ

MD

DEL

The TREATY of PARIS

The Seven Years' War formally ended in 1763 when Britain and France signed the TREATY OF PARIS. The treaty gave England all the French territory east of the Mississippi as well as the Spanish territory of Florida (Spain had sided with France).

PONTIAC'S REBELLION

British expansion made life a whole lot worse for Native Americans. Trade with the British was less profitable, and more settlers were seizing land and establishing farms.

BIOLOGICAL WARFARE

Some accounts claim the English invited Native American leaders to discuss peace, presenting them with a gift of blankets that had been intentionally contaminated with smallpox, causing a deadly outbreak of the disease.

An Ottawa chief named PONTIAC tried to unite Native Americans against the British. In early 1763, his forces took the fort at Detroit and attacked forts and settlements along the frontier. PONTIAC'S REBELLION, or PONTIAC'S WAR, continued until he was killed in 1769 and the British defeated his allies.

The PROCLAMATION of 1763

To prevent more clashes between settlers and Native Americans, KING GEORGE III issued the PROCLAMATION OF 1763, making it illegal for settlers to live west of the APPALACHIAN MOUNTAINS. This angered settlers, some of whom had already purchased land that was now out of bounds. They didn't understand why they couldn't just live wherever they wanted, and the proclamation was routinely disobeyed. The stage was set for more conflict between the colonies and Britain.

CHECK YOUR KNOWLEDGE

1. What did many French colonists do for a living?

2. Why did the French get along better with the Native Americans than the English did?

3. How did George Washington become a hero in Virginia?

4. What is the difference between the French and Indian War and the Seven Years' War?

5. What were the elements of the traditional European style of combat?

6. What were the terms of the Treaty of Paris?

7. How did Chief Pontiac respond to France's loss in the French and Indian War?

ANSWERS

CHECK YOUR ANSWERS

1. They were fur traders.
2. They traded with the Native Americans and did not settle on their land.
3. His bravery at the start of the French and Indian War, at Fort Duquesne, made him famous.
4. The French and Indian War became known as the Seven Years' War when it grew into a larger European conflict.
5. Organized ranks, usually wearing bright uniforms
6. The treaty gave England all the French territory east of the Mississippi as well as the Spanish territory of Florida because Spain had sided with France.
7. He attempted to unite Native Americans against the British.

Chapter 9

PARLIAMENT and PROTESTS
★ ★ ★

The END of SALUTARY NEGLECT

The French and Indian War had been very expensive, so Great Britain had a large debt. In addition, the expanding British territory meant that there were constant land conflicts with Native Americans. England sent a **STANDING ARMY** to America to protect the colonists, and those troops had to be paid, too. In order to pay off the war debt and maintain the standing army England had sent to America to protect the colonists, Parliament raised taxes.

MY FEET HURT!

> **STANDING ARMY**
> a professional army maintained even in peacetime

The SUGAR ACT ← SWEET! (NOT.)

The SUGAR ACT of 1764 actually LOWERED taxes on molasses that were brought into the colonies, hoping to minimize SMUGGLING. Because they were trying to stop smugglers, ships were searched by customs officers, and any suspected contraband could be taken away, even before the smuggler was convicted. Colonists believed that the Sugar Act violated their legal rights as British citizens by denying the right to trial—and some went even further: JAMES OTIS, a lawyer in Boston, argued that Parliament didn't have a right to tax the colonists at all, since the colonists didn't have representatives there to debate the tax.

YE DREADED → STAMP!

The STAMP ACT

In 1765, the STAMP ACT was passed. Any printed paper goods, including legal documents, had to be taxed and have a stamp proving the tax was paid. The Stamp Act was the first direct tax on individual colonists. Protests broke out, including **BOYCOTTS** in which colonists refused to purchase British goods at all.

BOYCOTT
a protest in which people don't purchase controversial items

STAMP AGENTS WERE TARRED AND FEATHERED, AND MOBS PREVENTED STAMP DISTRIBUTIONS.

NOOOO!

That October, the STAMP ACT CONGRESS—with representatives from nine colonies—met in New York. They wrote a petition explaining how the Stamp Act was a violation of their natural and political rights. In March of 1766, at the urging of British merchants who had been hurt by the boycotts, Parliament **REPEALED** the Stamp Act. But on the same day, they issued the DECLARATORY ACT, which basically reasserted Parliament's power to tax as it pleased.

REPEAL
to undo a law

SAMUEL ADAMS and PATRICK HENRY

Boston lawyer SAMUEL ADAMS agreed with Otis. He summed up Otis's position at a Boston town meeting in 1764 as "NO TAXATION WITHOUT REPRESENTATION." It became a rallying cry. Adams was a cofounder of a secret society called the SONS OF LIBERTY, which organized boycotts and protests, some of them violent. Women formed the DAUGHTERS OF LIBERTY, urging Americans to use homemade (rather than imported) clothes and household goods. This was some of the first political involvement by women in America.

PATRICK HENRY was a lawyer and member of the House of Burgesses. In 1765, he raised the cry of "No Taxation Without Representation" in Virginia and inspired the burgesses to protest the Stamp Act. Some people believed that these protests were headed toward **TREASON**. Henry said, "If this be treason, make the most of it," and implied overthrowing the king.

> **TREASON**
> a crime against a government to which one should be loyal

The TOWNSHEND ACTS

Parliament still wanted to raise more money to pay for British troops in America and the expenses of the French and Indian War. In 1767, it passed the TOWNSHEND ACTS, which taxed imports, including tea. Colonists were infuriated by another tax being passed without their permission. They were also angry about the WRITS OF ASSISTANCE, which gave customs officials permission to search for taxable goods without a search warrant. Soon tax collectors were among the most unpopular people in North America, and many went home to England to escape threats on their lives. The royal governor of Massachusetts asked England to send soldiers to maintain peace and enforce the law.

The BOSTON MASSACRE

In 1768, 1,000 Redcoats came to Boston. To the colonists, the Redcoats were not there to help, but were occupying troops. On March 5, 1770, a minor dispute broke out between a soldier and some Bostonians, who threw snowballs at him. More citizens and more soldiers came on the scene and formed a mob. In front of the customhouse, where the taxes were collected, stones were thrown and some citizens dared the soldiers to fire. A few soldiers panicked and did, killing five Boston citizens. The event came to be known as the BOSTON MASSACRE. The five victims became heroes of the colonial cause—notably CRISPUS ATTUCKS, son of African American and Wampanoag parents. JOHN ADAMS, a cousin of Samuel Adams, argued that everyone, including the soldiers, was entitled to a fair trial. He and JOSIAH QUINCY defended the soldiers, who were freed on the grounds of self-defense. The trial demonstrated to the world that the colonists were committed to justice.

BOSTON TEA PARTY

Parliament repealed all of the Townshend Acts in 1770 except one: the tax on tea. People in Massachusetts were able to purchase smuggled tea. However, in 1773, when the British East India Company faced financial ruin, Parliament passed the new TEA ACT, giving the company a **MONOPOLY** on selling tea directly to the colonists and making taxed tea cheaper than smuggled tea. That reinforced taxes on the colonies and hurt local merchants who had made their living from tea.

Many colonists began to drink coffee to replace tea.

At midnight on the night of December 16, 1773, while three East India Company ships were docked in Boston, the Sons of Liberty, disguised as Native Americans, boarded the ships and dumped 342 chests of tea into Boston Harbor. This was dubbed the BOSTON TEA PARTY. Because they considered themselves loyal British citizens, the colonists attempted to pay England back for the tea in exchange for a repeal of the Tea Act. However, the king and Parliament had finally had enough and were determined to punish the colony of Massachusetts.

The INTOLERABLE ACTS

King George III acknowledged that England would either need to "master" the colonists or "leave them to themselves." He picked "master." In 1774, Parliament passed the COERCIVE ACTS, known in the colonies as the INTOLERABLE ACTS because . . .

Boston Harbor was closed until colonists compensated the East India Company for its lost tea.

INTOLERABLE!

Most town meetings were banned.

The charter of Massachusetts was revoked.

The Massachusetts legislature was put under the control of the new governor, General Thomas Gage. In effect, Boston was put under martial law.

INTOLERABLE!

Royal officials who committed crimes in the colonies couldn't be tried in colonial courts.

The Quartering Act forced colonists to let British soldiers stay in their homes.

VERY ANNOYING... I MEAN, INTOLERABLE!

Land the colonists thought belonged to them was given to Quebec (the Quebec Act).

The goal was to exert control in the colonies, but the Intolerable Acts had the OPPOSITE effect.

CHECK YOUR KNOWLEDGE

1. Why did England send a standing army to the colonies?

2. Which key American idea was developed by Bostonian James Otis and coined by Samuel Adams?

3. How does a boycott work?

4. How were women involved in political protests in the 1760s?

5. What was the verdict in the case of the Boston Massacre deaths?

6. Who was responsible for the Boston Tea Party?

7. What was the reasoning behind the Coercive Acts?

ANSWERS

CHECK YOUR ANSWERS

1. To protect the colonists from Native Americans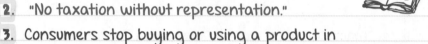
2. "No taxation without representation."
3. Consumers stop buying or using a product in order to encourage those who sell it to make a change.
4. They encouraged Americans to use homemade (not imported) goods.
5. The soldiers were found not guilty.
6. The Sons of Liberty
7. They were intended to help England maintain control over the colonies.

COERCIVE ACTS?
MORE LIKE...
INTOLERABLE!

☆ Chapter 10 ☆

The BRITISH

★ ★ ★ ★ ★ ★ ★ ★ ★ ★ ★ ★ ★ ★ ★ ★

ARE COMING!

OOH, IS IT THE
BEATLES?

I BELIEVE THEY
MEAN US, SIR.

The FIRST CONTINENTAL CONGRESS

Seeing the Coercive Acts as truly intolerable, the colonies sent representatives to meet in Philadelphia in September of 1774 to figure out how to respond. This was the FIRST CONTINENTAL CONGRESS.

Debate was about how to best oppose British policy or negotiate with Parliament.

"CONGRESS" today is the legislative branch of the U.S. government. But back then, "congress" was just a fancy word for a meeting. It was the first time delegates from all over the continent got together.

Georgia was the only colony that didn't send representatives to the First Continental Congress. Later, Georgia agreed with its decisions.

95

Patrick Henry—who told the Second Virginia Convention in 1775,

"GIVE ME LIBERTY OR GIVE ME DEATH"

—argued on the side of war.

Congress decided to put on a different kind of pressure. They escalated the boycotts. They sent a petition, the VIRGINIA DECLARATION OF RIGHTS, to King George, informing him of the rights to "life, liberty, and property" they deserved as Englishmen. And they endorsed the SUFFOLK RESOLVES by the leaders of Suffolk County, Massachusetts, calling on colonists to form militias and declaring the Intolerable Acts null and void. The delegates were hoping for the best and preparing for the worst.

The SONS of LIBERTY STRIKE AGAIN

Instead of repealing the Intolerable Acts, King George III sent more troops to Boston. So many people were spying for both sides that it wasn't long before General Gage, governor of Massachusetts, learned that the colonial militia was storing an arsenal of weapons in Concord, just outside Boston. In April of 1775, he ordered his men to head there to destroy it and to arrest Samuel Adams and John Hancock (who also helped found the Sons of Liberty) in nearby Lexington.

On April 18, 1775, a Sons of Liberty spy came across a British regiment preparing to march. He ran to tell PAUL REVERE and

William Dawes, also members of the Sons of Liberty. Revere asked a man named Robert Newman to keep watch from the steeple in the Old North Church in Boston. Newman was told to light one lantern if the British troops were coming by land, and two if by sea.

THE REGULARS ARE COMING OUT!

When they saw two lanterns, Dawes took an overland route and Revere rowed across the harbor and took a MIDNIGHT RIDE through Charleston and on to Lexington and Concord. As he rode, he shouted, "The regulars are coming out," secret code words to warn the colonists that the British were coming.

LEXINGTON and CONCORD

The local militia, called MINUTEMEN (they could be READY IN A MINUTE), heard Revere and grabbed their weapons. When the 700 Redcoats reached Lexington around dawn, about 70 minutemen were waiting. Both sides were ordered not to fire unless fired upon, and to this day no one knows who shot first, but it was "THE SHOT HEARD 'ROUND THE WORLD," starting the BATTLE OF LEXINGTON AND CONCORD.

BANG!

BLIMEY, DID YOU HEAR THAT?

The British quickly defeated the outnumbered minutemen, killing eight of them, and marched on to Concord.

97

As the British were leaving Concord, they were surprised by more minutemen at the North Bridge. The colonists killed almost 200 Redcoats, using the bright red jackets as targets. The British retreated to Boston, and both sides pondered their next move.

Colonists who supported independence were called **PATRIOTS**, while those who remained loyal to Britain were called **LOYALISTS**. Many Loyalists fled the colonies, often heading to Canada.

The SECOND CONTINENTAL CONGRESS

Initially most Native Americans didn't take sides in the Revolutionary War, but the majority of those who fought supported the British. The British convinced many tribes to fight against colonials settling in frontier regions.

Since King George III continued to ignore the Declaration of Rights, the colonial leaders from all 13 colonies met on May 10, 1775, in a SECOND CONTINENTAL CONGRESS. They began to set up their own post office, make treaties with Native Americans, and serve as an impromptu governing body. They formed the CONTINENTAL ARMY with the Virginian George Washington as its commander. The colonial leaders, who were mostly from Massachusetts, chose a Virginian as commander to make the resistance appealing to Southerners.

The BATTLE of BUNKER HILL

COLONEL WILLIAM PRESCOTT set up the Massachusetts militias on BUNKER HILL and BREED'S HILL, across the harbor from Boston. On June 17, 1775, over two thousand Redcoats

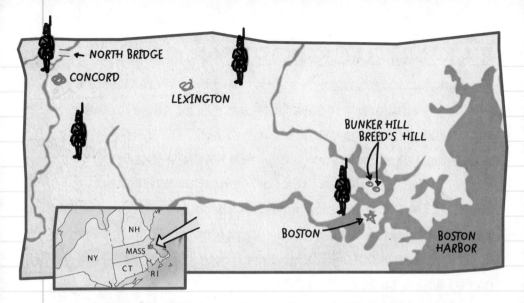

marched up the hill. According to legend, the militias were short on ammunition, so Prescott ordered them not to fire at the Redcoats until they could see "the whites of their eyes." Twice, the militias drove back the powerful British army. Although the British eventually forced them off Bunker Hill, the inexperienced colonial armies proved that they wouldn't be easily defeated.

The OLIVE BRANCH PETITION

On July 5, the Second Continental Congress sent King George III one last shot at peace, the OLIVE BRANCH PETITION. They still wanted to be part of England if the king would protect their rights. They urged the king to negotiate on disputed issues with recognition that the colonies should rule themselves on most matters. King George III rejected the petition and instead hired 30,000 German "Hessian" (or mercenary) troops to fight with the British.

TAKING BACK BOSTON

Washington took control of militias and began creating
the Continental army to take back Boston. He came up with
a plan to retrieve the weapons from FORT TICONDEROGA,
which the Vermont militia (the GREEN MOUNTAIN BOYS,
led by ETHAN ALLEN) and the Connecticut militia (led by
BENEDICT ARNOLD, most famous for turning traitor and selling
information to the British army) had captured from the British
earlier. Colonel HENRY KNOX and his troops
hauled heavy cannons from the fort
over 300 miles by foot in the middle of winter.
The Redcoats, under the command of SIR WILLIAM HOWE,
saw that defeat in Boston was inevitable. On March 17, 1776,
the British retreated, fleeing north to Canada.

COMMON SENSE

In January 1776, a recent immigrant from England named
THOMAS PAINE wrote an anonymous pamphlet arguing for
democracy and independence titled *COMMON SENSE*. Paine
blamed King George III personally—not just Parliament.
Pretty radical for a time when most countries
were ruled by kings (who claimed to have God
on their side), *COMMON SENSE* sold hundreds of
thousands of copies throughout the colonies and
convinced many to support independence.

COMMON SENSE

ADDRESSED
TO THE
INHABITANTS
OF
AMERICA

The DECLARATION of INDEPENDENCE

The Second Continental Congress came up with the national motto **E PLURIBUS UNUM**, meaning "out of many, one" in Latin.

JUNE 7, 1776:

Richard Henry Lee of Virginia introduced a **RESOLUTION** in the Second Continental Congress calling the colonies free and independent states.

RESOLUTION
a formal expression of an opinion

Congress created a committee to draft a Declaration of Independence that included Benjamin Franklin, John Adams, and Thomas Jefferson. Jefferson wrote it within two weeks, drawing on the ideas of **JOHN LOCKE**. It was meant to explain the LEE RESOLUTION.

JULY 2, 1776:

Congress unanimously passed Lee's resolution. John Adams figured this date would become a national holiday.

JOHN LOCKE wrote that all individuals have the right to "life, liberty, and property." "Property" became "the pursuit of happiness" in one of the most famous lines of the Declaration of Independence.

JULY 4, 1776:

The delegates adopted the Declaration of Independence. The United States of America was born . . . provided the colonists won the war.

. . . and now we celebrate July 4th every year as Independence Day!

101

The DECLARATION

ACTUAL WORDS

The Declaration of Independence has four parts:

1. **PREAMBLE** (introduction)
2. Declaration of Natural Rights
3. List of **GRIEVANCES** Against the King
4. Resolution of Independence by the United States

> **PREAMBLE**
> introductory section
>
> **GRIEVANCES**
> complaints

From the Preamble

"When in the Course of human events, it becomes necessary for one people to dissolve the political bands...they should declare the causes which impel them to the separation."

People must state their reasons for a revolution.

From the Declaration of Natural Rights

"We hold these truths to be self-evident, that all men are created equal, that they are endowed by their Creator with certain unalienable Rights, that among these are Life, Liberty, and the pursuit of Happiness...."

Some rights come from the fact of just being human and can't be taken away by a king. When they said "equal," the Founding Fathers didn't initially include Native Americans, slaves, or women.

# of INDEPENDENCE

THE COLONIES' JUSTIFICATION FOR SEPARATION

From the List of Grievances

"The history of the present King of Great Britain is a history of repeated injuries and usurpations, all having in direct object the establishment of an absolute **TYRANNY** over these States."

TYRANNY
rule by an often harsh absolute power

The grievances, or complaints, the colonists had against King George III, followed by a lot of examples

RESTATES THE LEE RESOLUTION

From the Resolution of Independence

"We, therefore, the Representatives of the United States of America, in General Congress...do, in the Name, and by Authority of the good People of these Colonies, solemnly publish and declare, That these United Colonies are, and of Right ought to be Free and Independent States..."

"We're independent!"

The DECLARATION of INDEPENDENCE in 40 WORDS

Government is a social contract. If the ruler doesn't protect the people and their natural rights, the contract is broken and the people can overthrow him. King George III broke the contract, so now the U.S. is its own nation.

PUT YOUR JOHN HANCOCK RIGHT HERE

John Hancock, president of the Congress, was the first to sign the Declaration of Independence. His signature was so large and stylish that people sometimes still call a signature a "John Hancock."

actual size

CHECK YOUR KNOWLEDGE

1. What did the First Continental Congress debate about?

2. What was declared in the Declaration of Rights?

3. How did Paul Revere know which way the British were coming from?

4. What were the colonial militiamen nicknamed?

5. Who fired first at the Battle of Lexington?

6. What was the Olive Branch Petition?

7. What was the importance of the pamphlet COMMON SENSE?

ANSWERS

CHECK YOUR ANSWERS

1. They debated about how to best oppose British policy or negotiate with Parliament.

2. That the colonies didn't want independence—they just wanted their rights

3. Robert Newman lit two lanterns in the steeple of the Old North Church in Boston to indicate the British were coming by sea.

4. The Minutemen

5. Nobody knows!

6. It was the last attempt by the Continental Congress to make peace with King George III and remain part of England.

7. Many people were convinced by Thomas Paine's pamphlet that independence was a good idea.

Unit 3

American Revolution and the Early Republic
1776–1791

Once the Declaration of Independence was signed, the United States was born, but Americans still had work ahead. First, they needed to win a war against one of the best armies and the most powerful navy in the world. Next, they had to invent a whole new form of government.

☆ Chapter 11 ☆

The AMERICAN REVOLUTION

TIMELINE to (REAL) INDEPENDENCE

Americans declared independence, but they weren't independent yet.

Washington was put in charge of the Continental army in 1775, but it was less an army than a collection of part-time volunteer militias only contracted to fight for one year. The Continental Congress suggested a **DRAFT**, but not everyone participated. The wealthy paid slaves, apprentices, or others to serve in their place.

> **DRAFT**
> a mandatory call of duty to serve in an army

The British—masters of a well-trained, professional army and rulers of a great empire—were confident of victory.

The BATTLE of LONG ISLAND

Summer of 1776: Over 30,000 British soldiers under GENERAL WILLIAM HOWE arrived in New York City. Washington's troops were outnumbered.

August 1776: In the BATTLE OF LONG ISLAND, the Patriots were driven out of New York and then New Jersey, and forced to take refuge in Pennsylvania across the Delaware River.

The British were so sure the war would be over soon that they left the defense of New Jersey up to the HESSIANS, a group of German mercenaries, while the British army spent the winter in comfort in New York.

Thomas Paine, the author of *Common Sense*, also wrote a series of pamphlets called AMERICAN CRISIS. The first one, published in 1776, begins with the line, "These are the times that try men's souls."

WASHINGTON CROSSES the DELAWARE

Christmas Day 1776: During a terrible storm, Washington and thousands of his troops secretly rowed across the Delaware River while the Hessians were celebrating Christmas. The next morning, while the Hessians were camped out at Trenton and still sleeping, the Continental army attacked and won an important victory.

January 2, 1777: British general CHARLES CORNWALLIS, in charge of the British troops, tried to stop the Continental army, but Washington was a step ahead. His troops lit campfires near Princeton to make it look like they were resting. Instead, they followed the British troops and made another surprise attack.

The BATTLE of SARATOGA

Spring of 1777: The British plan was to capture the city of Albany and take control of the Hudson River to cut off New England from the other colonies. General William Howe would move north up the Hudson. GENERAL JOHN BURGOYNE would head south from Canada and recapture Fort Ticonderoga on the way. LIEUTENANT COLONEL BARRY ST. LEGER would travel down the Mohawk Valley. All three would meet in Albany. That was the theory, anyway.

DON'T HATE HIM BECAUSE HE'S BEAUTIFUL

GENERAL BURGOYNE was affectionately called "Gentleman Johnny Burgoyne" by his troops for his kindness. And maybe also for his good looks and fashion sense.

FORT TICONDEROGA

NEW HAMPSHIRE

SARATOGA

MOHAWK RIVER

MOHAWK VALLEY

ALBANY

MASSACHUSETTS

HUDSON RIVER

NEW YORK

CONNECTICUT

PENNSYLVANIA

NEW YORK CITY

LONG ISLAND

NEW JERSEY

DELAWARE RIVER

VALLEY FORGE

CROSSING

NEW ENGLAND 1777

PHILADELPHIA

Howe decided it'd be better to capture Philadelphia. He forced the Continental Congress to flee the city. Burgoyne recaptured Ticonderoga, but Gentleman Johnny didn't know Howe wasn't on his way up the Hudson and was trapped in the woods by American militias. St. Leger was forced back en route to the Mohawk Valley by American General Benedict Arnold.

← TRAITOR! SPY! NOT-GOOD GUY!

Burgoyne eventually made it to Saratoga, New York, where he was met by the American forces of GENERAL HORATIO GATES. The British had no reinforcements and no escape route. On October 17, they surrendered, and the BATTLE OF SARATOGA became the first major American victory of the Revolutionary War.

> The victory also led the French to get involved in the revolution. The French and British were bitter enemies, so the French began supporting the Patriots when they saw that the Americans could win and wouldn't be satisfied with anything less than independence.

WINTER at VALLEY FORGE

Winter of 1777: The Continental army suffered through one of the worst winters on record. While the British were comfy in Philadelphia, the Continental army was camped 20 miles west at VALLEY FORGE. The 12,000 troops had almost no food, clothing, or supplies. About a quarter of them died before spring. Those who survived had spent the winter training under Prussian Officer Baron von Steuben. They became a small but very skilled new Continental army.

HIRED BY CONGRESS FOR HIS MILITARY EXPERTISE

HELP from OVERSEAS

1778: The French had been secretly providing supplies and their navy to the Patriots. The victory at Saratoga, plus the charm of Benjamin Franklin as American diplomat in France, convinced the French to support the U.S. publicly. In 1778, King Louis XVI decided that France would officially become an ally and declare war on Great Britain.

> **PRIVATEER**
> a privately owned ship commissioned by the government to fight the enemy; in exchange, the ship could keep whatever they found on enemy ships.

1779: Spain joined the war against England. Louisiana Governor BERNARDO DE GÁLVEZ helped Spain take Natchez, Baton Rouge, and other cities from the British. Holland also helped the Patriots with loans and funding.

The **MARQUIS DE LAFAYETTE**, a young French nobleman, became a trusted aide to George Washington. Lafayette was such a strong believer in the Revolutionary War that he paid the troops under his command out of his own pocket!

WAR on the WESTERN FRONT

The British army had to spread out to cover a lot of land.
West of the Appalachian Mountains, the British gained
Native American allies like Mohawk chief JOSEPH BRANT.
This area had been made more accessible thanks in part to
DANIEL BOONE, who had **BLAZED** the WILDERNESS ROAD
in 1775. GEORGE ROGERS CLARK, a lieutenant colonel in the
Virginia militia, captured the British outposts and FORT
SACKVILLE in modern-day Indiana.

> **BLAZED**
> cut a trail—as in, he was a trailblazer!

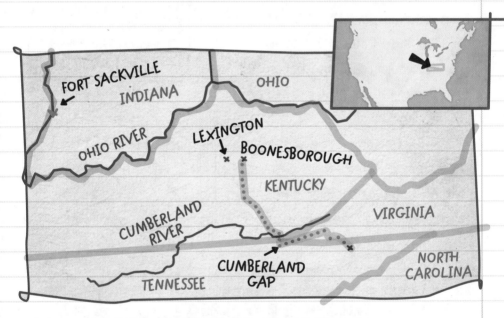

WILDERNESS ROAD ····

WAR in the SOUTH

1778–1780: The British offered freedom to the slaves of Patriots if they would run away and join the British troops. In December of 1778, British commander HENRY CLINTON captured Savannah, Georgia (and eventually the entire state of Georgia). In May of 1780, Clinton also gained control of Charleston, South Carolina, in a battle that destroyed most of the American army in the South. GENERAL CORNWALLIS was put in charge of maintaining a British stronghold in the South.

Congress appointed GENERAL HORATIO GATES, who had led troops to victory in Saratoga, to create a new Southern army. Unfortunately, they were quickly defeated by Cornwallis.

1781: Congress replaced Gates with a new Southern general, NATHANAEL GREENE. Greene's army (under Patriot Daniel Morgan) defeated the British at the battle at Cowpens, South Carolina. It was the first time that militia units were deployed in battle.

GUERRILLAS and the SWAMP FOX

Instead of using the traditional European style of lining up for combat, Southern Patriots used their knowledge of the terrain by attacking supply and communication centers in small groups and escaping before they could be caught.

It was a new kind of warfare: **GUERRILLA WARFARE**. The most famous guerrilla of the South was FRANCIS MARION, leader of MARION'S BRIGADE. He was so difficult to catch that the British called him the "SWAMP FOX." Eventually, the British fled the Carolinas.

> **GUERRILLA WARFARE**
> system of warfare in which the soldiers fight using techniques such as surprise, ambush, and disruption

SWAMP FOX!

The BATTLE of YORKTOWN

Early 1781: Cornwallis moved his troops to YORKTOWN, Virginia, on the banks of the York River. Supplies and money were running low and he needed a port to resupply his troops. Philadelphia and New York were controlled by the British. It was discovered that Benedict Arnold had been plotting to turn over the critical military fort, West Point, and conspiring to capture George Washington. Morale was low.

> Benedict Arnold wasn't the only spy around. **NATHAN HALE**, a young soldier for the Continental army, volunteered to go behind enemy lines and report on British troop activities during the Battle of Long Island. When he was caught and sentenced to hang in 1776, Hale's famous last words were this:
> **"I ONLY REGRET THAT I HAVE BUT ONE LIFE TO LOSE FOR MY COUNTRY."**

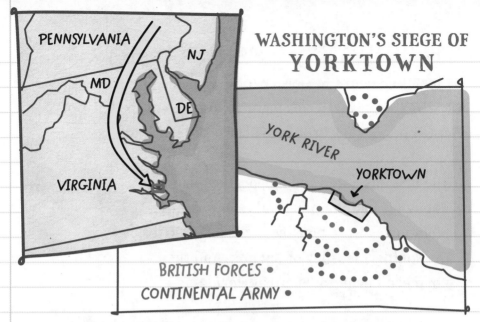

WASHINGTON'S SIEGE OF YORKTOWN

PENNSYLVANIA

NJ

MD

DE

VIRGINIA

YORK RIVER

YORKTOWN

BRITISH FORCES •
CONTINENTAL ARMY •

When Washington learned that Cornwallis had moved into Yorktown, he saw an opportunity. After a fast and top-secret march south, the Continental army (with the help of 7,000 French troops under Lieutenant General Rochambeau) surrounded the city of Yorktown. French ships had already blocked Chesapeake Bay, making it impossible for Cornwallis to escape or get reinforcements.

On October 19, 1781, after weeks of fighting, Cornwallis surrendered.

There were several small battles left to fight, but the war was over. Benjamin Franklin, John Jay, and John Adams began negotiations with the British in Paris to end the conflict. The last British troops left New York Harbor. Washington left for his home in Mount Vernon, Virginia.

The TREATY of PARIS (Again)

It took two years to finish negotiating the 1783 TREATY OF PARIS, but the terms were favorable for the U.S. On September 3, 1783, Britain officially agreed that:

The U.S. was a free and independent nation. Though it had the potential to expand, its boundaries were now the Mississippi River, the southern border of Canada, and the northern border of Spanish Florida.

Americans could fish the waters of British Canada.

Debts would be repaid.

Captured slaves would be returned.

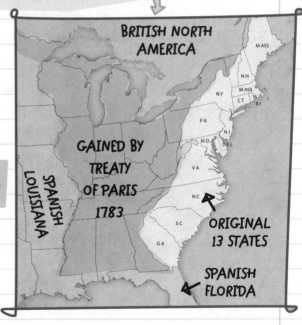

BRITISH NORTH AMERICA

MASS

NH
NY MASS
CT
RI

PA
NJ
MD DEL

VA

GAINED BY TREATY OF PARIS 1783

SPANISH LOUISIANA

NC

SC

ORIGINAL 13 STATES

GA

SPANISH FLORIDA

The Congress agreed to RECOMMEND that property taken from Loyalists be returned. However, many Loyalists fled to New Brunswick and Nova Scotia. Also, Spain got Florida back.

The **1763 TREATY OF PARIS** ended the Seven Years' War.
The **1783 TREATY OF PARIS** ended the Revolutionary War.
A completely different **TREATY OF PARIS**, in 1898,
ended the Spanish-American War.

HOW the WAR WAS WON

So if the British army was better trained and better supplied,
how did the Patriots win?

HOME-FIELD ADVANTAGE

KNOWLEDGE OF THE TERRAIN

MOTIVATION FOR THE CAUSE

CIVILIAN SUPPORT

GREAT LEADERSHIP

HELP FROM FRANCE AND SPAIN

WOMEN IN THE REVOLUTIONARY WAR

With the men away, women took more responsibility for the home front. They also supported the cause of independence: They sewed clothes and made supplies for the army, or became nurses. A few even disguised themselves as men to fight or became spies. One famous example, Mary Ludwig Hays McCauley, was nicknamed **MOLLY PITCHER** because she brought pitchers of water to the soldiers. Although many historians doubt Molly Pitcher existed, her name symbolizes the many women of the Revolutionary War.

AFRICAN AMERICANS IN THE REVOLUTIONARY WAR

At first, African Americans weren't allowed to fight in the Continental army, mainly because the Southern states didn't want to give weapons to slaves. After the British recruited slaves, attitudes changed. A lot of free African Americans served in the army; for example, the **FIRST RHODE ISLAND REGIMENT** consisted of 140 African Americans out of 225 soldiers. By the end of the war, every state except South Carolina included African Americans in their troops.

CHECK YOUR KNOWLEDGE

1. How did people get out of the draft for the Revolutionary War?

2. How long were most American troops contracted to fight at the time of the Revolutionary War?

3. What was the significance of the Battle of Saratoga?

4. What is a privateer?

5. Why was Francis Marion called the "Swamp Fox"?

6. What were the terms of the 1783 Treaty of Paris?

7. How did women participate in the American Revolution?

ANSWERS

1. They paid slaves or apprentices to go instead.

2. One year

3. It was the first major American victory and led to French intervention.

4. A privately owned ship asked by the government to attack the enemy in exchange for whatever they can take

5. He used guerrilla tactics and was hard to catch.

6. American independence and borders were determined. Debts were to be repaid and slaves returned. Americans could fish in British Canada, too.

7. Women made supplies for the army and became nurses. A few also fought, helped soldiers, or became spies.

SWAMP FOX!

AND SWAMP RAT!

WAIT, WHO?

Chapter 12

A NEW GOVERNMENT

Nobody wanted a new tyranny, but they needed a national government.

The ARTICLES of CONFEDERATION

Congress appointed a committee to form a national government.

> **SOVEREIGNTY**
> authority or power

A new national constitution was drafted and called the ARTICLES OF CONFEDERATION. It established a CONFEDERATION CONGRESS, a national legislature responsible for borrowing and creating money, settling arguments between states, dealing with Native Americans, and making treaties. The Congress could ask the states to provide money and soldiers. States could refuse, because they maintained their **SOVEREIGNTY**. Furthermore, each state had one vote regardless of size or population, so they were all equal.

The Continental Congress approved the Articles of Confederation on November 15, 1777, but the Articles still needed to be **RATIFIED**, or confirmed, by the states. Maryland was the last, and in March 1781, the Articles of Confederation became the constitution of a new nation.

> **RATIFY**
> to approve or confirm

The NORTHWEST TERRITORY

It was important for Congress to take control of the western lands, because the U.S. was in debt. It hadn't paid its soldiers yet and needed to sell land to make money. The LAND ORDINANCE OF 1785 split land into TOWNSHIPS that could be sold off. The NORTHWEST ORDINANCE OF 1787 made these plots of land (parts of present-day Illinois, Indiana, Michigan, Ohio, Minnesota, and Wisconsin) the NORTHWEST **TERRITORY**.

NORTHWEST TERRITORY

Territories within the Northwest Territory could apply to become states once they reached a population of 60,000 people and drafted a state constitution. Slavery was banned in them. Land there was cheap; the population quickly increased.

> **TERRITORY**
> in this context, a subdivision of land that is not a state but is governed by the U.S.

DIPLOMATIC and ECONOMIC PROBLEMS

> **LEVY**
> impose, raise

The Articles of Confederation didn't give the government much power. It couldn't **LEVY** taxes to cover the war debt or build a unified army. Britain realized this. They refused to follow through on the terms of the Treaty of Paris and wouldn't allow American ships into its ports. Spain closed the lower Mississippi to U.S. shipping and trade with foreign lands. Other European countries placed high **TARIFFS** on American goods. The war had seriously damaged harvests, particularly in the South, so these states had few crops to trade.

> **TARIFF**
> a charge or duty imposed by the government on imports or exports

Another problem was **INFLATION**. The paper money printed by the Continental Congress during the Revolutionary War had little value, because the states didn't have gold or silver to back it up. The states lowered the

> **INFLATION**
> an economic condition characterized by high prices and a decrease in the value of money

value of paper currency by printing their own bills. The combination of inflation and **TRADE DEFICITS** led to a **DEPRESSION**.

> **TRADE DEFICIT**
> when more goods are coming into the country than going out of it
>
> **DEPRESSION**
> an economic condition characterized by low employment and little economic activity

SHAYS' REBELLION

To pay its war debts, the state of Massachusetts decided to raise taxes on land. Farmers tended to own a lot of land but earn little money, and those who couldn't pay were forced to give up their land or go to jail.

In August of 1786, a farmer and former captain of the Continental army named DANIEL SHAYS began SHAYS' REBELLION.

> **ARSENAL**
> a place where weapons are stored

He and a group of farmers closed down the state courts and marched on the federal **ARSENAL**. The Massachusetts militia finally stopped him and his men. Although Massachusetts had requested federal assistance, it did not receive any, because Congress didn't have the authority to help. If ordinary farmers could launch a revolt, it was clear that the national government needed more power.

The CONSTITUTIONAL CONVENTION

In May 1787, delegates met at a CONSTITUTIONAL CONVENTION in Philadelphia. After electing George

Washington as the president of the convention, they discussed whether to **AMEND** or ditch the Articles of Confederation.

> **AMEND**
> to modify or change, usually by a formal procedure

DON'T MIX UP THESE MEETINGS:

THE CONTINENTAL CONGRESS
↳ signed the Declaration of Independence

THE CONFEDERATION CONGRESS
↳ created by the Articles of Confederation

THE CONSTITUTIONAL CONVENTION
↳ met to fix the Articles of Confederation and ended up creating a whole new Constitution

 ☆ **THE FOUNDING FATHERS OF THE UNITED STATES** ☆

The men who attended the Constitutional Convention, signed the Declaration of Independence, framed the Constitution, and/or helped with the American Revolution are called the **FOUNDING FATHERS** of **THE UNITED STATES**. No women or minorities were invited to sign documents or attend conventions.

The GREAT COMPROMISE

Congress couldn't agree on how states should be represented: a **BICAMERAL** legislature (two houses with votes per state based on the population—the VIRGINIA PLAN) or a **UNICAMERAL** legislature (one house with equal votes for each state—the NEW JERSEY PLAN). The Virginia plan appealed to large states that would have many representatives; smaller states like New Jersey wanted state size not to matter in terms of how much representation you got.

> **BICAMERAL**
> consisting of two chambers as a legislative body
> **UNICAMERAL**
> consisting of a single chamber as a legislative body

Roger Sherman of Connecticut proposed the CONNECTICUT COMPROMISE (the GREAT COMPROMISE), which created the bicameral federal legislature we know today: a SENATE with two votes per state and a HOUSE OF REPRESENTATIVES with representation proportional to each state's population.

VIRGINIA PLAN
BICAMERAL: TWO HOUSES WITH VOTES PER STATE BASED ON POPULATION

NEW JERSEY PLAN
UNICAMERAL: ONE HOUSE WITH EQUAL VOTES PER STATE

CONNECTICUT COMPROMISE
SENATE: TWO VOTES PER STATE
+
HOUSE OF REPRESENTATIVES:
REPRESENTATION BASED ON STATE POPULATION

RECOGNIZING SLAVES... OR NOT

Southern states, which had large slave populations, preferred a system in which slaves counted for representation by size of population—but not taxation. Northern states, which had few slaves, argued that if slaves were considered property, they should count for taxation but NOT representation. The delegates agreed that three-fifths of the slave population would count for both things—a clause called the THREE-FIFTHS COMPROMISE.

HEY, WHAT ABOUT US?

Allowing slaves in a nation founded on the principles of liberty and equality didn't make sense to some delegates. Many Northern states had already banned slavery and wanted to extend that to all the states. Southern states whose wealth depended on slaves disagreed. Georgia and South Carolina threatened to leave the Union if their right to own slaves was taken away. The delegates settled on the SLAVE TRADE COMPROMISE: Importing slaves could not be restricted or abolished until 1808.

The CONSTITUTION

On September 17, 1787, 39 of the 42 delegates who assembled in Philadelphia signed the Constitution. However, it still needed to be ratified so it could take effect. Those who refused to sign, including George Mason of Virginia, felt that a bill of rights—a formal summary of citizens' freedoms—was necessary.

The CONSTITUTION

The new government still operates today. It is based on the principle of **FEDERALISM**: balancing power between the national government and the state governments in a **DIVISION OF POWER**, and balancing strong central authority with **POPULAR SOVEREIGNTY**.

The three branches of federal government are:

THE LEGISLATIVE BRANCH		THE EXECUTIVE BRANCH		THE JUDICIAL BRANCH
the Senate and House of Representatives, where laws are made	**+**	the president and his office, where laws are applied	**+**	the courts, where laws are interpreted

 A system of **SEPARATION OF POWERS** and **CHECKS AND BALANCES** keeps any one branch from getting too powerful.

 The Constitution is the **SUPREME LAW OF THE LAND** and no state can create a law that goes against it.

 The Constitution **CAN BE AMENDED** so that it stays flexible and is a "living document."

FEDERALISM
system of government in which power is shared by the national government and the states

POPULAR SOVEREIGNTY
authority of the people

Just as the Declaration of Independence was inspired by John Locke, the Constitution was influenced and based on Enlightenment philosophy, the Magna Carta, the English Bill of Rights, and Thomas Jefferson's Virginia Statute for Religious Freedom.

FEDERALISTS and ANTIFEDERALISTS

Those who were in favor of ratifying the Constitution called themselves FEDERALISTS. The Federalists promoted their views in a series of essays called the FEDERALIST PAPERS. Written by Alexander Hamilton, James Madison, and John Jay, but published under a pseudonym of "Publius," the FEDERALIST PAPERS argued that the Constitution would protect people from tyranny. The ANTIFEDERALISTS felt that the Constitution gave too much power to the federal government.

In 1788, the Antifederalists published a pamphlet called "**Observations on the New Constitution**." It was written by a woman, **MERCY OTIS WARREN**, the sister of James Otis, the Boston lawyer who argued for no taxation without representation. Warren became a well-respected historian, playwright, and poet.

RATIFICATION of the CONSTITUTION

The Constitution required only nine states to ratify it for it to go into effect. Delaware was the first state to ratify, in December 1787, and when New Hampshire became the ninth in June 1788, the new government had been approved. Virginia and New York, two of the largest and most influential states, had not yet agreed to it. James Madison argued that the Constitution had to be approved as written; no changes could be permitted because it would mean each state was signing a different document. Virginia agreed, and New York soon followed. Two years later, in May 1790, Rhode Island became the last state to ratify. The BILL OF RIGHTS, the first 10 amendments to the Constitution, was ratified in December of 1791.

CHECK YOUR KNOWLEDGE

1. What were the powers of the Confederation Congress?

2. According to the Northwest Ordinance, how could a territory become a state?

3. What was the state of the American economy in the 1780s?

4. Why did Daniel Shays lead a rebellion in Massachusetts?

5. What was the Three-Fifths Compromise?

6. What are the three branches of government?

7. What was the difference between the Federalists and the Antifederalists?

ANSWERS

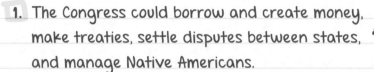

1. The Congress could borrow and create money, make treaties, settle disputes between states, and manage Native Americans.

2. Once it had 60,000 people and a draft of a constitution, it could apply for statehood.

3. Trade was decreasing and there was a lot of inflation. Congress could not raise revenue.

4. Because the state of Massachusetts was taking farmers' land if they could not pay their taxes

5. A clause that stated three-fifths of a slave population would count for both taxes and representation

6. Executive, legislative, and judicial

7. Federalists supported ratifying the Constitution and Antifederalists didn't, believing the new constitution would give too much power to the federal government.

The CONCISE CONSTITUTION

The Constitution is divided into seven ARTICLES, each of which includes SECTIONS. The Constitution also includes a BILL OF RIGHTS, as well as more AMENDMENTS added since it was originally framed.

> You should read the whole thing to get all the details. Considering how **COMPLICATED** government is, the Constitution is really **SHORT**.

The PREAMBLE

The Preamble sets out the reasons for a constitution. It states that the people are establishing the new government. The whole thing:

"**WE THE PEOPLE** of the United States, in Order to form a more perfect Union, establish Justice, insure domestic Tranquility, provide for the common defense, promote the general Welfare, and secure the Blessings of Liberty to ourselves and our **POSTERITY**, do ordain and establish this Constitution for the United States of America."

> **POSTERITY**
> future generations

The ARTICLES

ARTICLE I describes the LEGISLATIVE BRANCH. The Legislature of the U.S. is bicameral: the House of Representatives and the Senate. The vice president of the U.S. is the president of the Senate, but doesn't vote except in a tie. If a majority of the Congress is present, a **QUORUM** is reached, but if not, they can **ADJOURN**. Each **BILL** must be signed by the president before becoming law. If the president **VETOES** the bill, it could still become law if two-thirds of the Congress **OVERRIDES** the veto. Congress has the right to make any laws "necessary and proper" to carry out its power.

QUORUM
the required number of people needed to legally do business

VETO
the power to cancel the actions of another branch of government

ADJOURN
to postpone a meeting to another time

BILL
a draft of a law

Article I, Section 8:18: The "**necessary and proper**" clause is also known as the "elastic clause" because it gives Congress the ability to stretch its powers.

OVERRIDE
to have the final authority

Before the Constitution, government positions were unpaid, and this favored wealthy people who could afford to work for nothing. The Constitution says that congressmen are paid a salary out of the treasury, which is important, because when that wasn't the case, government attracted only wealthy people.

SECTION 8: The powers of Congress are: Levying taxes and tariffs as long as they are uniform throughout the states, paying debts, borrowing money, regulating commerce with other countries/between states/with Native Americans, deciding how people become citizens, making money and regulating it, punishing counterfeiters, making a post office, regulating copyrights, establishing federal courts inferior to the Supreme Court, punishing crimes against international law, declaring war, raising an army or navy and paying them, summoning militias, regulating law in the District of Columbia, and making any other laws "necessary and proper" to do all of that.

SECTION 9: But: No discussing slavery until 1808, no overriding the WRIT OF HABEAS CORPUS (can only arrest a person for a specific cause) except in wartime suspension, no passing a BILL OF ATTAINDER (a law targeting one person or group without a trial), no passing an EX POST FACTO law (a law that applies to people who broke it before it was written), no levying export taxes, no favoring one state in any way, no levying direct taxes on people (aka CAPITATION, no set amount that everyone has to pay in taxes, only taxes determined by income or money spent), no taking money from the treasury without a specific budget being passed as law, and no creating a titled aristocracy.

ARTICLE II describes the EXECUTIVE BRANCH: the president and his duties. The president, like the vice president, serves a four-year term. He receives a salary and takes an oath to protect the Constitution. The powers of the president include serving as COMMANDER-IN-CHIEF of the armed forces; **PARDONING** criminals; nominating ambassadors, judges, and officers; and making treaties, provided that two-thirds of the Senate approves. The president, vice president, and other civil officers may be **IMPEACHED** for treason, bribery, or other misdemeanors and "high crimes."

> **PARDON**
> to release or excuse a person from being punished for an offense

> **IMPEACH**
> to bring an accusation against a government official

ARTICLE III describes the JUDICIARY BRANCH, or the courts, and it establishes a Supreme Court. All judges appointed under Article III (such as judges on the Supreme Court, the federal courts of appeals, and district courts) can hold their jobs for life. In all cases involving ambassadors or entire states, the Supreme Court has **ORIGINAL JURISDICTION**, meaning it's the first court to hear the case.

> **JURISDICTION**
> the authority to administer justice

There is a reason judges hold their jobs for life—it's to prevent them from having to run for reelection or be influenced by politics.

ARTICLE IV defines the relationship between the states and says that the federal government guarantees each state a "REPUBLICAN FORM OF GOVERNMENT."

In the *FEDERALIST PAPERS*, James Madison described a republican form of government as a representative democracy as opposed to a direct democracy. That is, people have control via representatives. Also, a monarch cannot rule the government. The Constitution created a republic—NOT a democracy.

ARTICLE V explains how AMENDMENTS to the Constitution can be proposed and passed.

An amendment requires two-thirds of both the House and Senate and three-fourths of the state legislatures for approval. However, legislators can bypass Congress completely and pass an amendment if two-thirds of the state legislatures approve a call for a convention, which would convene to draft the amendment. Then, the amendment would need three-fourths of the states' approval. This method, however, has never been used.

ARTICLE VI states that the Constitution is the SUPREME LAW OF THE LAND.

ARTICLE VII confirms that the Constitution is established once nine states of the thirteen ratify it.

The AMENDMENTS

The first ten amendments are known as the BILL OF RIGHTS. Ratified in 1791, they protect individual liberties and limit the powers of the federal government.

1. Individual rights: freedom of religion, freedom of speech, freedom of the press, the right to assemble, and the right to petition.

2. The right to bear arms (meaning the right to own and carry weapons).

3. The right not to have soldiers quartered in a person's house without consent of the owner.

4. The right not to have **WARRANTS** issued without probable cause.

> **WARRANT**
> the authorization of an officer to make an arrest, seize property, or make a search

5. The right to due process, meaning that nobody can serve as a witness against himself, and capital crimes cannot be charged without a Grand Jury (except in wartime).

6. The right of the accused to have a speedy and public trial by jury, to know what crime they are charged with, to confront witnesses against them, and to be represented by a lawyer.

7. The right not to have a case reexamined in another court unless according to common law.

8. The right not to have to pay excessive bail or receive cruel or unusual punishments.

9. The right to other rights that may not be listed in the Bill of Rights.

10. The right for states to hold powers not specifically assigned to the federal government.

THE BILL OF RIGHTS CAN BE GROUPED LIKE THIS:

AMENDMENT 1 protects individual rights and minorities from majority rule.

AMENDMENTS 2–4 address mistakes made during the Revolutionary War.

AMENDMENTS 5–8 guarantee rights to people charged with crimes.

AMENDMENTS 9–10 maintain the rights of states and citizens.

Following the Bills of Rights, other amendments were made to the Constitution. There are 27 amendments in total.

Remember the **MAIN PRINCIPLES** of the Constitution:

Popular sovereignty
Limited government
Separation of powers
Checks and balances
Federalism
Republicanism
Individual rights

You can memorize these principles and the fact that Rhode Island was the last state to ratify with this mnemonic device:

Please,
Let's
Sign
Constitutions
Faster,
Rhode
Island.

☆ Chapter 13 ☆
PRESIDENT
PRECEDENTS

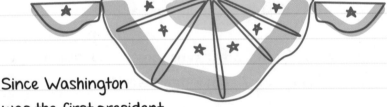

Since Washington
was the first president,
everything he (and FIRST LADY MARTHA WASHINGTON)
did became the start of a tradition, or a PRECEDENT.
For example, Washington chose to be called "Mr. President"
instead of "Your Highness," "Your Excellency," or "Your High
Mightiness" (someone seriously suggested that).

The FIRST PRESIDENT

In early 1789, the states that had
ratified the Constitution decided that an
ELECTORAL COLLEGE would meet and
elect a president. George Washington
was convinced to come out of retirement, and he received

> **ELECTORAL COLLEGE**
> a group that represents
> the people's vote in
> electing a president

ALL the electoral votes. According to the rules of the
Constitution, the person with the second-highest number of
votes was vice president, so
John Adams became the first
vice president. They were
inaugurated on April 30, 1789,
in New York City, then the
nation's temporary capital.

Each state legislature appointed
a certain number of "electors"
(based on its number of
congressmen) to represent their
state and elect a president.
The electoral college system has
changed a lot since then but is
still in practice today.

The CABINET

Congress created departments of the Executive Branch: the
State Department (to deal with other countries), the War
Department (to deal with defense issues), the Treasury (to
deal with the economy), the Justice Department (to deal with
administration of justice), and the Postal Service. Washington
chose these people to head these departments:

**Henry Knox (a general from the
Revolutionary War): Secretary of War**

Thomas Jefferson: Secretary of State

Alexander Hamilton: Secretary of the Treasury

Edmund Randolph: Attorney General

Samuel Osgood: Postmaster General

As a group, these heads of departments were THE CABINET.
The Cabinet (except the postmaster) began to advise the
president, as they do today.

143

The JUDICIARY ACT of 1789

ARTICLE III of the Constitution had few ⟵ ESTABLISHED THE JUDICIARY BRANCH

specifics about a federal court system, so Congress passed the FEDERAL JUDICIARY ACT OF 1789. This established federal courts consisting of thirteen DISTRICT COURTS and three CIRCUIT COURTS OF APPEAL. The states still maintained their own courts, but a federal court could overturn their decisions. The Supreme Court, the final federal court of appeals, would consist of six JUSTICES that were nominated by the president. President Washington nominated John Jay as the first CHIEF JUSTICE of the Supreme Court.

ALEXANDER HAMILTON and the NATIONAL ECONOMY

The new nation faced a huge war debt, with debts to foreign nations, individual citizens, and soldiers who'd been paid with BONDS rather than cash. Alexander Hamilton proposed a three-prong solution in 1790:

The U.S. would pay off all debts, including debts owed by states.

Revenue would be generated by raising tariffs, which should also encourage people to buy American-made goods.

A NATIONAL BANK would be established, owned jointly by the government and private investors, for the government to store money and make loans. A national mint would print paper money.

Hamilton ran into opposition:

The South had paid their few debts, so they saw Congress's decision as rewarding the North's failure to pay.

The South opposed tariffs, which don't benefit an economy that doesn't rely on manufactured goods.

People who lent money to the government in exchange for bonds often sold their bonds for cheap to **SPECULATORS**, who would now get a profit.

SPECULATORS
people who buy items at a lower price with the hope that their value will later increase and they can be sold at a profit

Some people argued that Congress didn't have the right to found a bank.

Hamilton supported a LOOSE CONSTRUCTION VIEW OF THE CONSTITUTION, noting that the ELASTIC CLAUSE of Article I gives Congress the authority to do what is "necessary and proper" to carry out its powers.

Thomas Jefferson and James Madison favored a STRICT CONSTRUCTION VIEW OF THE CONSTITUTION, arguing that the "necessary and proper" clause put stronger limits on what was truly necessary.

While Hamilton seemed to favor businessmen, Jefferson and Madison supported small farmers. While Hamilton advocated for a strong central government, Jefferson and Madison favored local and state governments. The disagreement between "Hamiltonians" and "Jeffersonians" over the scope and extent of federal powers laid the foundation for the first political parties in the U.S.

TWO AGAINST ONE, NO FAIR!

Partly by assuring Southern congressmen that the location of the nation's capital would move, Hamilton was able to convince them to accept his plan. Congress assumed the state debts, enacted low tariffs, and established the Bank of the United States in 1791. The bank had a 20-year charter that would have to be renewed, and states had the right to start their own banks. Washington had tried to stay neutral, but he agreed with Hamilton.

☆ WASHINGTON, D.C. ✳

New York City was a large and bustling metropolis, but some worried that keeping the capital there favored Northern interests. A piece of land on the Potomac River, between Maryland and Virginia but part of neither state, was chosen as the site of a new capital. In 1790, the capital moved temporarily to Philadelphia, and in 1800, Washington, the District of Columbia, became the new capital.

WASHINGTON, D.C.

VA

MD

1801 BORDER, NOW VA

The WHISKEY REBELLION

Alexander Hamilton also encouraged Congress to pass a tax on whiskey. In western Pennsylvania, farmers who grew the corn used to make the whiskey saw the tax as an attack. Many of them used whiskey as money.

In the summer of 1794, farmers attacked tax collectors in the WHISKEY REBELLION. That November, Washington personally led an army to stop the rebellion, and the farmers surrendered right away. Washington proved that the U.S. government was powerful and would use force if its people did not follow the law.

> The **WHISKEY REBELLION** is the only time in U.S. history that a sitting president has personally commanded an army.

The TREATY of GREENVILLE

Native Americans in the Northwest Territory united to fight American expansion into their land, with the support of the British. After many initial successes but a final defeat, 12 tribes signed the 1795 TREATY OF GREENVILLE, **CEDING** most of their land in the Northwest Territory to the U.S.

> **CEDE**
> to yield or formally surrender

The NEUTRALITY PROCLAMATION

In 1789, when the French Revolution began, Americans were supportive of a revolution that seemed similar in spirit to their own. But the French Revolution turned bloody and violent—a period that came to be known as the "Reign of Terror"—and war broke out between the French and other European nations. Jefferson felt that the U.S. shouldn't abandon its ally France—its people were fighting for liberty. Hamilton thought it was more important for the U.S. to protect relations with Britain, its biggest trading partner.

On April 22, 1793, Washington issued the NEUTRALITY PROCLAMATION. Americans wouldn't fight or help EITHER side, and foreign warships couldn't use American ports. Madison argued that only Congress had authority over foreign affairs. Jefferson resigned as secretary of state.

IMPRESSMENT and JAY'S TREATY

The British kidnapped American ships that traded in the French West Indies and forced the American sailors to fight for Britain. This practice, called IMPRESSMENT OF SEAMEN, pushed the U.S. closer to another war with England.

Washington sent Chief Justice John Jay to England to discuss the seized U.S. ships. In 1795, Jay was able to get the British to agree to pay for the losses. JAY'S TREATY prevented another war with Britain, and also:

- **improved trade between the countries**
- **withdrew British troops from western outposts in the U.S.**
- **established commissions to settle border disputes**

WASHINGTON'S FAREWELL

Concerned that he had too much power for one man, and overdue for retirement, George Washington announced in 1796 that he wouldn't be running for a third term (he could've run—there wasn't any precedent about how many terms a president got yet). In his FAREWELL ADDRESS, Washington warned against forming political parties, **FACTIONS**, or "permanent alliances" with foreign nations.

> **FACTION**
> a group that shares a common goal or belief

POLITICAL PARTIES FORM

The disagreements with Jefferson and Madison on one side and Hamilton on the other grew into the first full-fledged parties in American politics.

The DEMOCRATIC-REPUBLICAN PARTY (Jefferson and Madison) supported the ideas of REPUBLICANISM, including

- **strict construction view of the Constitution**
- **reliance on agriculture**
- **the ideal of a nation of small farmers**
- **sympathy for the French**

The Democratic-Republican Party was favored in the South and on the western frontier.

> The Democratic-Republican Party was also just called the Republican Party. It's not related to today's Republican Party. It actually evolved into today's Democratic Party.

The FEDERALIST PARTY (Hamilton) was named after those who had supported the Constitution from the beginning. This party supported:

- **strong, central representative government**
- **loose construction view of the Constitution**
- **reliance on trade (especially with England)**
- **the importance of urban merchants**

Most Federalists did business and lived in urban areas in New England.

CAUCUS
a meeting of party leaders to select candidates

The ELECTION of 1796

The Democratic-Republicans chose Thomas Jefferson to run for president and Aaron Burr to run for vice president at a **CAUCUS**. The Federalists chose John Adams and Charles Pinckney. Adams received the most electoral votes and became president. Jefferson, the runner-up, became vice president.

Jefferson and Adams were former friends who became bitter rivals.

The XYZ AFFAIR

France began attacking American ships, as England had. In 1797, President Adams sent Charles Pinckney, Elbridge Gerry, and John Marshall to Paris to negotiate. The French foreign minister,

This insult outraged Americans and led to the slogan, "Millions for defense but not one CENT for tribute."

TALLEYRAND, refused to meet. Instead, Talleyrand sent three agents to discuss a treaty for a huge bribe. Adams was furious. Referring to the agents as Agent X, Agent Y, and Agent Z, he urged Congress to prepare for war.

Congress expanded the navy, but Adams didn't REALLY want war.

CONSIDERED TO BE THE FATHER OF THE AMERICAN NAVY

The ALIEN and SEDITION ACTS

SEDITION
rebellion against the government

American citizens were now wary of new European immigrants, who might side with the French. Congress passed the **ALIEN AND SEDITION ACTS** in 1798. These controversial laws allowed the president to deport or imprison immigrants in wartime. They also made **SEDITION,** or opposing the government, illegal, taking away basic civil liberties such as freedom of speech and freedom of the press.

The KENTUCKY and VIRGINIA RESOLUTIONS

Democratic-Republicans thought the Alien and Sedition Acts were an abuse of power. Jefferson wrote a resolution for the Kentucky legislature in 1798, and Madison wrote one for Virginia in 1799 (although the authorship was kept secret). The KENTUCKY AND VIRGINIA RESOLUTIONS argued that the Acts were unconstitutional because they interfered with Constitutional rights granted to states. The Kentucky Resolution insisted that states could **NULLIFY** laws they found unconstitutional. The resolutions didn't change the law—Congress just let the Acts expire after Adams left office—but they showed that states could challenge the federal government.

> **NULLIFY**
> to cancel or make void

The CONVENTION of 1800

In 1800, Adams sent another set of delegates to Paris. In the CONVENTION OF 1800, France agreed to stop naval attacks. Adams was pleased, but many Federalists from his own party had wanted a war. And ever since the Alien and Sedition Acts, the Democratic-Republicans saw Adams as an enemy to their cause. When election season rolled around, Adams was in a bad position for reelection.

CHECK YOUR KNOWLEDGE

1. What is the role of the president's cabinet?

2. Who nominates federal justices?

3. Why did Alexander Hamilton support raising tariffs?

4. Why is Washington, D.C., the capital of the U.S.?

5. What caused most Americans to lose enthusiasm for the French Revolution?

6. What did Washington say in his Farewell Address?

7. What was the justification for the doctrine of nullification supported by the Kentucky Resolution?

FAREWELL AND DON'T FORGET MY WARNINGS!

ANSWERS

CHECK YOUR ANSWERS

1. To advise the president
2. The president
3. To raise revenue and encourage people to buy American goods
4. It was a compromise to move the capital closer to a neutral location that was not part of any state and between the North and South.
5. The Reign of Terror
6. He advised the nation to avoid forming political parties, factions, and permanent alliances with foreign countries.
7. That the states have rights that the federal government cannot alter, so the states can declare acts unconstitutional and nullify them

Unit 4

American Expansion
1801–1861

The first half of the nineteenth century was a period of expansion. The continental U.S. grew to fill the borders it has today, and the population skyrocketed. Changes created both new tensions and new opportunities.

☆ Chapter 14 ☆

PRESIDENT THOMAS
★ ★ ★ ★ ★ ★ ★ ★ ★ ★ ★
JEFFERSON

The ELECTION of 1800

Democratic-Republicans tried to paint Federalist candidate John Adams as a monarchist. Adams tried to label Thomas Jefferson, the Democratic-Republican candidate, as a radical and an **ATHEIST**. Adams clearly lost, but Jefferson tied with Aaron Burr, at 73 votes in the electoral college.

> **ATHEIST**
> a person who rejects the belief in gods

The House of Representatives (mostly Federalists) voted THIRTY-FIVE TIMES trying to break the tie. Finally, Alexander Hamilton convinced a congressman not to vote for Burr. Thomas Jefferson became the third president of the U.S.

Hamilton and Burr became bitter enemies.

> This was the first time in history that there was a peaceful transfer of power between opposing political parties.

> The mess of trying to break the tie led to the **TWELFTH AMENDMENT** in 1803, which made the election of the president and vice president two separate ballots.

JEFFERSON as PRESIDENT

Jefferson emphasized the central stances of the Democratic-Republican Party:

limited government with a **LAISSEZ-FAIRE** approach

focus on agriculture

political unity through individual independence

Taxes were repealed, the Alien and Sedition Acts expired, the military and military spending shrank, and the number of employees working for the federal government decreased.

> **LAISSEZ-FAIRE**
> French for "leave it alone," a theory, particularly in economics, that insists on minimal government intervention

The MIDNIGHT JUDGES

At the very end of Adams's presidency, Congress had passed the JUDICIARY ACT OF 1801, creating new federal judge positions. Once the judges were in office, they would keep their jobs for life, so Adams made sure to appoint them before he left. Because of the last-minute timing, they were called the "MIDNIGHT JUDGES."

When Jefferson became president, some of the judges hadn't yet gotten their COMMISSIONS, the documents that made it official. It was the job of the new secretary of state, JAMES MADISON, to deliver the commissions, but Jefferson told Madison, well, just not to deliver them. One of the judges left in limbo was WILLIAM MARBURY.

MARBURY v. MADISON (1803)

It gets complicated and there's *Latin*, but it's important. Marbury took his case straight to the Supreme Court, where he requested a WRIT OF MANDAMUS against James Madison, which basically asked the court to force Madison to give him his commission. The JUDICIARY ACT OF 1789 gave the Supreme Court the power to settle the case. Although CHIEF JUSTICE JOHN MARSHALL agreed that Marbury deserved his commission, he ruled against Marbury, saying the Supreme Court didn't have the power to grant the writ and settle the case because:

> Congress had no right to pass the Judiciary Act of 1789 in the first place.

> The Constitution is the "supreme law," so when the Constitution and the law were in disagreement, the Supreme Court could cancel out the law.

The case of *MARBURY v. MADISON* is important because it established **JUDICIAL REVIEW**: the power of the Supreme Court to nullify a law by

> **JUDICIAL REVIEW**
> the power to declare an act of Congress unconstitutional

declaring it unconstitutional. It made the Supreme Court equal in power and status to the executive and legislative branches. *MARBURY v. MADISON* strengthened the idea of checks and balances in the federal government and made the Supreme Court the final word on the constitutionality of the law.

WESTERN EXPANSION

KENTUCKY was admitted to the Union in 1792, TENNESSEE joined soon after in 1796, and OHIO in 1803. The Mississippi River was officially the western border, but Americans kept moving and kept pushing the limits. Merchants wanted to use the Mississippi River to conduct trade. Spain controlled the river and its major port, New Orleans . . .

The LOUISIANA PURCHASE

... but they didn't own it. Spain had secretly traded the Louisiana Territory (all of the land between the Mississippi and the Rocky Mountains, including New Orleans) to France in 1800. In 1802, Spain closed the port to American shipping. NAPOLEON BONAPARTE, the ruler of France, was planning to expand his empire in the Americas, using New Orleans as a critical point of entry for troops headed to the country. New Orleans also controlled the Mississippi River, which was a major port of exit for goods from the American West. France was essentially threatening the sovereignty and economic stability of the U.S.

Jefferson sent ROBERT R. LIVINGSTON and JAMES MONROE to France to meet with Minister Talleyrand ← ASKED FOR A BRIBE IN 1798

to discuss buying the territory of New Orleans, but they got a surprise. Haitian leader TOUSSAINT-LOUVERTURE led a slave revolt that forced the French out of Haiti. ← FRENCH TROOPS WERE ALSO DECIMATED BY YELLOW FEVER. France was losing interest in the Americas and needed to fund its war with England.

BURR v. HAMILTON

Concerned that the newly acquired lands would soon be filled with Democratic-Republicans, some Federalists discussed **SECEDING** and becoming a "Northern Confederacy," a separate union that would include New York. They encouraged Aaron Burr, who had been **OSTRACIZED** by his own party for not dropping out of the race during his tie with Jefferson, to run for governor of New York. Burr lost (he was sitting vice president at the time).

Burr blamed Alexander Hamilton for ruining his reputation and challenged Hamilton to a duel. In July 1804, Hamilton claimed he was opposed to dueling, and he may have chosen not to shoot at his opponent, or it may have been a mistake, but Burr shot Hamilton. Alexander Hamilton died from wounds from the duel 30 hours later.

SECEDE
to formally withdraw from an alliance or association

OSTRACIZE
to exclude by general consent

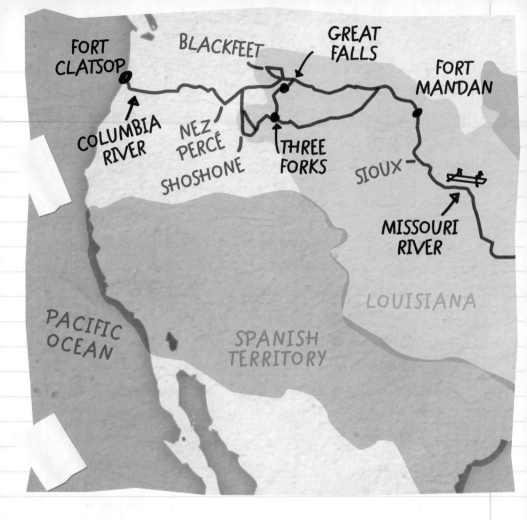

Talleyrand offered to sell them the whole Louisiana Territory, which was larger than the entire U.S.

The price of $15 million was a bargain (roughly 3 cents an acre). In October 1803, the LOUISIANA PURCHASE extended the borders of the U.S. to the Rocky Mountains (despite its questionable constitutionality).

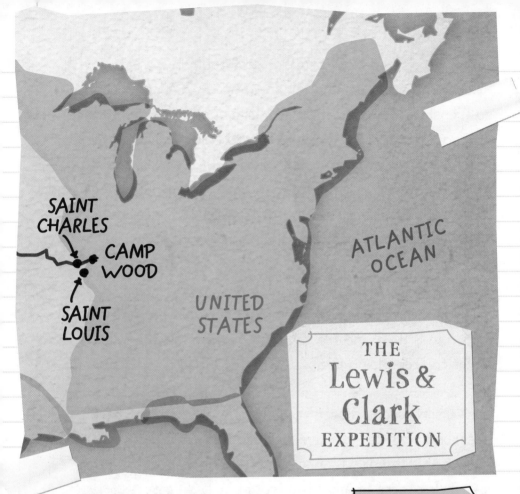

SAINT
CHARLES

CAMP
WOOD

SAINT
LOUIS

UNITED
STATES

ATLANTIC
OCEAN

THE
Lewis &
Clark
EXPEDITION

LEWIS and CLARK

Congress chose Captain Meriwether Lewis and Lieutenant William Clark to lead an exploration of the West. Their group of about 50 men—the "**CORPS**

CORPS
a group of people acting together under a common direction (the P and the S are silent)

OF DISCOVERY"—set out to map the new land. In May of 1804, the LEWIS AND CLARK EXPEDITION left St. Louis and followed the Missouri River. By winter, they had reached modern-day North Dakota.

When Lewis and Clark headed west again in the spring, a young Shoshone woman named SACAGAWEA, her husband (a French trader), and their newborn baby went with them. Sacagawea was the interpreter and guide. Following the Columbia River on the western side of the Rockies, they came into sight of the Pacific Ocean in November of 1805. Lewis and Clark returned home the next year filled with information. Their experiences inspired enthusiasm for the West.

TRADE TROUBLES

Even though the U.S. had remained neutral in the conflict between Britain and France, each of them tried to stop America from doing business with the other.

Jefferson, who had been reelected to a second presidential term, decided to punish England and France by cutting off their access to American trade altogether. In December 1807, Congress

EMBARGO
a government order prohibiting commercial ships sailing into or out of its ports

passed the **EMBARGO ACT**, ending all international trade between the U.S. and the rest of the world. Britain and France just traded with other countries instead. It was a disaster for American merchants and for Jefferson's image.

James Madison (Democratic-Republican) won the next presidential election.

CHECK YOUR KNOWLEDGE

1. How was the tie in the election of 1800 broken?

2. What were the central stances of the Democratic-Republican Party?

3. To whom does the term "midnight judges" refer?

4. What was the decision in the case *MARBURY v. MADISON*?

5. Why were the Mississippi River and the port of New Orleans important?

6. What did Napoleon Bonaparte intend to do with the Louisiana Territory?

7. How did Alexander Hamilton die?

8. Which route did Lewis and Clark take to the Pacific?

ANSWERS

CHECK YOUR ANSWERS

1. Hamilton convinced a congressman not to vote for Burr.

2. Limited government and laissez-faire economics, individual participation in government, and agriculture

3. It refers to the judges appointed by President Adams right before he left office.

4. Marbury had a right to his commission, but Congress had no right to extend the jurisdiction of the Supreme Court to apply to the case.

5. Because merchants wanted to use the Mississippi River to conduct trade

6. He would use it as a point of entry to gain holdings in America.

7. He was mortally wounded in a duel with Aaron Burr.

8. The Missouri River

☆ Chapter 15 ☆

The ☆ WAR ☆ of ☆ 1812 and OTHER FAILURES to COMMUNICATE

TECUMSEH and WESTERN WORRIES

Native Americans in the Northwest and Louisiana Territories were determined to hold on to their land. Led by Shawnee chief TECUMSEH, who was supported by Great Britain, several tribes united to fight settlers.

WILLIAM HENRY HARRISON, governor of Indiana Territory, sent a warning to Tecumseh, urging him to stick to the terms of past agreements. Tecumseh responded that the few chiefs who signed the treaties didn't have authority to represent other tribes and give away their land.

The BATTLE of TIPPECANOE

While Tecumseh headed south to convince the Creek Nation tribe to join his forces, Harrison attacked and defeated the

Shawnee people near the Tippecanoe River in 1811 at the BATTLE OF TIPPECANOE. Tecumseh crossed to Canada to join the British troops.

DEMANDS for WAR

Once again, war with the British seemed inevitable. **WAR HAWKS**, as they were called, were frustrated by the British practice of impressments and determined to acquire new land and more power for their new nation. The British were also inciting Native American unrest on the frontier. On June 18, 1812—the first time Congress had declared war—the WAR OF 1812 began. That fall, James Madison was elected to his second term as president.

The WAR of 1812 BEGINS

The first American plan of attack was to invade Canada, but the British and their Native American allies seized Detroit before the Americans could head north. It was also difficult to invade Canada because the British controlled Lake Erie. Commodore OLIVER HAZARD PERRY, the naval officer in charge of the Lake Erie forces, was ordered to seize the lake from the British. Even after his ship was destroyed, Perry continued to fight. The British eventually surrendered on September 10, 1813, making Perry a national hero and paving the way to invade Canada.

After his victory, Perry sent a message to Harrison: "We have met the enemy and they are ours."

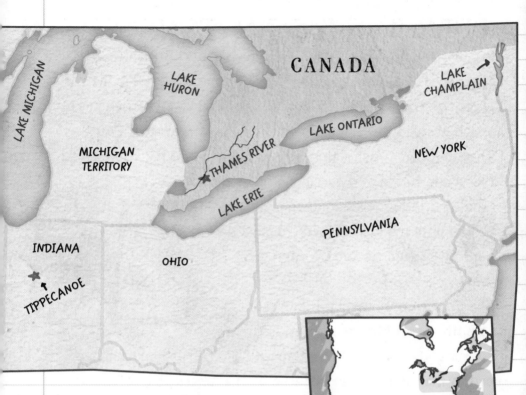

In October 1813, William Henry
Harrison—commanding the troops
in the area—defeated the British
and their Native American allies near the U.S.-Canadian
border. The BATTLE OF THE THAMES killed both Tecumseh and
any alliance with the Creek Nation. Although the Americans
had pushed the British out of the area, battles with Native
Americans, including the CREEK WAR, continued. In March
1814, ANDREW JACKSON, leader of the Tennessee militia,
defeated the Creek Nation in the BATTLE OF HORSESHOE
BEND, forcing them to sign the TREATY OF FORT JACKSON and
lose even more land.

ATTACK on WASHINGTON, D.C.

By 1814, Napoleon had fallen from power and British forces could focus on enemies to the west. On August 24, 1814, the American troops were defeated in the Battle of Bladensburg, which allowed the British to sail into the Chesapeake Bay. They invaded Washington, D.C., setting fire to the Capitol and the White House and forcing President Madison to flee. (The first lady, Dolley Madison, stayed behind until the last moment to save a portrait of George Washington.)

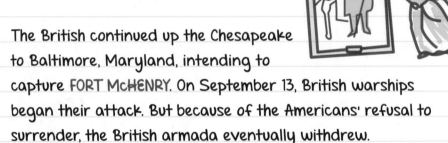

The British continued up the Chesapeake to Baltimore, Maryland, intending to capture FORT McHENRY. On September 13, British warships began their attack. But because of the Americans' refusal to surrender, the British armada eventually withdrew.

"The Star-Spangled Banner"

Before the British attack on Baltimore, Americans raised a large flag over Fort McHenry. When **FRANCIS SCOTT KEY**, a lawyer who had witnessed the night-long bombardment, saw at dawn that the flag was still there, he was so moved that he wrote a poem to it. The poem was later set to music, and it eventually became the U.S. national anthem.

CAPITAL VS. CAPITOL

A **capital** (with an "a") is a city or place that is the official seat of government of a country or state. The **Capitol** (with an "o") is a building in Washington with a famous dome and is named after an ancient Roman hill called the Capitoline.

The BATTLE of LAKE CHAMPLAIN and the BATTLE of NEW ORLEANS

In September 1814, British forces trying to seize the city of Plattsburgh, New York, faced the U.S. Navy at Lake Champlain. The Americans refused to surrender in the BATTLE OF LAKE CHAMPLAIN, and the British retreated.

The British forces in the South decided to attack New Orleans. As they advanced on Louisiana on January 8, 1815, an army organized by Andrew Jackson waited. Marching in their typical style across an open field, the British were easy targets. Winning the BATTLE OF NEW ORLEANS boosted Jackson's popularity. It was the final battle of the War of 1812—and it occurred after the war had officially ended.

NEW ORLEANS

The END of WAR

The British decided war wasn't worth the effort and reached an agreement with the Americans. But the news didn't reach Andrew Jackson or the Federalists. On December 15, 1814, Federalists met at the HARTFORD CONVENTION to show opposition to the war. Little did they know that on December 24, 1814, the British and Americans had signed the TREATY OF GHENT in Belgium. The Hartford Convention embarrassed the Federalists for opposing a war that was already won.

The Treaty of Ghent did not resolve border and trade disputes between the U.S. and Britain, but it increased patriotism. While the treaty returned the countries to the way things were before the war, Americans were proud to have held their own. Because the War of 1812 cemented America's independence, it is also called "America's Second War for Independence." American manufacturers profited, since British goods weren't available. The nation seemed destined for success.

CHECK YOUR KNOWLEDGE

1. How did Tecumseh try to protect Native American lands?

2. Who were the "war hawks" and what did they want?

3. What was the first time Congress ever declared war?

4. When did the U.S. push the British out of the Northeast?

5. What inspired "The Star-Spangled Banner"?

6. What was the last battle of the War of 1812?

7. What effect did the War of 1812 have on the national mood?

ANSWERS

CHECK YOUR ANSWERS

1. He led several united tribes to fight settlers.
2. They were people who wanted war with England.
3. The War of 1812, on June 18, 1812
4. After the Battle of the Thames, in October 1813
5. Francis Scott Key was inspired by troops at Fort McHenry defending Baltimore from the British.
6. The Battle of New Orleans, which took place after the war ended
7. Patriotism increased, as did confidence in the success of the nation.

A PEEK INTO
AMERICAN LIFE
★ in the ★
EARLY 1800s

The INDUSTRIAL REVOLUTION

The American Industrial Revolution is said to have begun in Rhode Island in 1793, when SAMUEL SLATER built the first American spinning mill, a factory that makes cloth. Rhode Island's geography was perfect for water-powered mills, and the War of 1812 made it tough to get imported goods, inspiring Americans to find more efficient ways to produce their own. The most famous factory was a textile mill started by Francis Cabot Lowell in 1814 and mostly employed young women. It was so successful that it led to the founding of an entire town, called LOWELL, MASSACHUSETTS. The "Lowell girls" were paid well, but they worked long hours in grueling conditions.

 The **INDUSTRIAL REVOLUTION** was the first time many people in America needed a clock. On a farm, you can plan your day by the movement of the sun; in a factory, not so much.

The Industrial Revolution was a time of great innovation.

NEW TECHNOLOGY
OF THE ERA INCLUDED:

INTERCHANGEABLE PARTS: First introduced by **ELI WHITNEY** (who invented the **COTTON GIN**) for muskets for the army, these pre-manufactured, identical parts created the possibility of **MASS PRODUCTION**.

The **TELEGRAPH**, invented by **SAMUEL F. B. MORSE** in 1837, improved communication. Using **MORSE CODE**, telegraphs sent short pulses of energy along a wire that were translated into letters that spelled out messages.

STEAM POWER:
The **STEAMBOAT**, perfected by **ROBERT FULTON** in 1807, improved river transportation.

The **STEAM LOCOMOTIVE**, created by **PETER COOPER** in 1830, improved land transportation and led to the development of railroads.

Once **STEAM ENGINES** were improved by JAMES WATT in 1780, factories no longer had to be located near rivers.

New technology helped people who were headed west. They could now use better agricultural tools, like the JOHN DEERE PLOW and the McCORMICK REAPER. Wheat became a cash crop, cities such as Chicago sprang up, farms in the Midwest began to supply the factory workers in the Northeast with food, and the Northeast began to supply the Midwest with manufactured goods. Large distances seemed to become smaller, thanks to American innovation.

One of the most significant inventions was the COTTON GIN. Invented by Eli Whitney in 1793, it could clean seeds from cotton quickly. It allowed plantation owners in the South to speed up harvests so that workers in the North could make more cotton goods.

On the flip side, however, the cotton gin also increased the use of slaves. Plantation owners, who only made up about three percent of the Southern population, made even more profit. In the Deep South, cotton was "king," and there was no incentive for anything else.

Other Southern whites earned livings as YEOMEN, small-scale farmers who owned land but no slaves, or TENANT FARMERS, who rented their land. These people tended to be poor.

SLAVE LIFE

By 1808, the international slave trade was abolished. The domestic slave trade increased to make up for it. By the early part of the century, almost every slave in the U.S. had been born into slavery.

Some slaves were determined to win their freedom. NAT TURNER, one of the most famous slave rebels, led a violent uprising in 1831 in Virginia. Turner was hanged, and NAT TURNER'S REBELLION scared many Southerners and hardened their position. Some states passed even harsher laws to control slaves.

Chapter 16

NEW AMERICAN BORDERS

After the War of 1812, feelings of **NATIONALISM** spread through the U.S.

> **NATIONALISM**
> patriotism; a sense of national identity

NATIONALISM and the ERA of GOOD FEELING

James Monroe was elected America's fifth president in 1816 with little opposition from the now-fractured Federalist Party. Monroe toured the country and was widely supported and welcomed everywhere he went. This era was marked by so little disagreement about national politics that it was called the ERA OF GOOD FEELING. In 1820, Monroe was reelected almost unanimously.

ERA OF GOOD FEELING? ANYONE WITHOUT THE RIGHT TO VOTE PROBABLY THOUGHT OTHERWISE...

The AMERICAN SYSTEM

In order to strengthen the national economy and further promote national unity, HENRY CLAY, Speaker of the House, proposed a program called the AMERICAN SYSTEM:

> A Bank of the United States would issue a single U.S. currency.

> Protective tariffs would be increased to encourage American manufacturing.

> Money generated from tariffs would be spent building roads and canals (public works).

The Bank, whose original charter expired in 1811, received a new charter in 1816 and was called the Second Bank of the United States, but it was still controversial. The South opposed tariffs because they hurt their economy. And some people argued that the Constitution did not say that Congress could spend money on public works within the individual states.

Congress had already approved the construction of the CUMBERLAND ROAD from Cumberland, Maryland, to Vandalia, Illinois (later called the NATIONAL ROAD). Congress also invested in the ERIE CANAL, built almost entirely by hand between 1817 and 1825, to connect New York City with the Great Lakes region. The Erie Canal led to increased trade and a population surge in the Midwest. It inspired the building of many more canals in pre-railroad era America.

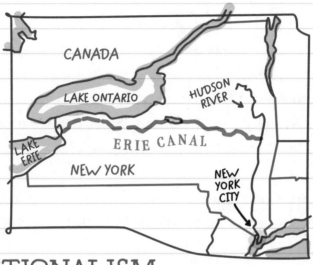

SECTIONALISM

As nationalism grew, SECTIONALISM, or the importance of regional and state identity, also grew. As always, the Northeast focused on factories and trade, the South relied on plantations, and now the West was a place for people to exploit new land.

This created regional politics: The North advocated for high tariffs so that people would buy American-made goods. The South supported slavery, and they also supported low tariffs, because they imported most of their goods.

Northerners wanted the government to sell its land at a high price to discourage poor workers from leaving the cities, but Westerners wanted the government to sell them land at a low price and give them roads and other public improvements.

The MISSOURI COMPROMISE

A conflict rooted in sectionalism happened when Missouri applied for statehood in 1817. At the time, the U.S. consisted of 11 slave states and 11 free states. If Missouri entered the Union as a slave state, as it wanted, it would upset a balance of power in the Senate between slave and free states.

In 1820, Henry Clay came up with a solution for the land from the Louisiana Purchase—the MISSOURI COMPROMISE.

Missouri would enter the Union as a slave state, but Maine, which was still a part of Massachusetts, would enter at the same time as a free state. In all future applications for statehood, slavery would be illegal north of the southern border of Missouri, at latitude 36°30'. The Missouri Compromise divided the land from the Louisiana Purchase into two different regions defined by slavery. Slavery was increasingly becoming an issue that divided the North and South.

RELATIONS with ENGLAND and SPAIN

The U.S. and Britain agreed that neither nation would maintain a navy in the Great Lakes region or along the U.S.-Canada border. A demilitarized border between the U.S. and Canada was created at the **49TH PARALLEL**, stretching as far west as the Rocky Mountains.

> **PARALLEL**
> another word for a line of latitude

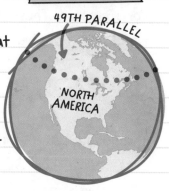

49TH PARALLEL

NORTH AMERICA

Relations between the U.S. and Britain improved, but tensions with Spain were high. The U.S. claimed western Florida belonged to the U.S. because it was part of the Louisiana Purchase. Spain disagreed. As American settlers moved into the Florida territory, the Seminole Indians native to the area raided the settlements and helped slaves escape.

In April 1818, without government permission, Andrew Jackson invaded Spanish territory and captured two Spanish forts,

UNITED STATES
FORT SCOTT
PENSACOLA
ST. MARKS
SUWANEE
SPANISH FLORIDA

starting the FIRST SEMINOLE WAR. Instead of punishing Jackson, and knowing that Spain could not fight back, Secretary of State JOHN QUINCY ADAMS (former President Adams's son) gave Spain two choices: They could police their territory or sell it. Spain sold Florida and their claims to part of the Pacific Northwest to the U.S. for $5 million. These military campaigns enhanced Jackson's reputation as a hero.

The MONROE DOCTRINE

Spain was losing territories not only in the U.S. but also throughout Latin America. SÍMON BOLÍVAR led revolutions to free people from Spanish rule. MIGUEL HIDALGO Y COSTILLA won independence for Mexico in 1821. When France, Russia, Prussia, and Austria discussed helping Spain regain their land, Monroe feared that European countries would also attempt to recolonize territories in the Americas.

On December 2, 1823, Monroe issued the MONROE DOCTRINE. It established American foreign policy for years to come and set the stage for America to become a world power.

Its three major points were that:

1. European interference in U.S. affairs would not be tolerated and the U.S. would stay **NEUTRAL** in European colonies or conflicts.

2. The U.S. wouldn't tolerate **NEW COLONIZATION** of the Americas.

3. Any attempt by Europe to further colonize the Americas would be considered an act of **AGGRESSION**.

The ELECTION of 1824

POPULAR VOTE
method of electing a candidate based on a majority of votes.

All of the candidates of the 1824 presidential election considered themselves to be in the same party. However, there was no agreed-upon way of nominating a candidate for the presidency. The North was in favor of John Quincy Adams, the South supported Andrew Jackson or William Crawford, and the West wanted Henry Clay or Andrew Jackson. Andrew Jackson won the **POPULAR VOTE** but didn't receive a majority of electoral votes.

Jackson got the most votes—about 40%—but **NOT** a majority.

ELECTORAL VOTES:	POPULAR VOTE:
JACKSON: 99	151,271
J.Q. ADAMS: 84	113,122
CRAWFORD: 41	40,856
CLAY: 37	47,531

NO CANDIDATE WON A MAJORITY OF THE ELECTORAL COLLEGE VOTE—THERE WERE TOO MANY CANDIDATES

According to the Constitution, the House of Representatives would decide the winner in that situation. Henry Clay, the Speaker of the House, who finished in last place, convinced his colleagues to vote for John Quincy Adams. When Adams became the country's sixth president and appointed Clay as his secretary of state, his opponents argued that a backroom deal had been made.

THE ELECTION of 1828 and JACKSONIAN DEMOCRACY

"OLD HICKORY"

The bitterness and anger over the 1824 election led to the development of two new political parties: The Democrats supported Jackson; the National Republicans supported Adams. Jackson was a hardworking national war hero nicknamed "OLD HICKORY" for his toughness. He won an overwhelming victory, and JOHN C. CALHOUN, who had been John Quincy Adams's vice president, became his vice president.

> **SUFFRAGE**
> the right to vote

One reason for Jackson's victory was that he promoted expanding democratic privileges to a wider population. Called JACKSONIAN DEMOCRACY, this movement included the extension of **SUFFRAGE**. Before, only white men who owned property or paid taxes could vote, but Jackson loosened these restrictions to include more white men—free blacks and women still couldn't vote. Jackson's win was considered a triumph for the common man.

Jackson began to replace government bureaucrats with his friends and supporters. Called the SPOILS SYSTEM, this was criticized as favoritism and political payback, but Jackson argued that it was good to clean house. Jackson appointed MARTIN VAN BUREN as secretary of state and depended on his advice. He also relied on his "KITCHEN CABINET," friends who gave him advice, often in the White House kitchen.

TARIFFS and the NULLIFICATION CRISIS

Before Jackson took office, Congress raised tariffs on raw materials and manufactured goods so much that the South called it the TARIFF OF ABOMINATIONS. The South argued that the tariff was unconstitutional because it favored one region over another. Also, the states could nullify laws that were unconstitutional because of the THEORY OF STATE SOVEREIGNTY, which says that the power of the federal government comes from the states and that the states are more powerful.

In the NULLIFICATION ACT OF 1832, South Carolina declared a federal tariff null and void, and threatened to secede from the Union. Jackson pushed for Congress to pass the FORCE BILL to allow him to use the army to enforce the tariff. In 1833, Henry Clay came up with a plan that would gradually reduce the tariff. South Carolina agreed to the compromise. When Jackson was reelected, he showed support for state rights by vetoing a renewal of the charter for the Second Bank of the United States, moving money to state banks.

None of this resolved the debate about states' rights, which has never ended.

The WHIG PARTY and the PANIC of 1837

MORE WIGS, FEWER CROWNS!

Partly in opposition to Jackson's destruction of the Second Bank of the United States, a new political party formed. The WHIG PARTY was formed in opposition to what they saw as a danger of majority parties. Led by Henry Clay, the Whig Party nominated three candidates for president in 1836 in hopes of throwing the election. They took their name from the English anti-monarchy party because they were opposed to the popular vote choosing electors. They felt it led to the tyranny of "King Andrew" Jackson. However, Van Buren, the presidential nominee for Jackson's supporters, now called the DEMOCRATS, still won and took office in 1837 as the eighth president.

By then the economic boom of Jackson's presidency was over. During the PANIC OF 1837, the values of land, cotton, and paper money decreased, leading to terrible inflation. The previous year, Jackson had attempted to make it illegal for people to use paper money to buy inexpensive land, demanding gold or silver instead, but this policy didn't work; nevertheless, he remained a national hero. Van Buren, not Jackson, was blamed for the depression that followed, particularly because he believed in laissez-faire economic policies.

"TIPPECANOE and TYLER TOO"

In 1840, the Whig Party nominated William Henry Harrison for president and JOHN TYLER for vice president. Using a log cabin as their symbol, the Whig Party tried to show that Harrison was a common man from the Ohio frontier while Van Buren was a man of privilege. (Harrison also came from a rich family, so...) Their personal attacks on Van Buren are called the LOG CABIN CAMPAIGN.

The Whigs also used the catchy slogan "TIPPECANOE AND TYLER TOO" to emphasize Harrison's past as a war hero at the Battle of Tippecanoe. The Whigs' plan worked, and William Henry Harrison was elected the ninth president.

On Inauguration Day, which was bitterly cold, Harrison (who was 68 years old) didn't wear a coat while he delivered his speech, probably to show he was a tough war hero.

LONGEST INAUGURAL ADDRESS IN HISTORY! BRRR!

He caught pneumonia and died about a month later. Tyler became president and went back to the beliefs of his former party, the Democratic Party. Like the other parties, the Whig Party was destined to fall victim to sectional differences.

FIRST TIME A PRESIDENT DIED IN OFFICE AND WAS SUCCEEDED BY HIS VICE PRESIDENT. ALSO SHORTEST PRESIDENCY!

???

BAH!

CHECK YOUR KNOWLEDGE

1. Why was the period after the War of 1812 known as the Era of Good Feeling?

2. What are the three major points of the Monroe Doctrine?

3. Name a factor behind increased sectionalism at the end of the Era of Good Feeling.

4. What were the terms of the Missouri Compromise?

5. What is the theory of state sovereignty?

6. How did Jackson try to stop the economic problems that led to the Panic of 1837?

7. What were the values of the Whig Party?

ANSWERS

CHECK YOUR ANSWERS

1. Nationalism increased and partisanship decreased during that time.

2. American neutrality, no more colonies in the future and that European intervention in the Americas would be considered an act of aggression

3. Each region's economy became even more specialized and different from the other's.

4. Missouri would be a slave state, Maine would be free, and all further states north of 36°30' would be free.

5. That federal power comes from the states, so states are the most powerful body in government

6. He tried to make it illegal for people to use paper money to buy inexpensive land—he demanded gold or silver instead.

7. They were against majority parties having too much power and potential presidential "tyranny."

☆ Chapter 17 ☆

WESTWARD ☆ ☆ ☆ HO! ☆ ☆ ☆

Americans looked west for new opportunities. New canals, railroads, and roads made travel easier, and LAND SPECULATORS, who had bought up large quantities of land, allowed families to make a fresh start by selling them parcels of that land (at a big profit). By the 1830s, a total of 26 states had been admitted to the Union, including Illinois, Alabama, and Michigan.

The INDIAN REMOVAL ACT

Native Americans already lived on the land settlers wanted. President Jackson believed that it was impossible for Native Americans to live as independent nations within what had become the borders of the U.S. He felt that they should either become U.S. citizens or leave.

In 1830, he encouraged Congress to pass the INDIAN REMOVAL ACT, which authorized the federal government to force the Native Americans of the Southeast, who lived on valuable farmland, off their land. The plan was to send them to the Great Plains, which Congress mistakenly believed was barren, worthless desert. Congress selected an area of modern-day Oklahoma to be INDIAN TERRITORY (also known as a RESERVATION). Within the next few years, Congress also established the BUREAU OF INDIAN AFFAIRS to manage the removal and transport of Native Americans.

The "FIVE CIVILIZED TRIBES" of the Southeast (Cherokee, Chickasaw, Choctaw, Creek, and Seminole) had already assimilated into American culture to varying degrees. They hoped that doing so would benefit them in some way, but they had little leverage against the U.S. government.

The TRAIL of TEARS

The Cherokee of Georgia were the most assimilated of the Southeast tribes, but the state of Georgia had motivation to DISPLACE them: In 1828, gold had been found on their land.

> **DISPLACE**
> to force people to leave their home or country

The Cherokees were part of a separate nation recognized in an eighteenth-century treaty, and they had a deep understanding of American law. They took their case to the Supreme Court. In 1832, in the case of WORCESTER v. GEORGIA, the Supreme Court ruled the Cherokees were a sovereign nation and that only the federal government (not Georgia) had the power to

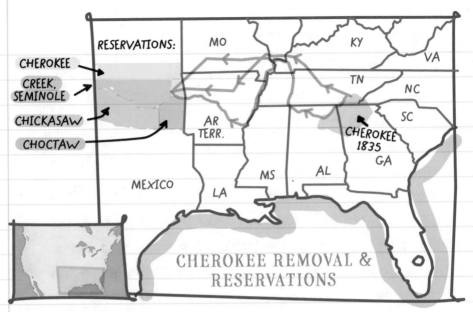

RESERVATIONS:

CHEROKEE

CREEK, SEMINOLE

CHICKASAW

CHOCTAW

MO

KY

VA

TN

NC

AR TERR.

SC

CHEROKEE 1835

GA

MS

AL

MEXICO

LA

CHEROKEE REMOVAL & RESERVATIONS

form a treaty with another nation (to move the Cherokees off their land). Both the state of Georgia and President Jackson decided to ignore the ruling. The Supreme Court had no power to enforce it.

In 1835, Congress was able to persuade a very small number of Cherokees to sign a treaty ceding their land, and the government decided that this counted as agreement of the entire tribe. President Van Buren sent GENERAL WINFIELD SCOTT and thousands of U.S. Army troops to invade the Cherokee Nation in 1838. Sixteen thousand Cherokees were moved into holding camps and then forced to go to their new land. During their 800-mile trek to Indian Territory, a quarter of the population died from disease, starvation, and harsh weather conditions. Their painful march became known as the TRAIL OF TEARS.

OTHER RESISTANCE to the INDIAN REMOVAL ACT

In Florida, the Seminoles also resisted being displaced. Although they were forced to sign removal treaties too, their chief, OSCEOLA, urged his people to go to war against the Americans, starting the SECOND SEMINOLE WAR. Even after Osceola was captured in 1837, his people hid in the Everglades, made surprise attacks, and used guerrilla tactics against the Americans. In 1842, the American army gave up, allowing those Seminoles who survived to remain in Florida. A Seminole population lives in Florida to this day.

OSCEOLA

OREGON COUNTRY

Back in Europe, hats made from beaver fur became a popular fashion accessory, prompting an explosion of the American beaver fur trade. It became so large that it nearly wiped out the Eastern beaver population.

People who made their living from beavers traveled to the Northwest to find more. A lot of these MOUNTAIN MEN immersed themselves in Native American culture and married into Native American families, choosing to live in the Northwest rather than return to the Northeast to make trades.

Instead, they met at a yearly **RENDEZVOUS**, where they socialized with other trappers and did business with Eastern merchants,

such as those working for the American Fur Company owned by JOHN JACOB ASTOR. As the beaver population in the Northwest also died out, and as beaver hats grew less fashionable, some mountain men started farming in Oregon, but many went back East and became guides to help other people make the journey West.

The land the mountain men settled in was called OREGON COUNTRY (modern-day Oregon, Washington, and Idaho, along with parts of Montana and Wyoming). The land had been claimed by the U.S., Britain, Spain, and Russia, but the 1819 Adams-Onís Treaty and another treaty between Russia and the U.S. in 1824 kept Spain and Russia out. The U.S. and Britain still both wanted the territory, but they decided not to go to war over it, instead choosing to control it jointly.

The Adams-Onís Treaty formally added Florida to the U.S. and defined Spanish-American borders. It also recognized the 42nd parallel as the southern boundary of the Oregon Territory.

The OREGON TRAIL

After the Panic of 1837 and at the height of the economic depression, many Americans chose to make the 2,000-mile trip from Independence, Missouri, to Oregon on the OREGON TRAIL. The difficult journey generally took six months in a wagon train of "prairie **SCHOONERS**" (wagons that looked like ships from a distance).

MISSIONARIES were among the first to travel the Oregon Trail. Their reports of the beautiful land of the West encouraged others to

MISSIONARY
someone who goes on a mission to a foreign place to spread his religion

follow. They believed that American expansion to the Pacific coast was part of MANIFEST DESTINY: the idea that the U.S. was chosen by God to spread across the continent and that the expansion of the United States was the people's "manifest," or obvious, destiny.

The SANTE FE TRAIL

The SANTA FE TRAIL also began in Independence, Missouri, and led to Santa Fe. After Mexico gained its independence and took control of New Mexico Province, which stretched from California to Texas, this area became an ideal place

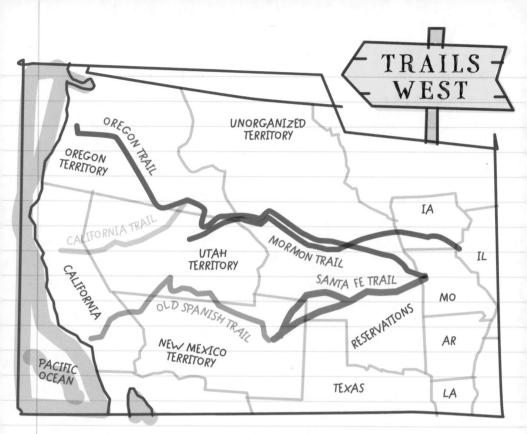

for trade. Although the 800-mile trip was long and often dangerous, the prospect of large profits inspired many traders.

The MORMON TRAIL

The Church of Jesus Christ of Latter-Day Saints had been founded by JOSEPH SMITH in 1830 in New York. The church's members, called Mormons, were persecuted because they practiced **POLYGAMY** and communal ownership of property, among other reasons. The Mormons moved to the Midwest (to Nauvoo, Illinois), but

POLYGAMY
having more than one spouse

conditions there were equally difficult and dangerous. Smith was murdered by an anti-Mormon mob in 1844. The new Mormon leader, BRIGHAM YOUNG, led his people in 1846 to an area they called DESERET. When Deseret became the UTAH TERRITORY in 1850, Brigham Young was appointed governor. Utah didn't become a state until 1896, nearly fifty years later.

CHECK YOUR KNOWLEDGE

1. How did speculators profit from cheap western land?

2. What were President Jackson's views on Native American rights?

3. Why was Indian Territory situated in Oklahoma?

4. How did the Cherokees resist being displaced?

5. What happened to the beaver population in the Northeast?

6. Why were wagons known as prairie schooners?

7. What is the idea behind Manifest Destiny?

8. Why did the Mormons go to Utah in 1846?

ANSWERS

201

CHECK YOUR ANSWERS

1. They bought it cheap and resold it in pieces for more money.

2. He thought they could not live as noncitizens within American borders.

3. The land was thought to be arid and uninhabitable.

4. They brought a case against Georgia to the Supreme Court (*WORCESTER V. GEORGIA*) and won (at least in court).

5. They were killed off to make hats.

6. Because they looked like ships sailing across the prairie

7. That God created the U.S. to spread across the continent, so American expansion was destiny

8. Because they were persecuted in the East, mostly for polygamy

☆ Chapter 18 ☆

The LONE STAR
★ ★ ★ ★ ★ ★ ★ ★ ★ ★ ★ ★ ★
NON-STATE

After Mexico gained its independence from Spain in 1821, it became a republic with a government based in Mexico City. Its territory included present-day Texas, which the Spanish called "Tejas."

SETTLERS in TEXAS

At the beginning of the nineteenth century, very few people lived in Tejas, aside from a few thousands TEJANOS, or Spanish Texans. To promote growth, the Mexican government offered large, inexpensive land grants to EMPRESARIOS, people who agreed to find settlers to purchase these grants. One of those settlers, STEPHEN F. AUSTIN, also received permission to start a new colony, on the condition that the new settlers follow Mexican law. Austin agreed, and, after arriving in Tejas in 1821, he recruited three hundred new families, who became known as the "OLD THREE HUNDRED," to settle in the area. These families encouraged many more Americans to move to Tejas in the upcoming years.

The new American settlers did not speak Spanish or practice Catholicism, and they kept illegal slaves. Within a decade, there were more Americans in Texas than Tejanos, and the U.S. decided to pressure the Mexican government to sell its land. In 1830, fearful of the growing, dissatisfied American population in Texas, the Mexican government outlawed immigration from the U.S. to Texas.

The TEXAS WAR for INDEPENDENCE

American Texans grew increasingly unhappy about following Mexican law. In 1833, Stephen Austin met with Mexico's vice president to urge Mexico to lift the ban on immigration. They agreed, but did not agree to Austin's request that Texas become an independent Mexican state. Instead, Mexico's new president, ANTONIO LÓPEZ DE SANTA ANNA, arrested Austin in Satillo and jailed him in Mexico City when he learned of Austin's plans for rebellion. Santa Anna also declared himself a dictator, thereby violating and subsequently abolishing Mexico's constitution, which protected the Tejanos' rights.

In 1835, Santa Anna gathered troops and sent them to GONZALES, Texas, with orders to seize its cannon. The Mexicans failed to confiscate the weapon, but the attempt set off the first battle in the Texas War for Independence.

The ALAMO

Having no army of their own, the Texans put out a call for volunteers. The 180-person volunteer militia (including free African Americans, rebel Tejanos, local residents, and adventure-seeking Americans like DAVY CROCKETT and JAMES BOWIE) occupied an abandoned mission called the ALAMO from February 23 to March 6, 1836. The volunteers were no match for Santa Anna, who had the entire Mexican military at his disposal. Mexican cannons broke down the walls of the Alamo, but the Texans did not surrender. The Mexicans captured and executed the remaining militia, who were stationed at a fort called Goliad, in the GOLIAD MASSACRE. But rather than become discouraged by these events, more Texans were inspired to join the militia.

The BATTLE of SAN JACINTO

AMBUSH
to attack unexpectedly

As Santa Anna remained on the attack, the Texas militia, now more than double in size and led by SAM HOUSTON, headed eastward. On April 21, 1836, Houston's troops **AMBUSHED** Santa Anna's army at their camp near the San Jacinto River. Shouting "REMEMBER THE ALAMO!" the Texans quickly defeated the Mexicans, taking Santa Anna captive and forcing him to sign a treaty recognizing Texan independence.

The LONE STAR REPUBLIC

During the siege of the Alamo, Texan leaders
met to draft their own constitution, which they
modeled on the U.S. Constitution. On March 2, 1836,
they declared their independence and established the
REPUBLIC OF TEXAS, or the "Lone Star Republic." After Santa
Anna signed the treaty, elections were held and Sam Houston
became president. Stephen Austin, whom the capital of Texas
was later named for, became secretary of state.

Because the Republic of Texas was in debt
and still in conflict with the Mexicans,

ANNEX
to attach or add on

Houston requested that the U.S. **ANNEX** Texas in 1836 so it
could apply for statehood. At the time, Jackson was president
of the U.S., and he feared admitting another slave state
to the Union, as well as provoking Mexico, so he denied the
request. Instead, he offered Texas diplomatic recognition
as its own nation. The next president, Martin Van Buren,
inherited the Texas issue from Jackson. Annexation debates
took place under the Van Buren administration. Mexico never
recognized the new nation, forcing Texas to create the
TEXAS RANGERS, a militia devoted to guarding the border.
Texas would not be admitted to the Union until 1845.

CHECK YOUR KNOWLEDGE

1. What was the form of government in Mexico following the 1821 revolution?

2. How did the Mexican government try to attract settlers to Texas?

3. How did General Santa Anna get control of the Mexican government?

4. Why was Stephen F. Austin jailed in 1833?

5. Why is Gonzales, Texas, famous?

6. What was the Alamo? Why should we remember it?

7. What was the Goliad Massacre?

8. What forced Santa Anna to recognize Texan independence?

9. Why was Texas's request to be annexed by the U.S. denied?

ANSWERS

CHECK YOUR ANSWERS

1. Republic
2. They offered land grants and hired empresarios to sell the land to people.
3. He overthrew the government and declared himself dictator.
4. Santa Anna jailed Austin because Austin was planning a rebellion.
5. The people of Gonzales did not allow Mexico to take their cannon, which began the Texas War for Independence.
6. It was an abandoned mission where a volunteer militia fought to their deaths.
7. It was when the remaining Texan militia were executed by the Mexican army, shortly after the fall of the Alamo.
8. He was taken captive by Sam Houston's troops.
9. Because it would have been a slave state and annexation might have provoked Mexican anger

OK, THIS IS DEFINITELY JAPAN!

THAT'S THE ALAMO.

☆ Chapter 19 ☆

THE MEXICAN-AMERICAN WAR

Even after Congress approved the U.S. annexation of the Lone Star Republic in 1845, Texas remained a disputed territory. A new Mexican government declared that the treaty Santa Anna had signed was not valid. Oregon Country and California also remained in question.

FIFTY-FOUR FORTY or FIGHT!

When John Tyler fell out of favor with the Whig Party, the Whigs nominated Henry Clay as their candidate in the 1844 presidential election. The Democrats nominated JAMES K. POLK, whose main campaign promise was in the slogan of "FIFTY-FOUR FORTY OR FIGHT!" That is, he supported setting the northern border of Oregon Country, which the U.S. jointly occupied with Great Britain, at latitude 54°40' north, giving the U.S. more land.

On this promise, and the popularity of Manifest Destiny, Polk was elected president. Because he was more interested in territory than war, Polk eventually compromised with Britain to extend the border to the 49th parallel, which

previous U.S. administrations had already proposed. THE OREGON TREATY of 1846 reset the borders between the U.S. and British-controlled Canada, creating the OREGON TERRITORY.

U.S.-MEXICO TENSIONS

Mexico eventually acknowledged that Texas was an American territory, but the border between the two nations was not yet settled. The U.S. government considered the Mexican border to be along the RIO GRANDE RIVER; the Mexican government believed the border was much farther north, along the NUECES RIVER.

The MEXICAN-AMERICAN WAR BEGINS

In 1845, President Polk sent Ambassador John Slidell to offer Mexico $30 million for the disputed areas of Texas, California, and New Mexico, but Mexico refused to negotiate. In a controversial move, Polk also sent GENERAL ZACHARY TAYLOR and his troops to Texas, with instructions to make camp in the disputed region between the Rio Grande and the Nueces.

Polk's stance was that this land was American land, so the U.S. was not invading Mexico. Mexico argued that the U.S. Army was making hostile moves. When Mexican troops engaged Taylor's men on April 25, 1846, Polk informed Congress that Mexico had attacked U.S. troops on U.S. soil without being provoked. In early May, Congress declared the MEXICAN-AMERICAN WAR. Public support for war with Mexico was mixed: Gaining another Southern territory would create more slave states in the Union. Still, the vote in Congress was a landslide since it would gain a lot of land at a very low cost.

THE SECOND DECLARED WAR UNDER THE CONSTITUTION

MEANWHILE, in CALIFORNIA

Mexico had taken control of California from Spain after its war for independence. The Mexican government replaced the Spanish mission system with RANCHOS (ranches), large parcels of land owned by wealthy rancheros and managed by *VAQUEROS*, or cowboys. The Hispanic Californians, called CALIFORNIOS, felt a stronger sense of local identity than of national identity. Given the distance between California and Mexico, it was tough for them to consider themselves Mexican. The American settlers, or ANGLOS, took this to an extreme: They felt that California shouldn't be part of Mexico at all.

The BEAR FLAG REVOLT

CALIFORNIA REPUBLIC

In June 1846, Anglos in California decided to declare independence and proclaimed themselves the REPUBLIC OF CALIFORNIA. Because of the bear motif on the flag they flew, California became known as the BEAR FLAG REPUBLIC. But by early 1847 California was firmly under the control of the U.S.

MEXICO DEFEATED

President Polk's plan for the Mexican–American War was to push the Mexican army out of Texas, take New Mexico and California, and then march on Mexico City. By the beginning of 1847, Zachary Taylor had accomplished the first step. Meanwhile, GENERAL STEPHEN KEARNY had occupied New Mexico and continued on to California, where the Bear Flag Revolt was under way. By September 1847, GENERAL WINFIELD SCOTT and his troops marched to Mexico City and took control. Mexico had no choice but to surrender.

The TREATY of GUADALUPE HIDALGO and the GADSDEN PURCHASE

The official end of the Mexican–American War came in February 1848 after the signing of the TREATY OF GUADALUPE HIDALGO. In what is known as the MEXICAN **CESSION**, Mexico gave up present-day California, Nevada, and Utah, along with parts of Arizona, New Mexico, Colorado, and Wyoming. Mexico also recognized the U.S. annexation of Texas and agreed to set the border between Texas and Mexico at the Rio Grande. In exchange, America gave Mexico $15 million and promised to protect those Mexicans who would now be living in the U.S.

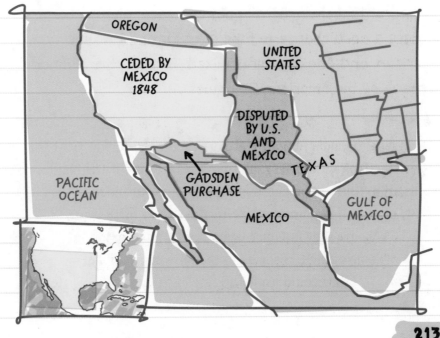

In 1853, Mexico also sold the U.S. a strip of land in present-day Arizona and New Mexico for $10 million. Negotiated by AMBASSADOR JAMES GADSDEN, the GADSDEN PURCHASE enabled the U.S. to build a potential Southern transcontinental railroad and set the final borders of the nation.

WAS NEVER BUILT—THE FINAL ROUTE WENT MUCH FARTHER NORTH THROUGH UTAH.

SETTLING the SOUTHWEST

After the U.S. took control of the Southwest, more Americans flocked there. Many followed the CALIFORNIA TRAIL, an offshoot of the Oregon Trail that ran through the Sierra Nevada Mountains. Although the Treaty of Guadalupe Hidalgo granted land rights to the Mexicans and Native Americans who already inhabited land in the Southwest, these grants were generally not enforced, giving new settlers a good chance to take over. Mexican, Native American, and Anglo cultures mixed, forming the distinct heritage of the American Southwest.

Maybe the most famous travelers on the California Trail were the **DONNER PARTY**, a group that set out for California, tried to find a shortcut, and then became stranded in the Sierra Nevada Mountains during the winter of 1846–1847. Why are they famous? When they ran out of food, some of them resorted to the only nourishment they could find: They ate each other.

Gold Rush

One of the first American men to settle in California was John Sutter, who founded SUTTER'S FORT in 1839. His homestead became a popular stop for people traveling or trading in the area near the Sacramento River, so he hired James Marshall, a carpenter, to build a sawmill. While he was working in January of 1848, Marshall discovered gold. It wasn't long before the entire country learned that there was **GOLD** in the rivers and mountains of California.

In 1849, tens of thousands of people flooded into California to try to strike it rich. Because most of them arrived that year, they became known as FORTY-NINERS. The miners usually agreed that the first person to begin looking for gold in a certain area could stake a claim to it, but conflicts often arose over mining rights. And while some people did get very wealthy, most miners ended up finding little or nothing of value.

BOOMTOWN LIFE

The sudden influx of people in California led to the creation of mining camps. These camps quickly became BOOMTOWNS, cities that came to life almost overnight. Few women lived in the towns, but those who did could earn money cooking and cleaning for the masses of young men. Merchants prospered in the mining towns, where there was little competition for their goods and services.

About eighty percent of the forty-niners were American, but a significant percentage also came from China. As gold supplies began to decline, a perception developed that the Chinese were taking American gold. In 1852, the FOREIGN MINERS TAX made mining too expensive for many Chinese immigrants, who were forced to find other work. Some founded successful businesses, and these became the foundations of thriving Chinese communities throughout California.

One of the most famous and successful boomtown merchants was Levi Strauss, a Jewish-German immigrant who sold miners sturdy work pants called "Levi's."

CALIFORNIA STATEHOOD

Even after the gold rush died down, many miners remained to farm or ranch. After just two years as a territory, California had a large enough population to apply for statehood. California wasn't granted statehood immediately: Because it was a free state, California would upset the Union's 30-year-long balance. It would also mean that the South would lose some of its power in Congress. In 1850, in another compromise between Northern and Southern interests, California became the thirty-first state to be admitted to the Union, but tensions between the North and South mounted.

CHECK YOUR KNOWLEDGE

1. What was the meaning of the phrase "Fifty-four Forty or Fight"?

2. Where did the U.S. think the Texas-Mexico border was? Where did Mexico think it was?

3. How did President Polk get Congress to declare war on Mexico?

4. What was the nickname of the Republic of California? Why?

5. What was the Mexican Cession?

6. What was the motivation behind the Gadsden Purchase?

7. What cultural heritages make up the culture of the American Southwest?

8. Who were the forty-niners?

9. Why did California institute the Foreign Miners Tax?

ANSWERS

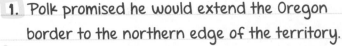

CHECK YOUR ANSWERS

1. Polk promised he would extend the Oregon border to the northern edge of the territory.

2. The U.S. thought it was the Rio Grande and Mexico thought it was the Nueces River.

3. He sent Zachary Taylor to camp in the zone between the disputed borders so it would be seen as an attack on American soil when the Mexicans defended what they thought was their territory.

4. The Bear Flag Republic, after the image on their flag

5. A land parcel including California, Nevada, Utah, and parts of Arizona, New Mexico, Colorado, and Wyoming

6. It would allow a cross-country railroad route in the South.

7. Mexican, Native American, and Anglo heritage are all combined into a unique culture.

8. They were the people who went to California during the gold rush of 1849.

9. Because of the perception that Chinese miners were taking American gold.

☆ Chapter 20 ☆

The MORE THINGS CHANGE:
REFORM

As the physical shape of the U.S. changed, so did its people and culture. Influenced in part by the Industrial Revolution, more immigrants poured into the country; those already here began movements to secure more rights.

IMMIGRATION

Millions of people immigrated to America in the mid-1800s. They often traveled in **STEERAGE**, but they made the journey in spite of the rough conditions. Many Irish people crossed the Atlantic due to the IRISH POTATO FAMINE in the 1840s. Mostly poor and uneducated, they settled in northeastern cities to work as laborers or domestics, which was preferable to famine and anti-Catholic persecution by the ruling Protestants in Great Britain.

> **STEERAGE**
> the lowest class on a ship

Driven out by an 1848 revolution in their homeland and general poverty, Germans made up another significant percentage of U.S. immigrants in the mid-nineteenth century. Germans tended to settle in the Midwest, where they found inexpensive land and the opportunity to farm. Most large groups of immigrants settled in clusters: Scandinavians tended to head for the northern Midwest, and the Chinese, who immigrated across the Pacific, went to California.

NATIVISM

NATURALIZATION
when a foreigner becomes a citizen

Americans were afraid the new arrivals would take their jobs for lower pay. Those who opposed immigration became known as NATIVISTS, and nativist politics soared in popularity.

In 1849, a secret society of nativists founded the American Party, though they were often called the KNOW-NOTHING Party because they refused to speak about the details of their organization. The Know-Nothings were anti-Catholic, and supported longer waiting periods for **NATURALIZATION** and a ban on foreign natives holding public office. Within a few years, however, the party fell apart over disagreements about slavery.

CITY LIFE

City life proved challenging for many immigrants. Most cities lacked adequate sewer systems, police and fire departments,

and enough housing
for a population boom.
Immigrants tended to live
in crowded **TENEMENT**

TENEMENT
a low-rent,
low-quality
apartment

apartment buildings, where disease spread easily. Others,
however, prospered as middle-class business owners.

The SECOND GREAT AWAKENING

The SECOND GREAT AWAKENING was a new religious revival
movement in the early nineteenth century, like the Great
Awakening, with millions of supporters. Preachers in the
movement:

> challenged traditional Protestant views

> encouraged an emotional attachment to religion

> emphasized the power of each man (rather than churches,
> priests, and rules) to control his own soul and salvation

> taught personal responsibility

> wanted to improve the world

REFORM MOVEMENTS

The Second Great Awakening's principles quickly spread
outside religion. Many Americans, particularly middle-class
women who had time and money to spare, developed a spirit

of reform. The popularity of reform movements was so great that the 1820s to 1860s became known as the AGE OF REFORM. Major reform movements of this time included:

THE TEMPERANCE MOVEMENT: This blamed society's problems on liquor and wanted a ban on alcohol.

THE PRISON-REFORM MOVEMENT: This was led by DOROTHEA DIX, who encouraged the creation of mental institutions so that the ill wouldn't be imprisoned with criminals anymore. The juvenile justice system also began in the same time period.

EDUCATION REFORM: This included the creation of the first teachers' training schools; CATHERINE BEECHER's first all-girls school; SAMUEL GRIDLEY HOWE's school for the blind; THOMAS GALLAUDET's school for the deaf; the expansion of public education; and the founding of liberal arts colleges, including Oberlin, the first college to admit women and African Americans.

CALLED "NORMAL SCHOOLS"

HELEN KELLER WENT THERE.

UTOPIAN SOCIETIES: These were attempts to create perfect communities based on religious or philosophical ideals. The SHAKERS, whose faith-based society prohibited marriage and having children, lasted longer than you'd expect, through converts and the adoption of orphans.

UTOPIA
a perfect place

ABOLITIONISM

ABOLISH
to do away with

Another major reform movement of the 1830s was the antislavery movement for **ABOLITION**. It firmly divided the pro-abolition North and the pro-slavery South. Not all Northerners agreed on how to end slavery. Some wanted to keep a racial hierarchy. Some thought sending African Americans to Africa was the only solution.

In 1821, the AMERICAN COLONIZATION SOCIETY founded the African nation of LIBERIA as a free home for African Americans. As it turned out, it wasn't feasible to send large numbers of people to Liberia. Also, most African Americans had lived their whole lives in the U.S. and wanted to stay.

In 1831, WILLIAM LLOYD GARRISON of Massachusetts began to publish *THE LIBERATOR*, an abolitionist newspaper. He also founded the AMERICAN ANTI-SLAVERY SOCIETY. Supporters included the Southern-born sisters ANGELINA AND SARAH GRIMKÉ, who wrote and lectured. Former slaves like FREDERICK DOUGLASS and SOJOURNER TRUTH traveled the nation and the world educating people about their lives as slaves.

Frederick Douglass wrote *Narrative of the Life of Frederick Douglass, an American Slave* and delivered one of the most important anti-slave orations on July 5, 1852, which became known as "What to the Slave Is the 4th of July?"

The UNDERGROUND RAILROAD

In the mid-1800s, a network of abolitionists, free blacks, and former slaves helped slaves escape to the North or to Canada. The UNDERGROUND RAILROAD (not an actual railroad) organized transportation and hiding places for **FUGITIVE SLAVES**. Its most famous guide, or "conductor," was HARRIET TUBMAN, a former slave who made more than a dozen trips to guide slaves to freedom.

FUGITIVE
a person fleeing from intolerable circumstances; a runaway

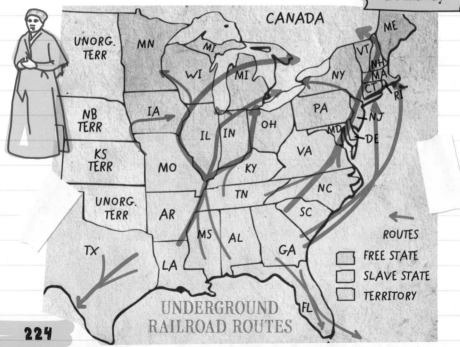

CANADA

UNORG. TERR | MN | MI | ME | VT | NH | MA | CT | RI
WI | MI | NY
NB TERR | IA | OH | PA | NJ
IL | IN | MD | DE
KS TERR | MO | VA
KY
UNORG. TERR | AR | TN | NC
MS | AL | SC
TX | GA
LA | FL

ROUTES
☐ FREE STATE
☐ SLAVE STATE
☐ TERRITORY

UNDERGROUND RAILROAD ROUTES

OPPOSITION to ABOLITIONISM

To Southerners, abolitionism was a threat to their way of life. Even in the North, some people worried that free blacks would take jobs from whites. Abolitionists faced violence and persecution.

The arguments against abolitionism and women's rights followed the same pattern:

↳ Some Southerners said blacks were incapable of taking care of themselves and were better off as slaves.

↳ Some people said women were incapable of taking care of themselves and were better off being protected from the world.

WOMEN'S RIGHTS

Around the same time, the women's rights movement was solidifying. Many supporters of abolition, such as the Grimké sisters, Sojourner Truth, and Frederick Douglass, also wanted equality of the sexes. Women couldn't vote; most weren't educated; they didn't receive equal pay for equal work; and if they did earn money, it belonged to their husbands or fathers.

In 1840, ELIZABETH CADY STANTON tried to attend an abolitionist convention in London, but women weren't allowed to participate. She and her friend LUCRETIA MOTT decided to organize a women's rights convention. The SENECA FALLS CONVENTION, in July 1848 in Seneca Falls,

New York, was the first meeting of its kind. Activists drafted a DECLARATION OF SENTIMENTS AND RESOLUTIONS, based on the Declaration of Independence, to lay out the injustices in gender relations. For example, it stated that "all men AND WOMEN are created equal." (Women didn't get the right to vote for another 70 years.)

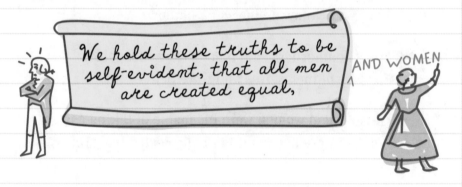

We hold these truths to be self-evident, that all men are created equal, AND WOMEN

The two pillars of the women's rights movement were abolition and temperance. Women could relate to the status of slaves, and they saw that alcohol abuse led to domestic issues.

LUCY STONE became a spokesperson for the Anti-Slavery Society. SUSAN B. ANTHONY encouraged New York State to pass laws allowing women to own property. The abolitionist movement and the women's rights movement had common roots, but they disagreed over which had greater priority.

CHECK YOUR KNOWLEDGE

1. What drove Europeans to immigrate to the U.S. in the mid-1800s?

2. What were the main values preached during the Second Great Awakening?

3. Who were most active in the reform movements of the mid-1800s?

4. What were the points of disagreement inside the abolitionist movement?

5. What was the Underground Railroad?

6. What were some of the ways that women were unequal in society?

ANSWERS 227

CHECK YOUR ANSWERS

1. Overcrowding, poverty, and persecution in Europe; opportunities in the U.S.

2. The Second Great Awakening challenged traditional Protestant views and taught personal responsibility. It also emphasized individual power of destiny and salvation, as well as an emotional attachment to religion. The preachers wanted to improve the world.

3. Middle-class women

4. People disagreed about whether African Americans should return to Africa, whether a racial hierarchy should exist, and how to go about advocating for change.

5. It was a network that organized transportation and hiding places for fugitive slaves.

6. Most women were not educated, could not vote, and did not receive equal pay for equal work. If they did work, the money they earned belonged to their husbands or fathers.

Unit 5

Civil War and Reconstruction
1850s-1870s

As the U.S. approached its seventieth year of independence, the relationship between the states and the federal government still wasn't resolved. Slavery remained a contentious issue. How would the North and South reconcile their differences? They couldn't, and the result was the Civil War.

☆ Chapter 21 ☆

NORTH VERSUS SOUTH

By the mid-nineteenth century, the U.S. stretched from the East Coast to the West Coast. As states continued to apply for statehood, the debate over abolition went on.

The WILMOT PROVISO

Representative David Wilmot of Pennsylvania had proposed the **WILMOT PROVISO**, suggesting that slavery be banned in any territory acquired through the Mexican Cession. It passed in the House, but Southerners prevented its passage in the Senate.

> **PROVISO**
> a part of a law that restricts something

The ELECTION of 1848

When the Wilmot Proviso failed, a new political party formed: the FREE-SOIL PARTY. They wanted to keep new territories and states free of slavery. They nominated former President Martin Van Buren against the Whig candidate

ZACHARY TAYLOR and Democrat Lewis Cass (a senator from Michigan). Taylor won the election. The Free-Soil candidates won some seats in Congress.

COMPROMISE of 1850

PROPOSED THE MISSOURI COMPROMISE, TOO

When California applied to the Union as a free state, some Southern states threatened to secede. Henry Clay had a compromise:

> California would be admitted as a free state.

> Texas would give up some of its land and the government would help pay off its war debts.

> Popular sovereignty would decide positions on slavery in territories and new states, which meant that settlers would decide the issue.

DON'T FORGET—THIS MEANS AUTHORITY OF THE PEOPLE

> The slave trade (but not slavery itself) would be banned in Washington, D.C.

> Congress would pass stronger laws to return runaway slaves.

After President Taylor died suddenly and his vice president, MILLARD FILLMORE, took his place, the Compromise of 1850 was passed into law.

The FUGITIVE SLAVE ACT

Maybe the most controversial part of the Compromise of 1850 was the FUGITIVE SLAVE ACT, which required Northern citizens to cooperate with and assist slave-catchers, and denied runaway slaves a fair trial (they were tried in a separate court). Many free blacks fled to Canada, and some Northern whites practiced CIVIL DISOBEDIENCE, refusing to follow the new law. In Massachusetts, abolitionist HARRIET BEECHER STOWE was inspired to write UNCLE TOM'S CABIN (1852), a story about the harsh realities of slavery. It became one of the most influential novels of the nineteenth century. The Fugitive Slave Act further divided the nation. The North hated it. The South felt vindicated. The North also passed Personal Liberty Laws, which basically negated the Fugitive Slave Act and proved to the South that the North was not enforcing the law.

> "CIVIL DISOBEDIENCE" was an essay written by Henry David Thoreau on the idea that people should refuse to follow the laws or commands of a government when they seem unjust.

The KANSAS-NEBRASKA ACT

In the presidential election of 1852, little-known Democratic candidate FRANKLIN PIERCE of New Hampshire defeated the Whig nominee, war hero Winfield Scott. At this time, some western land, including Kansas and Nebraska, was not yet organized, and Illinois senator STEPHEN A. DOUGLAS wanted to build a railroad that ran through it from Chicago to the Pacific. He initially proposed making KANSAS and NEBRASKA

DOCTRINE
a theory or position on an issue

U.S. territories that, under the terms of the Missouri Compromise, would be free. However, Douglas also knew that Southerners would object to this idea. Backed by President Pierce, he proposed the KANSAS-NEBRASKA ACT, which would invoke the **DOCTRINE** of popular sovereignty and allow the people there to determine the slavery issue. The act passed, and the Missouri Compromise was made obsolete.

BLEEDING KANSAS

During the March 1855 territorial elections in Kansas, thousands of so-called **BORDER RUFFIANS** crossed

the border to vote from the slave state of Missouri. In fact, about four times more people voted in Kansas than lived there. A pro-slavery local government took control. Antislavery settlers started their own government, creating two governments for one state.

RUFFIAN
a tough, lawless person; a bully

SACK
to pillage and plunder

In May 1856, the pro-slavery government sent a group to Lawrence, Kansas, to arrest the rival government, but they had fled. The pro-slavery group ransacked the city in the **SACK OF LAWRENCE**. In response, the passionate abolitionist JOHN BROWN led his group in the POTTAWATOMIE CREEK MASSACRE of pro-slavery

233

Kansans. Over the summer, hundreds of people were killed in "BLEEDING KANSAS" before federal troops restored order.

BLEEDING SUMNER

Violence also broke out in Congress after Senator CHARLES SUMNER of Massachusetts criticized people who were pro-slavery, specifically Andrew Butler of South Carolina. Butler's cousin, Representative PRESTON BROOKS, beat Sumner over the head with a cane in the Senate chambers. Sumner was badly injured.

The REPUBLICAN PARTY and the ELECTION of 1856

Both the Democratic and Whig parties were splitting on sectional lines. The antislavery Whigs decided to join the Northern Democrats and Free-Soilers to create the REPUBLICAN PARTY.

> Though some names have stayed the same, modern political parties are not the same as their roots.

The Republican Party nominated John C. Frémont of California for president, and the Democratic Party nominated JAMES BUCHANAN, a Pennsylvanian who favored compromise. The Know-Nothing Party nominated former president Millard Fillmore. Buchanan won the South and won the election.

> Frémont's campaign slogan was "Free Soil, Free Men and Frémont."

WASHINGTON TERRITORY

OREGON TERRITORY

MINNESOTA TERRITORY

NEBRASKA TERRITORY

WI

MI

NH

ME

VT

NY

MA

CT

RI

UTAH TERRITORY

IA

OH

PA

NJ

DE

IL

IN

CA

KANSAS TERRITORY

MO

VA

MD

NEW MEXICO TERRITORY

UNORG. TERR.

KY

TN

NC

AR

SC

MS

AL

GA

TX

LA

FL

DEMOCRATIC (BUCHANAN)

REPUBLICAN (FRÉMONT)

KNOW-NOTHING (FILLMORE)

DRED SCOTT

In 1857, a Supreme Court case about an enslaved man named DRED SCOTT fueled the abolitionist cause. Scott was a slave to an army doctor in Missouri, John Emerson, who brought him along on travels to Illinois, where slavery was illegal. After Emerson passed away in 1843, Scott petitioned his widow for freedom, but she refused. Scott continued living in slavery, but a few years later, with the help of lawyers from the North, he sued for his freedom, making the argument that he was free after having lived in a free place.

After a decade of appeals, the Supreme Court took on the issue in the case of DRED SCOTT v. SANFORD (also called the DRED SCOTT DECISION). Chief Justice Roger Taney wrote the 7-2 decision that ruled against Scott because:

1. Scott didn't have the right to sue because he was only a piece of property, not a citizen.

2. The government can't seize private property (Scott) from a citizen (Emerson) without due process of law.

3. Congress can't ban slavery in the territories, because that would violate the property rights of people bringing slaves there.

4. Therefore, the Missouri Compromise and other popular sovereignty decisions were unconstitutional.

The nation's highest court had ruled that abolishing slavery was unconstitutional.

The LINCOLN-DOUGLAS DEBATES

In the senatorial election of 1858, Senator Stephen A. Douglas of Illinois faced a new young challenger, ABRAHAM LINCOLN, a Republican lawyer who had served one term in the House of Representatives and eight years in the state legislature. Since Lincoln wasn't very well known, he challenged Douglas to a series of debates, the LINCOLN-DOUGLAS DEBATES. They were both against slavery, but they met seven times in cities and towns throughout Illinois to debate what to do about it.

Douglas was afraid that Lincoln believed in equality of the races. Lincoln said that blacks were entitled to the rights listed in the Declaration of Independence but also stated that they weren't equal to whites in every way. Lincoln gave his famous "House Divided" speech, while Douglas argued the FREEPORT DOCTRINE—a belief that territories could exclude slavery through local legislation. Douglas won the election, but Lincoln got national name recognition out of it.

The RAID on HARPERS FERRY

John Brown led another raid, this time in HARPERS FERRY, VIRGINIA. On October 16, 1859, his abolitionists raided an arsenal so they could arm slaves for an uprising. Local slaves feared joining his rebellion, and Brown and others were captured. John Brown was hanged for treason and murder, a **MARTYR** for Northern abolitionists. The raid had a huge impact on the South, which feared armed rebellion by slaves.

> **MARTYR**
> someone who dies for his or her beliefs

The ELECTION of 1860

Northern Democrats nominated Stephen Douglas, who supported popular sovereignty; Southern Democrats chose JOHN BRECKINRIDGE from Kentucky, who supported slavery. A new party, the CONSTITUTIONAL UNION PARTY (compromise and union at any cost), nominated JOHN BELL of Tennessee. Abraham Lincoln, who believed slavery should be banned in the territories, received the nomination from the Republican Party. Lincoln received only 40 percent of the popular vote and did not carry a single Southern state. However, he swept the North, along with California and Oregon, and became the sixteenth president of the U.S.

SECESSION

Although Lincoln did not favor abolishing slavery in states where it already existed, he had said that putting a stop to slavery's expansion would, sooner or later, cause the institution to fall apart. That idea made the South very worried about having him in the White House. Within days of Lincoln's victory, the South Carolina legislature met for a special session, arguing that, just as a state could choose to enter a union, it was possible for a state to choose to leave. On December 20, 1860, South Carolina seceded from the U.S. by repealing its ratification of the Constitution. While proponents of states' rights believed that secession was a legal right, there were those who believed that South Carolina's decision was a revolt. However, the South claimed that the government had violated its rights by not protecting slavery.

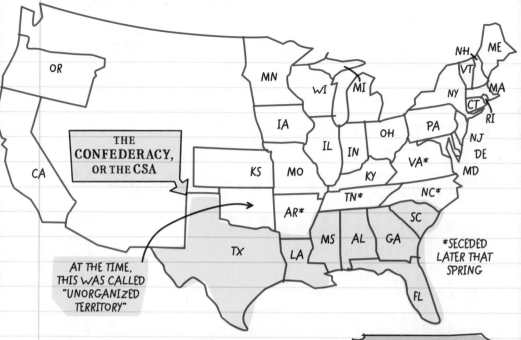

The map shows:

OR, CA, MN, WI, MI, IA, IL, IN, OH, PA, NY, NH, ME, VT, MA, CT, RI, NJ, DE, MD, KS, MO, KY, VA*, TN*, NC*, AR*, SC, TX, LA, MS, AL, GA, FL

THE CONFEDERACY, OR THE CSA

AT THE TIME, THIS WAS CALLED "UNORGANIZED TERRITORY"

*SECEDED LATER THAT SPRING

The CONFEDERATE STATES of AMERICA

CONFEDERATE
part of an alliance or confederacy

Following in South Carolina's footsteps, Texas, Louisiana, Mississippi, Alabama, Florida, and Georgia also seceded. On February 4, 1861, these states met to establish their own government as the **CONFEDERATE STATES OF AMERICA**. They elected JEFFERSON DAVIS as president.

LINCOLN'S FIRST INAUGURAL ADDRESS

INAUGURAL
having to do with an inauguration, the ceremony at which someone is sworn into office

Abraham Lincoln was inaugurated on March 4, 1861. The main points of his first **INAUGURAL ADDRESS** were:

Legal **REDRESS** and revolutionary actions are different; secession is not an acceptable choice.

The Union was perpetual, therefore the CSA doesn't actually exist and is a band of rebels living in the U.S.

Federal property in the South will remain federal property.

Slavery shouldn't be completely abolished, but it shouldn't spread.

War is not a reasonable option.

The people of the United States should all be friends, not enemies, because the United States is one country.

The address was meant to reassure Southerners that Lincoln would not interfere with slavery in the states where it already existed.

Lincoln's inaugural address is well known for its eloquence: "In your hands, my dissatisfied fellow-countrymen, and not in mine, is the momentous issue of civil war. The Government will not assail you. You can have no conflict without being yourselves the aggressors. You have no oath registered in heaven to destroy the Government, while I shall have the most solemn one to preserve, protect, and defend it. . . . I am loath to close. We are not enemies, but friends. We must not be enemies. Though passion may have strained it must not break our bonds of affection. The mystic chords of memory, stretching from every battlefield and patriot grave to every living heart and hearthstone all over this broad land, will yet swell the chorus of the Union, when again touched, as surely they will be, by the better angels of our nature."

CHECK YOUR KNOWLEDGE

1. What was the platform of the Free-Soil Party?

2. What did the Fugitive Slave Act require of Northern citizens?

3. What is popular sovereignty?

4. How was the Republican Party founded?

5. What was one reason given by the Supreme Court in the Dred Scott decision?

6. What were Lincoln's prewar opinions about racial equality?

7. What were the secessionists' arguments for the legality of their actions?

8. What did Lincoln think about the legality of secession?

ANSWERS

1. They believed that new states and territories ought to be free of slavery.

2. That Northern citizens had to cooperate with and assist slave-catchers and that slaves would be tried in special courts

3. The belief that states ought to let the people decide

4. Antislavery Whigs and Northern Democrats joined forces with the Free-Soilers.

5. Dred Scott did not have the right to sue because he was not a citizen.

6. He did not believe in equality but he thought slavery was wrong.

7. They believed that the Union got its power because all of the states independently agreed to participate, and they could choose to leave at any time.

8. Lincoln believed that secession was not legally possible and that the Confederacy was in rebellion.

#5 has more than one correct answer.

Chapter 22

The
CIVIL WAR

FORT SUMTER

Soon after his inauguration, President Lincoln learned that supplies for federal troops at FORT SUMTER, which was located in the harbor of Charleston, South Carolina, were running out. Sending more supplies could provoke war. After alerting the CSA, Lincoln sent unarmed supply ships. In response, on April 12, 1861, the Confederacy attacked Fort Sumter. The fort surrendered two days later. The **CIVIL WAR** had begun.

BORDER STATES

Lincoln called on state militias to supply troops for what he estimated would be three months of fighting. In response, North Carolina, Tennessee, Virginia, and Arkansas seceded—they refused to bear arms against their fellow Southerners and saw Lincoln's actions as unjust. Border states where

slavery was legal but not such a big part of the economy—
Delaware, Kentucky, Maryland, and Missouri—stayed in the
Union. In 1863, the part of Virginia loyal to the Union—WEST
VIRGINIA—became the USA's thirty-fifth state.

NORTH VERSUS SOUTH

The North (the **YANKEES**, or the **UNION**, who wore blue uniforms)
had a bigger population, more transport options (especially
railroads), more factories and production capacity, and more money.

The South (the **REBELS**, or the **CONFEDERATES**,
who wore gray uniforms) had better officers
and influence on the world's cotton market.

The South needed to fight a defensive war. They hoped
for foreign intervention and planned to hold out
until the North got weary of the war.

The North needed to fight a more active war
and subdue the Rebels.

Both armies consisted mostly of inexperienced volunteers
who signed up for only 90 days of fighting.

Together, North and South faced the scary reality of a war
that put brother against brother.

NORTH VERSUS SOUTH

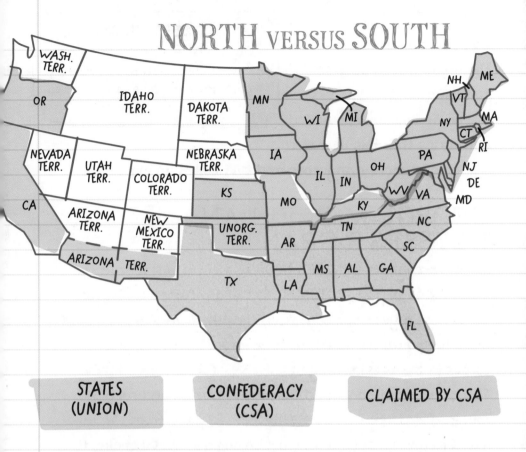

STATES (UNION) **CONFEDERACY (CSA)** **CLAIMED BY CSA**

The FIRST BATTLE of BULL RUN

In July of 1861, the Union army tried to take Richmond, Virginia, which had become the CSA capital. The Confederate troops met the Union army at MANASSAS, Virginia, which was a key railroad junction near BULL RUN CREEK. Neither side was ready. On July 21, the Union forces crossed the creek and pushed back all of the Rebels, except for the unit led by General Thomas Jackson, who received the nickname "Stonewall" for refusing to move. Under STONEWALL JACKSON, the

245

Confederate army pushed the Union troops back to Washington, D.C. The First Battle of Bull Run showed both sides that this war was going to be more dangerous and difficult than expected.

GEORGE McCLELLAN and ULYSSES S. GRANT

Lincoln brought in GENERAL GEORGE McCLELLAN to lead the Union ARMY OF THE POTOMAC. McClellan trained his troops for almost a year but, convinced that the Confederate troops were too powerful, hesitated to attack. Meanwhile, Union forces in the West, led by ULYSSES S. GRANT, were taking forts, gaining ground, and taking over trade and supply routes. ADMIRAL DAVID FARRAGUT led navy troops to take New Orleans, wrapping his wooden ships in heavy chains to protect them like IRONCLADS.

NEW MILITARY TECHNOLOGY

One of the most significant new inventions of the Civil War was the **IRONCLAD** warship, a ship that was armored with iron. Other major innovations were the **REPEATING RIFLE** (which could fire more than one bullet before it had to be reloaded) and the **MINIÉ BALL BULLET**; soldiers could shoot farther and more accurately. War became a whole lot deadlier.

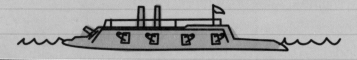

THE BIG BATTLES:

The BATTLE of SHILOH

The Confederacy's western troops retreated to Corinth, Mississippi. Grant's army followed closely behind, stopping near SHILOH CHURCH, in Tennessee, to wait for reinforcements. On April 6, 1862, Albert Sidney Johnston, leader of the Confederacy's western troops, and his soldiers ambushed Grant's camp. Over two days, the Union forces were able to push the Confederates back into Mississippi, but both sides lost huge numbers of soldiers in the BATTLE OF SHILOH.

The PENINSULA CAMPAIGN

As Lincoln was frustrated with McClellan's hesitations, McClellan finally announced a plan to move the entire army by boat to Virginia's Lower Peninsula—a huge and slow operation. He wanted to enter the James River Peninsula to attack Richmond from the south. By the time he got there, the Confederates were ready to attack.

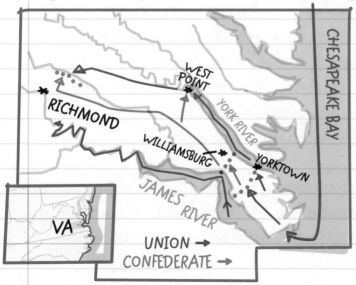

WEST POINT
CHESAPEAKE BAY
RICHMOND
YORK RIVER
WILLIAMSBURG
YORKTOWN
JAMES RIVER
VA

UNION →
CONFEDERATE →

McClellan's army suffered heavy losses and was forced to retreat by the CONFEDERATE ARMY OF NORTHERN VIRGINIA, led by ROBERT E. LEE.

The SECOND BATTLE of BULL RUN

In August 1862, in the SECOND BATTLE OF BULL RUN, the Rebels gained another victory.

ANTIETAM

Lee decided to attack the North. A victory there would take the war to Northern soil, encouraging Britain to join the war. (It was

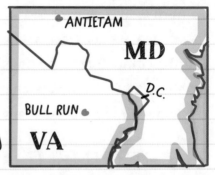

also designed to help Virginia farmers harvest their crops by moving the battle north.) In September 1862, the Confederate army crossed the Potomac into Frederick, Maryland.

Lee planned to divide his army into three units, which made him vulnerable to attack. A Union soldier found a copy of Lee's marching orders in an abandoned Rebel camp. When McClellan learned of the plan, he was slow to act when he could have used this secret information to get an advantage.

Two days later, on September 17, the two armies met near Sharpsburg, Maryland, at the BATTLE OF ANTIETAM, which became the single deadliest one-day battle in all of U.S. history.

After Lee retreated, McClellan didn't follow with an attack. Lincoln fired McClellan.

> COMBINED CASUALTIES WERE 23,000 KILLED, WOUNDED, OR MISSING.

The EMANCIPATION PROCLAMATION

> **EMANCIPATION**
> setting free

According to Lincoln, the Civil War wasn't being fought to end slavery. It was to preserve the Union. At first he didn't want to upset the border states.

The Union victory at Antietam gave him more confidence. On January 1, 1863, Lincoln issued the **EMANCIPATION PROCLAMATION**. He did not have the constitutional power to end slavery, but he had the authority to seize enemy property—including slaves. So this military order could free all slaves in any area that was in rebellion. The Emancipation Proclamation transformed the Civil War into a moral crusade against slavery and it encouraged some slaves to escape. However, the Union army could not actively ensure that slaves were freed. Nonetheless, it also prevented foreign intervention because no European power would fight to restore or preserve slavery.

Although many whites doubted black soldiers' courage and ability to fight, they—most famously the 54TH MASSACHUSETTS VOLUNTEERS regiment—proved their bravery after Congress allowed them to fight. There were 175 UNITED STATES COLORED TROOPS (USCT) regiments by the end of the Civil War, which constituted 10 percent of the entire Union army.

The HOME FRONT

Because so many men were away fighting, women took on more responsibility in farming, business, and manufacturing. Women also supported the war effort as nurses; nurse CLARA BARTON later founded the AMERICAN RED CROSS.

High demand for supplies bolstered the Northern economy. Shortages and inflation damaged the Southern economy and hurt Southern morale.

Both the Union and Confederate governments imposed an INCOME TAX and issued new currency; in the North, this money was called GREENBACK money.

The need for soldiers led to the institution of a draft on both sides. Because rich men could buy their way out of it, riots ensued in New York City, and over one hundred people died in the July 1863 draft riots.

HABEAS CORPUS

Concerned about the damage the opposition at home could do to Union morale, Lincoln suspended the WRIT OF HABEAS CORPUS. That is, he allowed people to be arrested without a specified cause. According to the Constitution, the president can ask Congress to suspend the writ of habeas corpus in an emergency but cannot act on his own. Lincoln's decision stirred controversy, but Congress validated it when it began its next session.

In Latin, "habeas corpus" means to "have the body." Literally, it means that a person can't be charged with murder unless a body is presented to prove that the crime took place. In law, the "writ" (or legal order) of habeas corpus means that a person can't be kept in jail unless those detaining him have the legal authority to do so.

FREDERICKSBURG and CHANCELLORSVILLE

After firing McClellan, Lincoln put AMBROSE BURNSIDE in charge. The Rebels and General Lee forced the Union to retreat in the December 1862 BATTLE OF FREDERICKSBURG. It was one of the worst defeats of the Union army, who lost more than 12,500 men. Burnside resigned. GENERAL JOSEPH HOOKER took his place.

Remember the not-so-great Union generals **McClellan**, **Burnside**, and **Hooker** with this mnemonic device:

MAKE
BETTER
HEROES.

In May of 1863, Hooker led the Union army in an attack on Chancellorsville, but they were again forced to retreat, even though Stonewall Jackson died of wounds from the battle. Hooker resigned. He was replaced by GEORGE MEADE.

CHANCELLORSVILLE WAS LEE'S GREATEST VICTORY, DESPITE LOSING JACKSON.

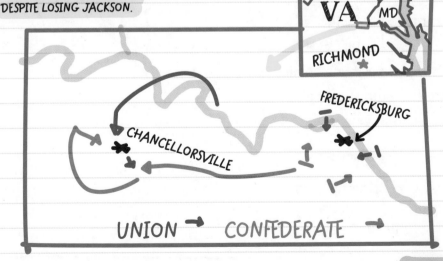

UNION ➡   CONFEDERATE ➡

THE BIG ONE: THE BATTLE OF
GETTYSBURG

Lee took another chance on invading the North. In June of 1863, Lee's army entered Pennsylvania and searched for supplies in the town of Gettysburg, unaware that Union cavalry was there as well. It was an accidental encounter that blew up into the most famous battle of the Civil War.

TIMELINE:

July 1: After the Rebels pushed the outnumbered Union forces back into the town, the Union troops regrouped on CEMETERY RIDGE and CULP'S HILL, strategic positions on high ground. Both sides called for reinforcements.

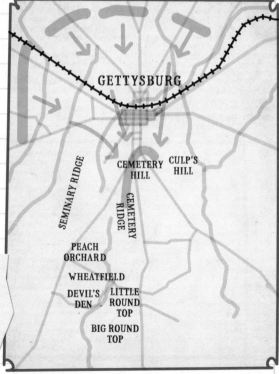

UNION →
CONFEDERATE →
RIVERS —   ROADS —
RAILROAD +++

GETTYSBURG

SEMINARY RIDGE

CEMETERY HILL

CULP'S HILL

CEMETERY RIDGE

PEACH ORCHARD

WHEATFIELD

DEVIL'S DEN

LITTLE ROUND TOP

BIG ROUND TOP

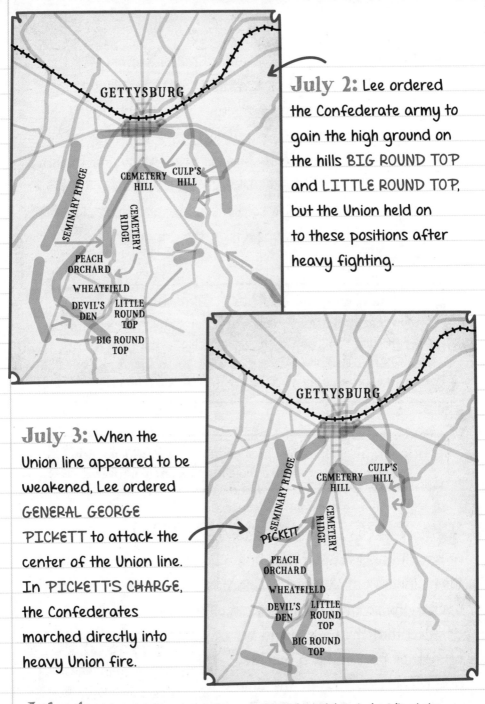

July 2: Lee ordered the Confederate army to gain the high ground on the hills BIG ROUND TOP and LITTLE ROUND TOP, but the Union held on to these positions after heavy fighting.

July 3: When the Union line appeared to be weakened, Lee ordered GENERAL GEORGE PICKETT to attack the center of the Union line. In PICKETT'S CHARGE, the Confederates marched directly into heavy Union fire.

July 4: Lee and his army began to retreat back to Virginia.

The BATTLE OF GETTYSBURG was a major victory for the Yankees and a turning point in the Civil War. Pickett's Charge became known as the "high-water mark of the Confederacy" because victory would never again be so close for the Confederates. Gettysburg is also famous as the site of Lincoln's GETTYSBURG ADDRESS. On November 19, 1863, during the dedication of a soldiers' cemetery there, Lincoln gave a two-minute-long speech on the importance of the Union's cause.

The first line of the GETTYSBURG ADDRESS, "Four score and seven years ago, our fathers brought forth, upon this continent..." is a clue to the year in which it was delivered. A "score" is 20, so four score and seven = 4 x 20 + 7 = 87 years. 1863 – 87 = 1776.

Vicksburg also fell to the Union on July 4, 1863, which meant that the North controlled the entire Mississippi River.

The VIRGINIA CAMPAIGN

After all the disappointing Union commanders, in early 1864, Lincoln put Ulysses S. Grant in charge of all military operations so the Union armies could act as one. Grant decided that the war would be an attack on Southern morale and resources. That is, the Union would practice **TOTAL WAR**.

TOTAL WAR
war that also uses/attacks civilians and nonmilitary resources

254

In the BATTLE OF THE WILDERNESS on May 5 and 6, 1864, Grant pushed into Virginia despite heavy losses, knowing that his army was larger than Lee's. He pushed on no matter how many casualties his army suffered. From June 9, 1864, to March 25, 1865, Lee was forced to defend Richmond and was vastly outnumbered in the SIEGE OF PETERSBURG. Grant broke through the Confederates' lines and forced Lee to abandon his fortifications. Lee's army had dwindled down to just 27,000 men, compared to Grant's force of 120,000.

SHERMAN in the DEEP SOUTH

In September 1864, GENERAL WILLIAM TECUMSEH SHERMAN marched with Union forces to Atlanta and destroyed the city. He continued on his MARCH TO THE SEA, capturing the city of Savannah, then moving north into the Carolinas. In this terrifying campaign, Sherman's army destroyed plantations and burned fields. He wanted to destroy the economy and morale of the South. He did—and he stirred up long-lasting resentment.

William Tecumseh Sherman was named after the Native American Shawnee chief Tecumseh. He wasn't proud of it; he became famous for stating later that "the only good Indian is a dead Indian."

The ELECTION of 1864

Until mid-1864, Lincoln had been in a bad position for reelection. After victories in Gettysburg and the South in the summer and fall of 1864, Lincoln won in a landslide against George McClellan. It was seen as a mandate (command) for emancipation. On January 31, 1865, Congress passed the THIRTEENTH AMENDMENT, banning slavery and making the Emancipation Proclamation a reality. It was quickly ratified by the states.

APPOMATTOX and the END of the WAR

On April 2, the government of the CSA fled, burning the city of Richmond behind them so that it wouldn't be any use to the Union army. Lee reluctantly decided he had no choice but to surrender.

On April 9, 1865, Lee and Grant met at APPOMATTOX COURT HOUSE. Grant offered the following terms of surrender: The Confederate soldiers would be fed and allowed to return home with their property and horses. Lee accepted. The last Confederate army surrendered on May 26. The Civil War was over with a victory for the Union—and now it was time to rebuild the country.

CHECK YOUR KNOWLEDGE

1. Which side did each border state take during the Civil War?

2. What did the North and South learn from the First Battle of Bull Run?

3. Why didn't President Lincoln like General McClellan?

4. Whom did the Emancipation Proclamation actually emancipate?

5. What is the writ of habeas corpus?

6. What is total war?

7. What does the Thirteenth Amendment signify?

ANSWERS

CHECK YOUR ANSWERS

1. Delaware, Kentucky, Maryland, and Missouri sided with the North. North Carolina, Tennessee, Virginia, and Arkansas sided with the South.

2. They saw that the war would be difficult and dangerous.

3. McClellan was too hesitant.

4. Slaves in states that were in rebellion (but the Union army could not actively ensure that it happened)

5. It legally guarantees that if you are arrested you must be given a specific cause.

6. Total war involves civilians and resources, not just soldiers.

7. A ban on slavery

☆ Chapter 23 ☆

RECONSTRUCTION

RECONSTRUCTION

Reconstruction was the name of the era after the Civil War ended, lasting from 1865 to 1877. The government and people struggled to find a balance between uniting the country and assisting former slaves.

The FREEDMEN'S BUREAU

Lincoln and Congress established the FREEDMEN'S BUREAU, an agency whose goal was to help the newly "freed men" by providing education, food, housing, and medical aid. The bureau was understaffed and lacked funding, but managed to set up schools and universities for former slaves.

> The Freedmen's Bureau was under General O. O. Howard and Howard University was named in his honor.

LINCOLN'S ASSASSINATION

On April 14, 1865, only a month after the Freedmen's Bureau was established and just days after Lee and Grant met at Appomattox to negotiate the South's surrender, President Lincoln and his wife attended a play at FORD'S THEATER in

Washington. During the play, Lincoln was shot in the head by Confederate sympathizer JOHN WILKES BOOTH

ASSASSINATE
to kill an important person, usually for political reasons

and died the following morning. President Lincoln was the first American president to be **ASSASSINATED**. Booth's coconspirators attacked the secretary of state, William Seward, and severely wounded him, and were also supposed to kill Vice President Andrew Johnson. Lincoln's death destroyed any hope for an orderly Reconstruction.

JOHNSON'S RECONSTRUCTION and BLACK CODES

Lincoln's vice president, former Democrat ANDREW JOHNSON, was sworn into office. Although Johnson followed Lincoln's agenda for Reconstruction per his presidential duties, he did not believe in racial equality, and his interpretation of Reconstruction was lenient toward the South. Every Southern state except Texas created new governments, and Johnson approved them. Their legislatures passed new laws. Many of the laws were BLACK CODES, **DISCRIMINATORY** laws that denied the **CIVIL RIGHTS** of blacks in the South and prevented the Freedmen's Bureau from doing its work.

DISCRIMINATORY
treatment against people based on the group or class to which they belong, such as race

CIVIL RIGHTS
rights that protect the ability to participate in activities granted to citizens, without discrimination; personal liberties

260

Some members of Congress—the RADICAL REPUBLICANS—decided that the federal government should intervene. Congress gave the Freedmen's Bureau more powers and passed the CIVIL RIGHTS ACT OF 1866, which confirmed that blacks were citizens and overturned the *DRED SCOTT* decision of 1857.

> **RADICAL**
> extreme

The FOURTEENTH AMENDMENT

> **DUE PROCESS**
> the normal way that the law is practiced; the process that is due to each citizen

The FOURTEENTH AMENDMENT to the Constitution was passed in June 1868. It ensured that any person (except Native Americans) born or naturalized in the U.S. was a citizen with full rights, such as **DUE PROCESS**. All of the states had to accept these amendments to reenter the Union. This led to:

riots in the South;

an influx of black voters; and

an unsuccessful attempt by Johnson to oppose it.

RADICAL RECONSTRUCTION

The Republicans initiated RADICAL RECONSTRUCTION. Congress, not the president, took charge of Reconstruction efforts. In March 1867, Congress passed the RECONSTRUCTION ACTS, which divided the South into five military districts that would be controlled by a military commander until the Southern states were readmitted to the Union.

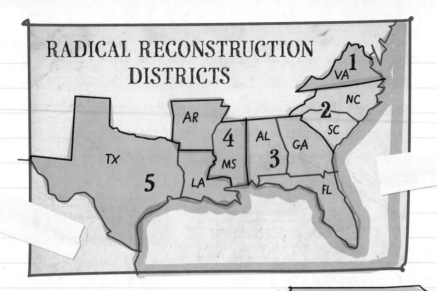

RADICAL RECONSTRUCTION DISTRICTS

IMPEACHMENT

Aware that Johnson opposed Radical Reconstruction, Congress also passed the **TENURE** OF OFFICE ACT, which limited executive power by requiring the president to secure congressional approval before he could remove members of his cabinet. During the summer of 1867, when Congress wasn't in session, President Johnson fired his secretary of war, Edwin Stanton. Congress voted to impeach Johnson for doing it without their approval (and, unofficially, for disagreeing with Congress). In February 1868, Johnson was tried in the Senate, but was acquitted by just one vote. He didn't run for reelection.

The ELECTION of 1868

In the presidential election of 1868, the Democratic former governor of New York, HORATIO SEYMOUR, ran against Republican war hero Ulysses S. Grant. Having garnered the support of Republicans in the North and newly **ENFRANCHISED** African Americans in the South, Grant won the election.

VIRGINIA, MISSISSIPPI, AND TEXAS WERE NOT ALLOWED TO PARTICIPATE BECAUSE THEY WEREN'T FULLY RECONSTRUCTED YET.

> **ENFRANCHISE**
> to set free or endow with a franchise, such as the right to vote

Because African Americans turned out in high numbers to vote in the presidential election, Republicans feared that Southern states would try to limit their voting in future elections. In 1869, Congress proposed the FIFTEENTH AMENDMENT, which made it illegal to deny citizens the right to vote based on race.

> The Fifteenth Amendment did not make any qualifications regarding gender. That is, women still could not vote.

LIFE for FORMER SLAVES

In 1870, HIRAM REVELS became the first African American in the U.S. Senate, representing Mississippi. In 1875, BLANCHE K. BRUCE, also from Mississippi, became the second black senator. Most former slaves remained poor. General Sherman had proposed a plan to divide plantations among freedmen (so everyone would literally get "40 ACRES AND A MULE"), but this was opposed by Congress. Most former slaves resorted to either contract work on plantations or the **SHARECROPPING**

> **SHARECROPPING**
> a system whereby farmers receive supplies and land in exchange for providing a share of the crop to the landowner

system, which often forced them into a lifetime of debt to landowners.

The KU KLUX KLAN

In 1866, a secret organization called the KU KLUX KLAN (the KKK) was organized in Tennessee with the purpose of opposing civil rights. Wearing disguises and hiding their faces, members attacked individuals, **LYNCHING** many. Local authorities often turned a blind eye. The FORCE ACTS passed by Congress and signed by Grant allowed the military to enforce the Fourteenth Amendment, which helped destroy the KKK. However, it would be resurrected in the 1920s.

CARPETBAGGERS AND SCALAWAGS

Northerners who came to work in the South as reformers were known as **CARPETBAGGERS**, after the luggage made of carpet that they used. Carpetbaggers were accused of trying to make a profit from Reconstruction. Southerners who supported the government were known as **SCALAWAGS**, or rascals. They were seen as traitors to the South.

The PANIC of 1873

In September 1873, a financial firm called JAY COOKE AND COMPANY went bankrupt, setting off the PANIC OF 1873. A major economic depression followed. Republicans were blamed.

The COMPROMISE of 1877

In the election of 1876, the Republican Party ran RUTHERFORD B. HAYES, the moderate governor of Ohio, against Democrat SAMUEL TILDEN, who fought corruption as governor of New York. Although it appeared that Tilden had won, the Republicans disputed electoral votes from the newly reconstructed states. Congress appointed a commission that led to the COMPROMISE OF 1877: Hayes would become president, but in return federal troops would leave the South and provide Southerners with aid for public projects. The Compromise of 1877 essentially ended Reconstruction.

SOUTHERN "REDEMPTION"

REDEEM
to recover or make amends for

Southern Democrats retook control of their state governments. Seen as the restorers of the "true South," they became known as **REDEEMERS**. They aimed to decrease taxes, decrease the size of government— and decrease racial equality. Although the Fifteenth Amendment guaranteed citizens the right to vote regardless of race, Southern states instituted POLL TAXES (requiring people to pay money to vote) and LITERACY TESTS (requiring a certain level of literacy to vote). These measures made it very difficult for former slaves to participate in government, but they did not have as much of an effect on whites: Most white men, even the poor and uneducated,

were **EXEMPTED** from both the tax and
the literary test by GRANDFATHER CLAUSES,
laws that protected men whose fathers or

> **EXEMPT**
> freed from
> responsibility

grandfathers voted before the Civil War (because they were
white). These laws weren't specifically based on race, so they
were allowed to continue. Southern states passed measures
known as the JIM CROW LAWS, which kept black citizens
and white citizens separate.

PLESSY v. FERGUSON

When Homer Plessy rode in a whites-only **SEGREGATED**
railroad car and was arrested, he sued the railroad company.
The Supreme Court ruled in the *PLESSY v. FERGUSON* decision
that segregation was legal as long as facilities for blacks
were "SEPARATE BUT EQUAL" to
those for whites. The Civil War was
over, but equality was still a long
road away.

> **SEGREGATION**
> the enforced separation
> of people, specifically on
> the basis of race

1. When was Reconstruction?

2. What does the Fourteenth Amendment do?

3. Why was President Johnson impeached?

4. To what does the phrase "40 acres and a mule" refer?

5. What was the Compromise of 1877?

6. What was a grandfather clause?

7. What was *PLESSY v. FERGUSON*?

CHECK YOUR ANSWERS

1. 1865–1877
2. It guarantees the right to due process and equal protection under the law.
3. He broke the Tenure of Office Act by firing a cabinet member without Congress's approval.
4. General Sherman proposed giving these things to former slaves, to be taken from plantations that would be split up, but Congress didn't agree to it.
5. Hayes would become president, but in return federal troops would leave the South and provide Southerners with aid for public projects.
6. A grandfather clause gave those whose grandfathers could vote exemption from other voting criteria, such as literacy tests and paying taxes.
7. The Supreme Court case that ruled that segregation was legal as long as facilities for blacks were "separate but equal" to those for whites

Unit 5

Reshaping the Nation
1850–1917

The developments that started before the Civil War continued after it. There was even more **EXPANSION**, more **MINING**, and more **INDUSTRY**. In between the Civil War and World War I, the U.S. turned into the modern nation we recognize today—but getting there took work.

Chapter 24

TRAINS, BONANZAS,
★ ★ ★ ★ ★ and ★ ★ ★ ★ ★
BUCKAROOS

EAST MEETS WEST

In the early 1860s, the PONY EXPRESS, a mail relay system using horses, connected the East and West. The telegraph was much faster and rendered the Pony Express obsolete. But the telegraph couldn't carry people or packages.

The TRANSCONTINENTAL RAILROAD

Between 1862 and 1864, Congress passed the PACIFIC RAILWAY ACTS. It **SUBSIDIZED** the CENTRAL PACIFIC and UNION PACIFIC railroad companies to build a transcontinental railroad.

> **SUBSIDIZE**
> to provide financial help, usually used when a government helps a business

They relied on cheap immigrant labor to lay tracks through harsh conditions and rugged terrain, and were especially reliant on the Chinese and Irish, who finished the dangerous work.

The Central Pacific line started in Sacramento, California, and the Union Pacific line started in Omaha, Nebraska. On May 10, 1869, the two railroads met in the middle at PROMONTORY, Utah, where Leland Stanford, president of the Central Pacific railroad and former governor of California, drove a GOLDEN SPIKE into the railroad to connect the two lines.

> The **golden spike** was a giant nail used to attach the metal rail of a railroad to the wooden ties (the slats that run perpendicular to the rails) underneath.

TRAIN-ING the NATION

The railroad routes built during the late 1800s led to an explosion in the population of the West. Steel, cattle, and coal industries also grew, and locomotive technology expanded. To make rail travel more uniform, in 1883 the railroad industry created four standard American time zones. (Before that, individual communities kept their own time according to the sun's position.) The railroad affected the life of every American.

COWBOYS
and the
"WILD WEST"

Post–Civil War prosperity in the Northeast created a demand for beef, so RANCHERS (particularly in Texas) raised a lot of cows, using the Great Plains's abundant amount of grass.

Cows need COWHANDS, or COWBOYS. Cowboys adopted the techniques and clothing of the Mexican vaqueros. When they arrived in a town, they had a reputation for being wild. The need for local lawmen or **VIGILANTES** to control cowboys and outlaws led to the myth of the WILD WEST—even though the West was no more wild than the rest of the country.

> **VIGILANTE**
> a person without legal authority who takes the law into his or her own hands

One of the most famous peace officers of the western frontier was **WYATT EARP.** He was also a farmer, buffalo hunter, and gambler, and his participation in a gunfight at the O.K. Corral made him an iconic figure of the Wild West.

HOME on the RANGE

The HOMESTEAD ACT, passed in 1862, opened up the land for any **HOMESTEADERS** who wanted to farm it, including women and African Americans. It gave settlers 160 acres of land to get started. Originally seen as a desert that couldn't be farmed, the Great Plains proved valuable to farmers who were determined to make use of the land.

> **HOMESTEADERS**
> people who claimed and agreed to settle on land promised to them by the Homestead Act

> Barbed wire was patented by Joseph Glidden in 1871. It created hardships for Native Americans, but settlers could now fence in their property and contain cattle.

The FARMERS ORGANIZE

Population growth

More demand for food

More need for farming

More profits for farmers

More farmers

More food

Too much food

Lower prices

Farmers began to lose money. They blamed high shipping fees, high costs for supplies, and high interest.

In 1867, Oliver Hudson Kelley led farmers in creating the NATIONAL **GRANGE** OF THE PATRONS OF HUSBANDRY, an organization that provided social services and set up cost-cutting **COOPERATIVES** for farmers, although the cooperatives weren't successful. The National Grange also lobbied for state regulation of railroad fees and prices.

> **GRANGE**
> a place where grain is stored; an association of farmers

> **COOPERATIVE**
> an organization in which people share costs and profits

SILVER AND GOLD

In 1873, the nation put its currency on the GOLD STANDARD, meaning that the amount of paper money available was determined by the amount of gold in the treasury. Gold was scarce, so less money was in circulation; prices fell because each individual dollar was worth more. The FREE SILVER movement appealed to farmers because as prices fell, so did their profits. The Free Silver movement advocated adding silver into the mix to produce more money, which would lead to INFLATION.

POPULISM and the ELECTION of 1892

> SECOND PRESIDENT ASSASSINATED—THE ASSASSIN WANTED ARTHUR TO BE PRESIDENT!

Following Presidents JAMES GARFIELD and CHESTER A. ARTHUR, GROVER CLEVELAND was elected in 1884. During Cleveland's presidency, Congress passed the INTERSTATE COMMERCE ACT in 1887, regulating the railroad industry.

In 1892, during PRESIDENT BENJAMIN HARRISON's term, the political activism of farmers and the Free Silver movement led to the formation of the **POPULIST PARTY**, a new political faction with a platform of federal regulation, Free Silver, and workers' rights. In the 1892 presidential election, the Populist Party ran James B. Weaver, but Grover Cleveland decided on another (nonconsecutive) run for president and won. Still, another economic crisis (called the PANIC OF 1893) strengthened the Populist cause.

> **POPULIST**
> having to do with populism, the political philosophy of focusing on "average" people

Remember: The **PANIC OF 1837** took place during the Jackson and Van Buren administrations.

AAAAHHHH!!!

The **PANIC OF 1873** took place during the Grant presidency.

The **PANIC OF 1893** took place in Cleveland's presidency.

WAIT, WHICH PANIC IS THIS?!

The ELECTION of 1896

In 1896, an anti-silver candidate, WILLIAM McKINLEY, ran on the Republican presidential ticket. WILLIAM JENNINGS BRYAN, a Free Silver politician, ran on the Democratic ticket and was endorsed by the Populist Party. McKINLEY won the 1896 presidential election, and the Populist Party fell apart.

The END of the FRONTIER

Free land for homesteaders began to run out. The U.S. government was under pressure to make more land available. On April 22, 1889, it opened up an area in what is now Oklahoma to non-Native American settlers. Previously designated "Indian Territory," it was the last place in the Continental U.S. that was considered "unsettled." At noon that day, thousands of settlers rushed into the territory to stake their claims to new land. According to the historian FREDERICK JACKSON TURNER, the **FRONTIER** was finished.

EVEN THOUGH MANY NATIVE AMERICANS LIVED THERE

FRONTIER
the border of a
settled territory

YEE-HAW!

Oklahomans are known as **SOONERS** because although the land that would eventually become Oklahoma officially opened up on April 22, some ambitious farmers and ranchers rushed into the territory sooner to claim the best land.

CHECK YOUR KNOWLEDGE

1. Why was the Pony Express first needed, and why did it later become obsolete?

2. Which two railway companies collaborated on the first transcontinental railroad?

3. Which industries were most affected by the railroad expansion?

4. Why were time zones invented?

5. Why was the West known for being "wild"?

6. What was the gold standard?

7. Who were the Sooners?

8. Was the territory now known as Oklahoma empty of people when it was opened to American settlers?

ANSWERS

CHECK YOUR ANSWERS

1. It was needed to communicate with the West, and it was made obsolete by telegraphs.

2. Union Pacific and Central Pacific

3. Steel, cattle, and coal

4. In order to coordinate train schedules

5. Cowboys and outlaws led to a need for local policing, and thus to the myth of the Wild West—even though the West wasn't more wild than the rest of the country.

6. A system where the amount of paper money available was determined by the amount of gold in the treasury

7. Eager farmers and ranchers who rushed into the Oklahoma territory to claim land before it was officially open

8. No, Native Americans lived there.

☆ Chapter 25 ☆

NATIVE AMERICAN
★ ★ ★ ★ ★ ★ ★ ★ ★ ★ ★ ★
RESERVATIONS

LAND CONFLICT... AGAIN

Now the U.S. government was allowing American settlers onto land that was previously set aside for Native Americans. As miners and ranchers traveled west, they competed with the Native Americans for resources along the way. The U.S. built forts on **SIOUX** land to protect the travelers.

> **SIOUX**
> is pronounced "soo"

MORE RESERVATIONS

In 1866, Sioux warriors led by RED CLOUD began a series of attacks against those forts. In one attack, Sioux military leader CRAZY HORSE and his men ambushed American soldiers. The U.S. government agreed to abandon its forts and create a reservation for the Sioux, overseen by the Bureau of Indian Affairs.

The previous year, the TREATY OF MEDICINE LODGE had created reservations for the Comanche, Apache, Cheyenne, and several other peoples. Most of the Plains Indians didn't like the idea of living on a reservation, which would destroy their culture of nomadic hunting. However, they had little choice but to accept the terms of the treaties and move because the U.S. government wanted to use their land.

Conflict between the U.S. government and Native Americans continued throughout the 1860s. In 1863, the U.S. Army burned Navajo villages to force the people to make the "LONG WALK," a painful 300-mile trek to their appointed reservation in New Mexico, which killed many Navajos along the way. In 1864, the Colorado militia opened fire on a Cheyenne camp in the SAND CREEK MASSACRE. Although the Cheyenne, led by CHIEF BLACK KETTLE, retaliated, they eventually agreed to stop fighting.

CUSTER'S LAST STAND

In 1874, soldiers led by LIEUTENANT GENERAL GEORGE ARMSTRONG CUSTER found gold on the Sioux reservation in the Dakotas, tempting the U.S. to abandon the terms of the Second Treaty of Fort Laramie and purchase the land. However, Sioux CHIEF SITTING BULL refused to sell. Instead, he and Chief Crazy Horse encouraged their people to fight, beginning the most famous Native American act of resistance of the time. On June 25, 1876, Custer and a few hundred of his men faced thousands of Sioux and Cheyenne in the BATTLE OF THE LITTLE BIGHORN, near the Little

Bighorn River in Montana. The battle is also known as CUSTER'S LAST STAND, because Custer's entire unit was killed, including Custer.

Although Little Bighorn was a major Sioux victory, it was also their last. The U.S. government stepped up its military action, and the following year, in 1877, Crazy Horse surrendered. Although Sitting Bull initially fled to Canada, in 1881, he also surrendered and was sent to a reservation, where he was later killed by reservation authorities.

Still, many Native American groups continued resistance movements. In 1877, CHIEF JOSEPH attempted to lead the Nez Percé from present-day Oregon to Canada, rather than to their appointed reservation in Idaho, though he gave in after the U.S. Army threatened to attack. GERONIMO led the Apache resistance from the 1870s until his surrender in 1886.

The buffalo were virtually hunted into extinction between 1850 and 1880. This hurt the Native American people by eliminating the most essential animal in their hunting culture. Buffalo were hunted for meat and hides, as well as hunted for sport from trains. The railroads wanted fewer buffalo because large herds caused delays in schedules.

The DAWES ACT

To make Native Americans assimilate into American culture instead of maintaining their own, Congress passed the DAWES GENERAL ALLOTMENT ACT in 1887, splitting Native

American land into **ALLOTMENTS**, private plots of land that were to be used as farms, destroying the Native American culture of

> **ALLOTMENT**
> a portion or share, as of land

communal property. The government reclaimed "leftover" land and sold it to American settlers. The government also took many Native American children away from their families, sending them to schools like the CARLISLE SCHOOL in Pennsylvania to make them more "American," restricting their clothing, how they wore their hair, and what language they could speak.

OLYMPIAN JIM THORPE GRADUATED FROM HERE.

WOUNDED KNEE

Many Native Americans longed for the old way of life. They wanted to be nomadic hunters again, but the food demands of the American settlers and railroad crews had decimated the bison population. Many turned to a religious movement led by a prophet called WOVOKA, who spoke of a future time when the buffalo would return. Part of Wovoka's teachings included a ceremony called the GHOST DANCE, a peaceful religious gathering that the U.S. government interpreted as a threat and tried to suppress. On December 29, 1890, American troops attacked and killed hundreds of Sioux who were gathered for a Ghost Dance in the WOUNDED KNEE MASSACRE. This became the last major clash between the U.S. government and the Native Americans of its time.

NOT A GOOD CHAPTER.

CHECK YOUR KNOWLEDGE

1. Why were Indian reservations created?

2. Why did Native Americans sign treaties forcing them onto reservations?

3. How did reservation life change Native American cultures?

4. What was the "Long Walk"?

5. Who won at the Battle of the Little Bighorn?

6. How did the U.S. government make money from the Dawes Act?

7. Why were Native American children taken away from their families?

8. What were Ghost Dance ceremonies?

ANSWERS

CHECK YOUR ANSWERS

1. The U.S. government wanted to use Indian land.
2. They had no choice.
3. They could no longer follow buffalo herds or hunt freely, which destroyed their traditional nomadic way of life. Allotments also destroyed their culture of communal property.
4. It was the journey of the Navajo from their homeland to their reservation.
5. Crazy Horse and Sitting Bull led the Sioux and Cheyenne to a victory.
6. Land on the reservations that was not used for allotments was sold.
7. They were sent to schools to be "Americanized."
8. Religious gatherings of Native Americans who hoped for a future in which the buffalo would return

☆ Chapter 26 ☆

The SECOND INDUSTRIAL

★ ★ ★ ★ ★ ★ ★ ★ ★ ★ ★ ★ ★ ★

REVOLUTION

The SECOND INDUSTRIAL REVOLUTION

In the late 1800s, industry was revolutionized for a second time, creating a SECOND INDUSTRIAL REVOLUTION. After the Civil War, the U.S. became one of the leading industrial powers in the world, and businesses such as steel and railroads grew by leaps and bounds. Business tycoons, notably the RAILROAD BARONS, those who rose to prominence in the railroad industry, flourished, and life changed for people of every income level.

INVENTIONS GALORE

Industrial growth, especially in the railroad sector, fueled a demand for new technology, and each new innovation led to others. Many of America's most significant technological developments came about in the late nineteenth century.

AMERICAN INVENTIONS GALORE

BEEP! BEEP!

1851: ISAAC SINGER improved on the original 1845 SEWING MACHINE design, enabling the garment industry to begin to replace at-home clothing construction.

1866: The first TRANSATLANTIC TELEGRAPH wire was put in place.

1867: The first commercially successful TYPEWRITER was invented by Christopher Sholes, Carlos Glidden, and Samuel W. Soule.

1876: ALEXANDER GRAHAM BELL invented the TELEPHONE and started by the Bell Telephone Company, launching the telecom industry.

1876: THOMAS EDISON opened a lab in Menlo Park, New Jersey, and went on to patent more than 1,000 inventions. In 1879, he invented the first electric LIGHTBULB.

1886: GEORGE WESTINGHOUSE founded the Westinghouse Electric Company, which expanded the power grid created by Edison.

1888: The ADDING MACHINE, an early calculator patented by William Seward Burroughs, facilitated business transactions, and the KODAK CAMERA brought snapshot photography to the mainstream thanks to George Eastman.

1903: ORVILLE AND WILBUR WRIGHT made the first airplane flight at KITTY HAWK, NORTH CAROLINA, on December 17.

1908: HENRY FORD devised the Model T car. Created by his innovative assembly line system, the car was affordable enough for many middle-class Americans to own.

ASSEMBLY LINE → If everyone on the line does one job over and over (specialization and division of labor), people working together can produce more in a shorter time period. Those workers are also paid less because they have fewer skills.

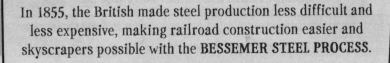

In 1855, the British made steel production less difficult and less expensive, making railroad construction easier and skyscrapers possible with the **BESSEMER STEEL PROCESS.**

With new inventions also came a higher demand for fuel. After Edwin L. Drake's 1859 discovery of CRUDE OIL (which could be turned into kerosene for lighting lamps and used as fuel) underground in Pennsylvania, the petroleum industry began to skyrocket.

The CORPORATION

As businesses grew, many of them became too expensive or risky for one person to own. Instead, CORPORATIONS owned them and SHAREHOLDERS controlled them, meaning less risk, as well as the promise of **DIVIDENDS**. Selling **STOCK** was an easy way for corporations to raise **CAPITAL**, and banks could make a profit through involvement in corporate finances.

> **DIVIDENDS**
> sums of money paid to shareholders of a corporation from its earnings
>
> **STOCK**
> a share of a corporation, entitling the owner to a portion of the company's profits
>
> **CAPITAL**
> in this context, financial assets

HORIZONTAL and VERTICAL INTEGRATION

Some individual businessmen were so successful that they gained worldwide recognition, like JOHN D. ROCKEFELLER. Rockefeller founded an oil refinery in 1863, which became the STANDARD OIL COMPANY of Ohio in 1870. Before long, Standard Oil controlled almost the entire American petroleum industry, because Rockefeller created a **MONOPOLY** by driving his competition out of business.

In 1882, he founded the Standard Oil **TRUST**, a corporate board that bought stock in and controlled many companies in the industry. Standard Oil then owned its competition and could set prices across the industry. Once Rockefeller controlled the industry, he found ways

> **MONOPOLY**
> when one company or person controls an entire market
>
> **TRUST**
> a group of companies controlled by a single corporate board

to make even more profit, including demanding that railroads charge him less to transport his products. The railroads complied; if they didn't, they would lose too much business.

Another famous businessman of the time was the Scottish-born steelmaker ANDREW CARNEGIE, who began his career as a railroad employee and, after making smart investments in steel and iron, founded the CARNEGIE STEEL COMPANY. Carnegie controlled every step of the manufacturing process, a tactic known as VERTICAL INTEGRATION: He owned not only the steel mills, but also the mines, the transportation,

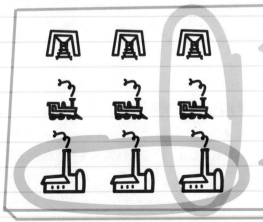

VERTICAL INTEGRATION
(Carnegie)

HORIZONTAL INTEGRATION
(Rockefeller)

and the warehouses. He was able to cut costs and ensure a better product. Unlike Rockefeller, Carnegie did not intend to take over his competition (that tactic is known as HORIZONTAL INTEGRATION).

ROBBER BARONS and PHILANTHROPISTS

> **GILDED**
> covered in gold, but not made of it

There was so much inequality that the period between 1869 and 1896 became known as the **GILDED AGE**, because it looked like gold on the outside but was something crude on the inside. People like Rockefeller were called ROBBER BARONS, meaning that while they lived like nobility, they were also unethical men who had used trickery to become wealthy. In July of 1890, Congress passed the SHERMAN ANTITRUST ACT. Based on the concept that competition is necessary in free markets, it made trusts and monopolies illegal. It was difficult to enforce.

> Carnegie published an article that came to be known as "The Gospel of Wealth." He stated that it was the wealthy's responsibility to society to act philanthropically.

Regardless of how they obtained their wealth, Carnegie and Rockefeller both were **PHILANTHROPISTS**, giving away large amounts and founding establishments such as Carnegie Hall and the Rockefeller Institute.

> **PHILANTHROPIST**
> someone who gives to charity

LIFE in the FACTORY

Although many businessmen prospered, factory workers faced long hours, low pay, and unhealthy conditions. At this time, factory workers were not only adults but children as well. As automation increased and skilled labor was less necessary, workers themselves became part of the machine—and many bosses treated them as such.

UNIONS

Although unions and trade guilds had existed before, they grew in size and scope. The first national union, the KNIGHTS OF LABOR, was founded in Philadelphia in 1869. Originally established as a secret society to protect its members from employer retaliation, the organization went public, under the leadership of Terence V. Powderly, in the 1880s. Unlike most unions, the Knights of Labor welcomed women, African Americans, and unskilled laborers—but Asians were still excluded.

With its large membership, the Knights tried to use the tactic of **COLLECTIVE BARGAINING** to secure pay equality and other workplace rights. In 1886, SAMUEL GOMPERS founded the AMERICAN FEDERATION OF LABOR (AFL), a coalition of many smaller unions of skilled workers, which became a much more influential organization.

> **COLLECTIVE BARGAINING**
> the idea of workers acting together, or collectively—is the essence of a union, as it gives workers the power to convince the management to make a compromise

291

GOING on STRIKE

Although **STRIKES** sometimes helped unions fight businesses, they also sometimes damaged the reputation of the unions, some of which came to be seen as violent **ANARCHIST** groups.

> **STRIKE**
> when employees refuse to work, usually in an attempt to negotiate a change in working conditions
>
> **ANARCHIST**
> being opposed to government and/or law

The Haymarket Affair, Chicago, Illinois, 1886:
When the McCormick Harvester Company hired strikebreaking workers, a scuffle followed, killing a union member. This led to a protest at Haymarket Square in which several civilians and eight policemen were killed, and public opinion turned against the strikers.

The Homestead Strike, Homestead, Pennsylvania, 1892:
At Andrew Carnegie's Homestead steel mill, a strike led to a fight that resulted in ten deaths. The state militia was called in.

The Pullman Strike, Pullman, Illinois, 1894:
When **EUGENE DEBS**, the president of the American Railway Union, led a strike at the Pullman Palace Car Company over pay cuts, President Cleveland called in soldiers to put an end to the strike, which had shut down many railroads across the country. Debs went to prison.

CHECK YOUR KNOWLEDGE

1. How did the Bessemer Steel Process affect the steel industry?

2. Why are assembly lines important?

3. Why was crude oil in higher demand in the mid-1800s than it had been before?

4. How did the Standard Oil Trust help create a monopoly for Standard Oil?

5. Why was Rockefeller seen as a "robber baron"?

6. What were the terms of the Sherman Antitrust Act?

7. Why were the Knights of Labor originally a secret society?

8. How did violent strikes affect labor unions' reputations?

ANSWERS

CHECK YOUR ANSWERS

1. Steel got cheaper and easier to make.
2. They allow faster, cheaper production through division of labor.
3. New inventions needed fuel.
4. The trust owned shares in Standard Oil's competitors.
5. He lived like nobility and gained his wealth through unethical trusts and monopolies, which were (later) criminal.
6. Trusts and monopolies were made illegal to allow fair business competition.
7. In order to protect their members from being retaliated against by employers
8. Unions became unfairly associated with anarchist movements.

ANY THOUGHTS?

I GIVE IT A WEEK.

☆ Chapter 27 ☆

NEW IMMIGRANTS,
★ ★ ★ ★ ★ ★ ★ ★ ★ ★ ★
NEW CITIES

The NEW IMMIGRANTS

Previous immigrants had come mostly from Western and Northern Europe, but the "NEW IMMIGRANTS" in the 1880s were from Eastern Europe and Southern Europe, as well as Asia and Mexico.

The reasons for both waves of immigration were mostly the same. Immigrants strived to escape the overcrowding, religious and political persecution, and economic problems of their homelands. They hoped for a better life in America.

ELLIS ISLAND

After immigrants completed the often-treacherous journey to the U.S., they had one last hurdle to cross: the immigration processing center, where their health, legal status, and destination were confirmed. Many people had their names respelled, shortened, or otherwise "Americanized." The most famous immigration processing center was ELLIS ISLAND in New York Harbor. Most of those who came through Ellis Island were European; Asians usually entered the U.S. through the Bay Area's ANGEL ISLAND, and Mexican immigrants tended to arrive through an immigration center in El Paso, Texas.

The **STATUE OF LIBERTY**, installed in New York Harbor in 1886, was a gift to the U.S. from France. The poem on the base of the statue includes the famous lines **"Give me your tired, your poor, Your huddled masses yearning to breathe free"** (from "The New Colossus," by **EMMA LAZARUS**). To many immigrants, the first sight of the statue represented a new beginning and the American dream.

BECOMING "AMERICAN"

Like previous immigrants, the new immigrants tended to settle in ethnic neighborhoods where they could continue speaking the language and practicing the religion, cuisine, and traditions of their homelands. However, the new immigrants were more recognizably different, and the diversity they brought to cities was often seen as a negative. Some U.S. citizens feared the immigrants would "take" jobs away from citizens by working for less, while others thought that the immigrants should

ASSIMILATE into American culture as quickly as possible. NATIVISM, an opposition to immigration, was on the rise again.

> **ASSIMILATE**
> to blend in

As it turned out, many immigrants, including women and children, ended up working in factories or **SWEATSHOPS** under harsh

> **SWEATSHOP**
> a factory defined by its poor working conditions and low wages

conditions for very low pay. Immigrant farmers could not afford to purchase their own land in America, so they had no choice but to accept the work.

In 1882, Congress passed the CHINESE EXCLUSION ACT, which banned immigration from China for ten years (the act was renewed twice, for a total of thirty years). Congress also limited immigration from Japan and (unsuccessfully) attempted to restrict all immigration by illiterate persons. Convicts and people with certain illnesses were banned from coming to the U.S.

> Although immigrants were encouraged to **AMERICANIZE**, the notion of being "American" was difficult to define. As immigrants assimilated, they changed what it meant to be American. America was becoming a "**MELTING POT**": a blending of cultures.

URBANIZATION

Most immigrants moved to cities. As machinery reduced the need for farm labor, those workers began coming to cities in the North for factory work, as did many African Americans from the South. It was a time of great URBANIZATION, or growth of cities.

CITY LIFE

Turn-of-the-century cities were places of innovation and excitement:

The steel industry and the invention of the **ELEVATOR** (patented by **ELISHA OTIS**) allowed buildings to be taller; building up rather than out conserved city space. The first **SKYSCRAPER** was a ten-story building constructed in Chicago in 1884.

Next time you're in an elevator, look for a logo. The **OTIS ELEVATOR COMPANY** is still a major producer of elevators.

Public transportation enabled travel. San Francisco installed its **CABLE CARS** in 1873, and Richmond introduced **TROLLEYS**, electric cars that would replace horse-drawn streetcars. Boston opened up its subway system in 1897, and New York City's followed in 1904.

Construction of **CENTRAL PARK** was completed in 1873. Designed by **FREDERICK LAW OLMSTED**, the park was built when New York recognized the importance of having a green space; other major parks were built during this same time period.

Cities were still in need of development. The working class often lived in dangerous tenements that were unhygienic and overcrowded. Areas with many tenements became SLUMS, which led to increased crime. City sewage systems were not equipped to handle so many people. Earthquakes and fires could destroy large sections of cities at a time because of unsafe building standards. These problems encouraged the growing MIDDLE CLASS to move to the SUBURBS, now easier to reach because of better transportation.

REFORMING the CITIES

Local governments did little to address the problems of the cities, especially for immigrants. However, individual activists tried to make a difference. Photojournalist Jacob Riis took photos of slums to expose their terrible conditions. Others set up SETTLEMENT HOUSES to provide social services to the poor. New York's NEIGHBORHOOD GUILD, founded in 1886 by Charles Stover and Stanton Coit, was the first. The most famous settlement house was Chicago's HULL HOUSE, founded in 1889 by JANE ADDAMS and Ellen Gates Starr.

CHECK YOUR KNOWLEDGE

1. What was new about the new immigrants?

2. Why did the new immigrants make the trip to the U.S.?

3. What was the point of immigration processing centers?

4. Why did some people want to stop immigrants from coming to the U.S.?

5. How does the concept of a "melting pot" apply to the assimilation of immigrants in the U.S.?

6. What were the causes of urbanization during the Second Industrial Revolution?

7. How did certain areas of American cities become slums?

8. What led to the growth of the suburbs?

9. Why did Jacob Riis take photographs of people in the slums?

10. Why were settlement houses necessary?

ANSWERS

CHECK YOUR ANSWERS

1. They were from Southern and Eastern Europe rather than Northern and Western Europe. There were also Asian and Mexican immigrants.

2. Economic problems, religious and political persecution, overcrowding, poverty, and the hope of a better life

3. To determine the health, destinations, and legal status of each immigrant

4. They were afraid immigrants would take jobs by working for less.

5. When immigrants become part of American culture, they also add their own heritage to the mix.

6. Many people (especially African Americans) were moving North, as fewer farm workers were needed to do the same amount of work.

7. Too many people lived there without adequate public services.

8. Bad housing, transportation improvements, and the growth of the middle class

9. To educate others about the way those people lived

10. The government was not providing for the poor.

Chapter 28

PROGRESS! (ivism)

CONSUMERISM and LEISURE TIME

> **CONSUMERISM**
> increasing consumption; focus on consumption and purchasing

Industrialization led to long hours in the factories, but unlike farmers, factory workers (and the wealthy) often had days off. In the late 1800s, as LEISURE TIME became more common, so did activities such as

{ shopping in **DEPARTMENT STORES**, which encouraged **CONSUMERISM** via advertisements }

{ amusement parks, such as **CONEY ISLAND** in New York }

{ **VAUDEVILLE**, circuses, and other theater }

{ **WORLD'S FAIRS**, where consumers, merchants, and innovators came together }

303

{ BASEBALL and other spectator sports, including basketball and college football, as well as participatory sports such as tennis, golf, and cycling }

{ new kinds of American music, such as RAGTIME and early JAZZ }

CORRUPTION in the GILDED AGE

Political parties used illegal means (like bribes and extortion) and legal means (like convincing the poor to vote a certain way by promising them jobs) to control elections. These organizations were called POLITICAL MACHINES, and their leader was the BOSS. The most famous political machine was New York's Democratic TAMMANY HALL, led by WILLIAM MAGEAR "BOSS" TWEED, who is said to have stolen millions of dollars from the city.

The PROGRESSIVE MOVEMENT

President Garfield, who took office in 1881, saw that reform was needed, but he was assassinated before he could implement reforms. Some people, known as SOCIALISTS, believed that government should take complete ownership of corrupt businesses. Others, known as PROGRESSIVES, thought the government should regulate, not control. They aimed to democratize American society, and many of their reforms were to give the people a greater say in government. The PROGRESSIVE MOVEMENT in the 1890s aimed to fix social and economic problems, particularly in cities.

MUCKRAKERS

The Progressives gained support for their cause from journalists known as MUCKRAKERS, who exposed the "muck" of society. Famous muckrakers included IDA TARBELL, who exposed the oil trusts in her book *THE HISTORY OF THE STANDARD OIL COMPANY* (1904); UPTON SINCLAIR, who wrote about the meatpacking industry in his novel *THE JUNGLE* (1906); and JACOB RIIS, who displayed tenement life in his book of photographs *HOW THE OTHER HALF LIVES* (1889). Another muckraker, LINCOLN STEFFENS, exposed political machines.

REFORMERS and THEIR PROJECTS

Many of the most active Progressives in the country were middle-class women who were well educated but were expected to stop working when they got married. By the turn of the century, families tended to be smaller, and technology (like the vacuum cleaner) helped with housework, freeing up more of women's time to create change.

POLITICAL REFORM:

Supported by President Arthur, the PENDLETON CIVIL SERVICE ACT (1883) created a civil service exam to evaluate job candidates on the basis of merit, putting an end to the spoils system at the federal level.

Wisconsin held the first PRIMARY ELECTION in 1903, prompting voters to become more involved in national politics.

Oregon introduced VOTER INITIATIVES (to propose laws), REFERENDA (to approve laws), and RECALLS (to remove officials before the end of their term), allowing voters more control over state politics.

Adopted in 1913, the SIXTEENTH AMENDMENT allowed Congress to levy an income tax, which gave government funding to do, in the Progressives' view, great things; ratified in 1913, the SEVENTEENTH AMENDMENT gave the people the right to elect their senators directly rather than through the often-corrupt state legislatures.

EDUCATION REFORM:

Progressives like JOHN DEWEY advocated changes in public education to place greater emphasis on understanding rather than on rote memorization.

Settlement houses offered some of the first kindergarten classes.

Compulsory education laws were designed to not only educate children but to eliminate child labor.

ANTI-ALCOHOL REFORM (TEMPERANCE):

Organizations like the WOMAN'S CHRISTIAN **TEMPERANCE** UNION and the ANTI-SALOON LEAGUE worked to prohibit alcohol, which they saw as the cause of social problems.

TEMPERANCE abstaining from drinking alcohol

PROHIBITION time period in American history when alcohol was illegal

Temperance activist CARRIE NATION charged into saloons and destroyed liquor bottles with an ax.

Ratified in 1919, the EIGHTEENTH AMENDMENT began **PROHIBITION**, the period during which the production, sale, and transport of alcohol became illegal in the U.S.

LABOR REFORM:

Since children could be paid less than adults, CHILD LABOR was commonly used. Many people advocated placing limits on child labor, but congressional limits were deemed unconstitutional.

In 1905, a Socialist union called the INDUSTRIAL WORKERS OF THE WORLD was established, and it welcomed women, minorities, and others who could not join the American Federation of Labor (AFL).

Following the 1911 TRIANGLE **SHIRTWAIST** COMPANY factory fire in New York, which killed nearly 150 workers (mostly young women) who were locked inside by the company owners to prevent theft, the INTERNATIONAL LADIES' GARMENT WORKERS UNION advocated for increased workplace safety.

In 1912, Massachusetts created the first minimum wage law.

SHIRTWAIST
the common term for a lady's shirt during the early twentieth century

WOMEN'S RIGHTS

Once slavery was banned, many former abolitionists turned their attention to women's SUFFRAGE. In 1869, the NATIONAL AMERICAN WOMAN SUFFRAGE ASSOCIATION (NAWSA) was formed, and some of its leaders included Elizabeth Cady Stanton, Susan B. Anthony, Anna Howard Shaw, and Carrie Chapman Catt.

The NINETEENTH AMENDMENT was ratified in 1920; at last, women had the right to vote.

FINALLY!!!

SUSAN B. ANTHONY

One of most famous female reformers of the time was Mary Harris Jones, better known as **MOTHER JONES**, who helped organize numerous labor strikes.

Antidiscrimination Movements

The American Jewish Committee and the ANTI-DEFAMATION LEAGUE fought anti-Semitism, the SOCIETY OF AMERICAN INDIANS advocated for Native American rights, and the Mexican-American **MUTUALISTAS** assisted those living in the BARRIOS (labor camps or predominantly Spanish-speaking neighborhoods). Other groups facing discrimination included Catholics, Asians, and African Americans.

> **MUTUALISTAS**
> community-based
> aid groups

Within the African American community, two major schools of activism emerged. One was led by BOOKER T. WASHINGTON, who believed that education and financial stability were the keys to equality; that is, if African Americans persevered, equality would automatically follow. Washington struck the ATLANTA COMPROMISE with Southern white leaders, which stated that African Americans would resign to white political rule as long as they could receive education and economic equality. On the opposite side of the spectrum was W.E.B. DU BOIS, who believed that legal equality for African Americans would put an end to injustice.

Du Bois used the term "The Talented Tenth" to describe a class of leaders in the African American community that he believed would help create social change.

In 1881, Washington founded the TUSKEGEE INSTITUTE, an agricultural and industrial school in Alabama, and in 1909, Du Bois helped found the NATIONAL ASSOCIATION FOR THE ADVANCEMENT OF COLORED PEOPLE, or NAACP (pronounced "N-double A-C-P," it remains one of the most influential civil rights organizations in the U.S.).

Another significant African American figure of the time was GEORGE WASHINGTON CARVER. A member of the Tuskegee faculty, Carver revolutionized Southern agriculture by developing hundreds of uses for peanuts and other crops that were alternatives to cotton.

CHECK YOUR KNOWLEDGE

1. What is a political machine?

2. What is the main difference between Socialist beliefs and Progressive beliefs?

3. Who was Ida Tarbell?

4. Why were many reformers middle-class women?

5. What happened during the Triangle Shirtwaist Company factory fire?

6. When was suffrage granted to women?

7. What did Booker T. Washington and W.E.B. Du Bois disagree about?

ANSWERS

CHECK YOUR ANSWERS

1. Political machines are political parties that use illegal and legal means to control election outcomes.

2. Socialists believed that government should take complete ownership of corrupt businesses. Progressives thought the government should regulate, not control.

3. She exposed the oil trusts in her book *THE HISTORY OF THE STANDARD OIL COMPANY*.

4. They were well-educated and had time but were expected not to work.

5. Nearly 150 workers (mostly young women) were killed because they were locked inside by the company owners to prevent theft.

6. Suffrage was granted to women in 1920.

7. They disagreed about whether African Americans ought to focus on economic freedom or political freedom first.

☆ Chapter 29 ☆

EXPANSIONISM
★ ★ ☆ ★ ☆ and *★ ☆ ★ ★ ☆*
IMPERIALISM

Alongside progressivism, old ideas persisted. These ideas included Manifest Destiny, even though it seemed as though there was nowhere left for Americans to spread.

> **SOCIAL DARWINISM**
> was a major factor in imperialism. It was a popular idea that technologically advanced societies should rule over and control less advanced societies.

The continental U.S. had taken shape following the Gadsden Purchase, but some Americans advocated expanding overseas. In Europe, **IMPERIALISM** was at its height as European powers took over nations in Asia

> **IMPERIALISM**
> the policy of gaining authority over other nations or of acquiring colonies

and Africa. Many Americans believed that imperialism would bring prosperity and prestige to the U.S. and would allow Americans to spread Western ideals. Since Washington's Farewell Address, the U.S. had steered clear of foreign problems, as Washington had advised—but its agenda was about to change.

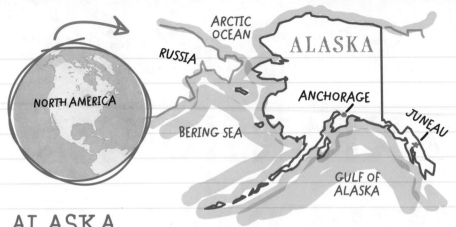

ARCTIC OCEAN

RUSSIA

ALASKA

NORTH AMERICA

BERING SEA

ANCHORAGE

JUNEAU

GULF OF ALASKA

ALASKA

Shortly after the Civil War, Secretary of State WILLIAM SEWARD purchased ALASKA from Russia for $7.2 million. Considering how cold Alaska was, many people considered this a foolish purchase, calling it "Seward's Folly" and referring to Alaska as "Seward's Ice Box." As it turned out, Alaska was rich with natural resources, and the U.S. officially annexed it in 1884.

The U.S. in the PACIFIC

The U.S. was becoming increasingly interested in the Pacific to open foreign markets to trade and American business interests. In 1854, COMMODORE MATTHEW PERRY used a combination of gifts and threats to convince Japan to enter into trade relations with the U.S. Japan was beginning a period of major modernization, and trade was seen as lucrative.

In 1867, the U.S. annexed the MIDWAY ISLANDS, islands midway between America and Asia where American ships could stop en route. Still, the U.S. wanted even more of a presence in the Pacific.

314

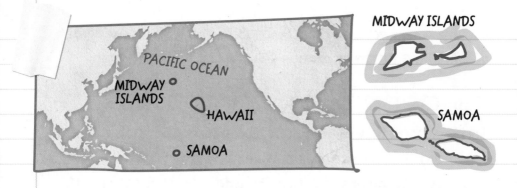

PACIFIC OCEAN

MIDWAY ISLANDS

MIDWAY ISLANDS

HAWAII

SAMOA

SAMOA

HAWAII

Since about the beginning of the nineteenth
century, the Hawaiian Islands, which were
unified, had been a source of sugar for the U.S.
Most of the sugar planters were Americans who
had moved there and forced the king of Hawaii to
grant them political power. In 1891, QUEEN LILIUOKALANI
came to power and attempted to limit American influence.
At about the same time, Congress imposed tariffs on imports
of Hawaiian sugar, angering the planters.

In 1893, planters staged a revolt with the help of the U.S.
Marines and the U.S. ambassador to Hawaii, forming their
own government. The new government asked to be annexed
by the U.S. President Benjamin Harrison agreed, but the
treaty he signed was not ratified before he left office.
President Cleveland, who succeeded him, opposed annexation
without the support of the Hawaiian people. It wasn't until
1900, during President McKinley's administration, that Hawaii

became a territory of the U.S. In 1899, the U.S. annexed part of SAMOA, a group of islands 2,500 miles south of Hawaii.

The OPEN DOOR POLICY

In the second half of the 1800s, European nations and Japan convinced the weaker nation of China to grant them SPHERES OF INFLUENCE, or areas within China to control. Since the U.S. didn't have a sphere of influence there, in 1899, Secretary of State John Hay suggested an OPEN DOOR POLICY of equal access for multiple imperial powers, including the U.S., to trade with China. There wasn't any reason for the other nations to agree—until the BOXER REBELLION of 1900, in which an antiforeign secret society known as the Boxers killed a number of foreigners living in China. Once the Boxers were defeated, the imperial powers agreed to Hay's policy and cooperated with one another.

However, Japan soon began ignoring the policy, which started the RUSSO-JAPANESE WAR with Russia. The TREATY OF PORTSMOUTH of 1905 ended the Russo-Japanese War, but Japan had become an even greater power, and U.S.-Japanese tensions began to rise.

CHECK YOUR KNOWLEDGE

1. What were the major arguments for imperialism in the U.S.?

2. What was Seward's Folly?

3. How did Commodore Perry convince Japan to enter into trade relations with the U.S.?

4. Why did the U.S. want territories in the Pacific in the late 1800s?

5. Who was Queen Liliuokalani?

6. Why did President Cleveland oppose President Harrison's plan to annex Hawaii?

7. What is a sphere of influence?

8. What convinced other nations to agree to an Open Door Policy with China?

ANSWERS

CHECK YOUR ANSWERS

1. People wanted to spread Western ideals, open trade, and increase the prestige of the U.S.

2. Secretary of State William Seward purchased Alaska from Russia for $7.2 million. Most people at the time thought there was nothing but cold up there, so they called the move "Seward's Folly."

3. Commodore Perry used a combination of gifts and threats to convince Japan to enter into trade relations with the U.S.

4. U.S. ships needed a place to stop on their way to trade with Japan.

5. Queen Liliuokalani was the queen of Hawaii who tried to limit American influence.

6. President Cleveland opposed annexation without the support of the Hawaiian people.

7. Area of control

8. The Boxer Rebellion of 1900 convinced other nations to agree to an Open Door Policy with China.

☆ Chapter 30 ☆
SPANISH-AMERICAN WAR

REBELLION in CUBA

While the U.S. was expanding, Spain—once the holder of a great empire in the Americas—was shrinking. Most Spanish holdings had declared independence, and those remaining were eager to be free of Spanish rule. In 1895, Cuban revolutionary JOSÉ MARTÍ returned from exile to lead the fight for Cuban independence. This worried many in the U.S., who were concerned about trade with Cuba and the island's proximity to Florida. However, neither President Cleveland, who was in his second term at the time, nor his successor, President McKinley, wanted to interfere.

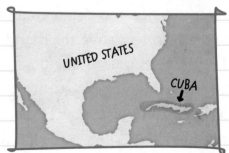

UNITED STATES

CUBA

YELLOW JOURNALISM

The fighting in Cuba became very violent, and Spanish troops treated Cuban prisoners terribly. The American public was shocked, but shock sold newspapers. In a tactic known as YELLOW JOURNALISM, Joseph Pulitzer and William Randolph Hearst exaggerated and sensationalized the stories, stirring up public fury. They were in competition with one another and scandals sold well.

REMEMBER the *MAINE*!

McKinley wished to avoid war. However, rioting in Havana, the capital of Cuba, put Americans in the area in danger. McKinley sent the ship U.S.S. *MAINE* to Havana in January of 1898 to protect them. With no warning, the ship exploded on February 15. Although evidence later suggested that it was an accident, Spain was blamed, and "REMEMBER THE *MAINE*!" became a rallying cry for war.

On April 20, Congress recognized Cuban independence and demanded that Spanish troops leave the island. In the TELLER AMENDMENT, the U.S. stated that it had no interest in controlling Cuba. On April 25, 1898, Congress declared war on Spain. The SPANISH-AMERICAN WAR had begun.

DEWEY in the PHILIPPINES

The Philippines were another holding of the Spanish empire, and like the Cubans, the FILIPINOS revolted in the 1890s. When COMMODORE GEORGE DEWEY led an American fleet to the Philippines on April 30, 1898, he had the support of the people there. On May 1, in the first battle of the Spanish-American War, Dewey destroyed the Spanish ships in Manila Harbor and then, with the help of Filipino rebels led by EMILIO AGUINALDO, took control of the city.

The ROUGH RIDERS and FIGHTING in the CARIBBEAN

Although the navy did much of the fighting, the army also played a role in the Spanish-American War. Many volunteers signed up to fight, including the FIRST U.S. VOLUNTEER CAVALRY, a diverse regiment of cowboys, students, and others organized by THEODORE "TEDDY" ROOSEVELT that became known as the ROUGH RIDERS. On July 1, 1898, the Rough Riders captured the hills around Santiago, Cuba. They helped the Americans win the BATTLE OF SAN JUAN HILL.

HAVANA
ATLANTIC OCEAN
CUBA
CARIBBEAN SEA
SAN JUAN HILL
GUANTÁNAMO
"TEDDY" ROOSEVELT

The TREATY of PARIS (AGAIN (AGAIN))

On August 12, only a few months after fighting had begun, **ARMISTICE** was declared. The Spanish empire was over, and the fighting had cost very few American lives. (In fact, many more Americans died of tropical diseases than of battle wounds.) In the 1898 TREATY OF PARIS, signed on December 10, Spain ceded control of Cuba, Puerto Rico, Guam, and the Philippines to the U.S.

PHILIPPINES

GUAM

PUERTO RICO

CUBA

Remember: The 1763 **TREATY OF PARIS** ended the Seven Years' War, the 1783 **TREATY OF PARIS** ended the Revolutionary War, and the 1898 **TREATY OF PARIS** ended the Spanish-American War.

EXPANSIONISM EXPANDS

Once the Spanish left, Americans needed to decide what to do with their new lands. Many, including the founders of the ANTI-IMPERIALIST LEAGUE, thought that the islands should be given their independence—to do otherwise would be **ANATHEMA** to American democratic ideals and betray America's own history fighting for independence from British colonialism. Others argued that colonies would provide the U.S. with markets, resources, naval stopovers, and places to spread those democratic ideals. Although each island nation was treated differently, in the end imperialist reasoning prevailed.

> **ANATHEMA**
> something hated

> Puerto Rico and Guam became territories, meaning that they remained under U.S. control. In 1917, Puerto Ricans gained citizenship.

> Cuba became an American **PROTECTORATE**, an independent country with American oversight. When Cuba rewrote its constitution in 1901, the PLATT AMENDMENT specified that the U.S. still had a right to make decisions for the Cuban government and that the U.S. could maintain a military presence at GUANTÁNAMO BAY.

> **PROTECTORATE**
> a country that is protected and controlled by another, more powerful country

The Philippines became an American colony, prompting Aguinaldo to lead another fight for independence. This second struggle in the Philippines was much more challenging for the U.S., but the U.S. managed to capture Aguinaldo in 1901. In 1946, the Philippines became independent by allowing the U.S. to retain military bases there and agreeing to trade agreements favorable to the U.S.

CHECK YOUR KNOWLEDGE

1. Why did the Cuban revolution worry many people in the U.S.?

2. Why did American newspapers sensationalize the conflict in Cuba?

3. Why were people supposed to remember the *MAINE*?

4. How did the Filipinos react to Commodore George Dewey's arrival in the Philippines?

5. Who were the Rough Riders?

6. What happened to the Spanish empire during the Spanish–American War?

7. Why did the Anti-Imperialist League oppose expansion?

8. What were some arguments for expansion?

ANSWERS

CHECK YOUR ANSWERS

1. Cuba is very close to Florida and many Americans traded with Cuba.
2. In order to sell papers
3. To remember why the U.S. needed to fight Spain
4. They welcomed him.
5. They were Teddy Roosevelt's First U.S. Volunteer Cavalry.
6. It fell apart after Spain's defeat.
7. They thought imperialism was opposed to American democratic values.
8. Colonies would provide the U.S. with markets for trade and allow the spread of democratic ideals.

☆ Chapter 31 ☆

A MAN and HIS PLAN:
✱ ✱ ✱ ✱ MORE ✱ ✱ ✱ ✱
PROGRESSIVISM

Hero of the Spanish-American War TEDDY ROOSEVELT became governor of New York and vice president during PRESIDENT McKINLEY's second term. When McKinley was assassinated by an anarchist in 1901, Roosevelt, who was 42, became the youngest person to be a U.S. president.

Roosevelt became known as the first conservationist president, founding the U.S. Forest Service. For his work helping negotiate the Treaty of Portsmouth to end the Russo-Japanese War, Roosevelt also won the Nobel Peace Prize.

Roosevelt was the inspiration for the **TEDDY BEAR**. He loved to hunt, but during a hunting trip in 1902, he decided not to shoot a bear captured by others in his party. A toy maker heard this story and named the stuffed bear toy he was making after the president.

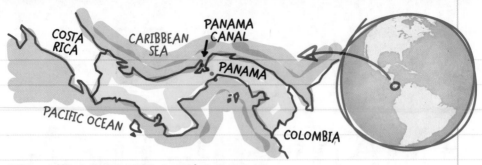

The PANAMA CANAL

The distance between U.S.-controlled land in the Pacific (the Philippines and Hawaii) and in the Atlantic/Caribbean (Cuba and Puerto Rico) made it difficult for U.S. ships to travel from place to place. The **ISTHMUS** of PANAMA seemed like the perfect place for a canal connecting the two oceans.

> **ISTHMUS**
> a narrow piece of land connecting two larger land masses

The narrow piece of land was owned by Colombia. Knowing that the people of Panama were planning a revolution against Colombia, Roosevelt sent a warship to block Colombian troops from reaching the uprising. The Panamanian revolution was successful. Roosevelt quickly recognized the new nation and negotiated a 99-year lease on the 10-mile-wide CANAL ZONE. The HAG–BUNAU–VARILLA TREATY established the canal zone and the right of the U.S. to protect it.

Construction on the PANAMA CANAL began in 1904. The work was dangerous, mostly due to malaria and yellow fever carried by mosquitoes, and many workers died before construction was completed ten years later. On August 15, 1914, the *ANCON* was the first ship to make the crossing.

SPEAK SOFTLY and CARRY a BIG STICK

Roosevelt believed that the U.S. had the right and the responsibility to act in Panama as it did. Roosevelt was famous for saying that one ought to "SPEAK SOFTLY AND CARRY A BIG STICK." That is, as the U.S. took greater charge of the western hemisphere, Roosevelt saw the nation's role as that of a police officer and reminded other nations of the power of the American military (the "big stick").

The ROOSEVELT COROLLARY

The Monroe Doctrine had warned European nations not to interfere in the western hemisphere. At that time, the U.S. didn't have the military power to support that warning. By 1900, that was no longer the case. When several Latin American nations defaulted on debts to European countries, Roosevelt forced them to pay, to prevent European interests from getting involved.

This was the **ROOSEVELT COROLLARY** to the Monroe Doctrine: It barred Europe from interfering in Latin America and it gave the U.S. the right to intervene and settle disputes instead. The U.S. took charge of the Dominican economy in 1905 and stopped a revolt in Cuba in 1906 as well.

> **COROLLARY**
> a conclusion that follows naturally from another proposition

ROOSEVELT and the SQUARE DEAL

Roosevelt viewed the presidency as a "bully pulpit," or powerful platform, to advance his political agenda. He was the first president to enforce the Sherman Antitrust Act, fighting trusts that he singled out for working against the public good, a practice that earned him the name "trustbuster."

In 1902, during a UNITED MINE WORKERS strike, Roosevelt was the first president to threaten to use the army to break a strike on *behalf of the union* (he convinced the company to agree to **ARBITRATION**).

> **ARBITRATION**
> deciding on a question by presenting it to an "arbitrator," a third party; usually used to avoid going to court or having a strike

In his bid for reelection in 1904, Roosevelt ran on the platform that every American deserved a "Square Deal," and easily won. His Square Deal program included:

controlling corporations and fighting corruption

protecting consumers (He passed the Meat Inspection Act and the Pure Food and Drug Act of 1906.)

conserving natural resources

TAFT: A PROGRESSIVE?

Roosevelt wanted Republican WILLIAM HOWARD TAFT to succeed him as president. In 1908, Taft defeated the

Democratic nominee, William Jennings Bryan, and Eugene V. Debs, who ran on the Socialist ticket. Taft supported the SIXTEENTH AMENDMENT (to establish federal income taxes) and the SEVENTEENTH AMENDMENT (to establish the direct election of U.S. senators). However, Taft didn't lower tariffs or support conservation.

DOLLAR DIPLOMACY

While Roosevelt's big stick was the military, Taft preferred a big wallet. He encouraged DOLLAR DIPLOMACY, using business investments and international loans to increase American influence in Latin America and East Asia. Taft was reluctant to resort to violence, but did sometimes use the military to protect American investments, which led to resentment in South and Central America.

The PROGRESSIVE PARTY

A rift developed between Roosevelt and Taft, and Roosevelt chose to run again for president in 1912, even though the Republican Party still supported Taft. Roosevelt formed the PROGRESSIVE PARTY (also known as the BULL MOOSE PARTY because of the strength Roosevelt attributed to it), but he succeeded only in splitting the Republican vote. As a result, the Democrat WOODROW WILSON was elected president.

A BULL MOOSE IS JUST A MALE MOOSE, NOT SOME WEIRD MUTANT BULL-MOOSE THING.

PROGRESSIVISM UNDER WILSON

Except when it came to segregation, which he supported, Wilson was progressive in his policies. During his two terms, progressive advances included:

The CLAYTON ANTITRUST ACT of 1914, which further limited the ability of companies to form monopolies and increased government regulatory power

The FEDERAL RESERVE ACT of 1913, which created the FEDERAL RESERVE BOARD (the FED) to oversee the federal banks and control interest rates

The UNDERWOOD TARIFF of 1913, which decreased tariffs

The creation of the FEDERAL TRADE COMMISSION in 1914, which enforced trade laws

The KEATING-OWEN ACT of 1916, which limited child labor (though it was later struck down)

The MEXICAN REVOLUTION and PANCHO VILLA

President Wilson was more opposed to imperialism than his predecessor. His policy of MORAL DIPLOMACY involved doing business only with countries that were free and democratic.

However, when the Mexican Revolution began in 1910, Wilson decided to use military force. Because of the many economic ties between the U.S. and Mexico, the revolution affected the U.S.

1911:

The reformer Francisco Madero overthrew dictator Porfirio Díaz.

1913:

General Victoriano Huerta overthrew Madero.

1914:

Wilson refused to recognize Huerta's government and sold weaponry to Venustiano Carranza, his rival. With help from the U.S., which granted him diplomatic recognition, Carranza took power.

Then, in January 1916, FRANCISCO "PANCHO" VILLA, a prominent Mexican Revolutionary general who had sought **DIPLOMATIC RECOGNITION** from the U.S. for years, protested Carranza's administration by killing 15 Americans in Chihuahua, Mexico. When this didn't provoke conflict, he crossed into New Mexico and killed about 20 people in Columbus, a border town.

> **DIPLOMATIC RECOGNITION**
> when a nation is acknowledged by other governments and other countries

Wilson sent GENERAL JOHN J. PERSHING and his troops, who chased Pancho Villa for a year, until World War I called them away. The Mexican Revolution ended in 1920.

CHECK YOUR KNOWLEDGE

1. How did Roosevelt intervene in Colombian politics in order to get the Canal Zone lease?

2. What did Roosevelt mean by "speak softly and carry a big stick"?

3. What is the Roosevelt Corollary?

4. How does dollar diplomacy work?

5. What did the Federal Reserve Act of 1913 do?

6. How did President Wilson's views about Latin America differ from those of Taft and Roosevelt?

7. Why did General Pershing stop chasing Pancho Villa?

1. He blocked the Colombian army from reaching Panama.

2. Roosevelt meant that the U.S. should act like a police officer and remind other nations of America's military power.

3. The Roosevelt Corollary to the Monroe Doctrine allowed the U.S. to intervene in Latin American disputes.

4. Taft used business investments and loans, rather than the army, as his first tool to influence Latin America.

5. The Federal Reserve Act of 1913 created the Federal Reserve Board (the Fed) to oversee the federal banks and control interest rates.

6. Wilson wanted to spread democracy but did not want to control other nations.

7. World War I started and he was needed elsewhere.

Unit 7

World Wars and Modern America
1900s–1930s

It's impossible to separate American history from
world history. George Washington instructed politicians
to avoid foreign entanglements, and they tried and tried.
The beginning of the twentieth century put an end to that.
It was hard to hide on the other side of an ocean.
The U.S. affected and was affected by the rest of the world.

Chapter 32

THE GREAT WAR

WHAT THEY WERE FIGHTING ABOUT

The exact cause of World War I (WWI), initially called the Great War, is hard to pinpoint. Peace in Europe was so fragile that anything could have set off a conflict—it was a powder keg waiting for a spark from:

MILITARIES
 An arms race was happening

IMPERIALISM
 Especially in Africa

NATIONALISM
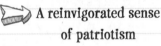 A reinvigorated sense of patriotism
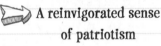 Countries wanted to prove their might
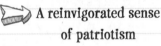 Ethnic groups wanted to form their own nations

ALLIANCES
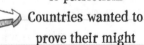 THE TRIPLE ALLIANCE: Germany, Austria-Hungary, and Italy
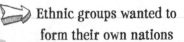 THE TRIPLE **ENTENTE**: Britain, France, and Russia

ENTENTE
an understanding or agreement

Remember the **MAIN** reasons for World War I using this mnemonic device:

MILITARIES
ALLIANCES
IMPERIALISM
NATIONALISM

Millions of Slavic people who lived under the AUSTRO-HUNGARIAN EMPIRE wanted to become part of Serbia. On June 28, 1914, a Serbian nationalist named GAVRILO PRINCIP assassinated the ARCHDUKE FRANZ FERDINAND (heir to the throne of the Austro-Hungarian Empire) and his wife, Sophie, in SARAJEVO. A month later, on July 28, 1914, Austria declared war on Serbia.

ALLIANCES

People defended their allies.

Germany, an Austro-Hungarian ally, declared war on Russia, which supported Serbia.

Germany also declared war on France, a Russian ally.

When Germany invaded Belgium, a neutral country between Germany and France, Britain, an ally of France and Belgium, declared war on Germany.

By early August 1914, a full-scale war had developed in Europe. The two sides were:

The **CENTRAL POWERS**	The **ALLIED POWERS, or the ALLIES**
Austria-Hungary	Serbia
Germany	Russia
The Ottoman Empire	France
Bulgaria	Great Britain
	Later, Japan and Italy

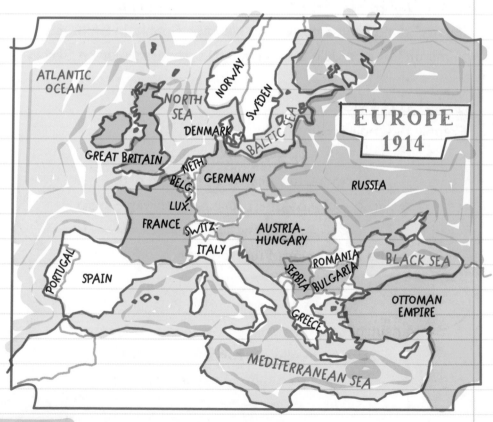

EUROPE 1914

ATLANTIC OCEAN

NORWAY

SWEDEN

NORTH SEA

BALTIC SEA

DENMARK

GREAT BRITAIN

NETH.

BELG.

LUX.

GERMANY

RUSSIA

FRANCE

SWITZ.

ITALY

AUSTRIA-HUNGARY

ROMANIA

BLACK SEA

PORTUGAL

SPAIN

SERBIA

BULGARIA

OTTOMAN EMPIRE

GREECE

MEDITERRANEAN SEA

AMERICAN NEUTRALITY

President Wilson was determined to follow George Washington's advice to steer clear of foreign conflicts. America planned to continue trading with both the Allies and the Central Powers.

The FIRST BATTLE of the MARNE

Germany was fighting a war on two fronts—Russia in the east and France and England in the west. The Germans tried to advance into France to knock France out of the war quickly, so they could focus on Russia. However, the small Belgian army held them off for nearly three weeks, giving France and Britain time to prepare to fight. The French and British stopped the Germans at the Marne River near Paris and declared victory in the FIRST BATTLE OF THE MARNE (September 6 through 12, 1914).

TRENCH WARFARE

The First Battle of the Marne proved that neither side would have an easy victory. The armies used a new style of fighting, TRENCH WARFARE: Soldiers stayed in dug-out trenches for long stretches of time, with a NO-MAN'S-LAND in between them. The soldiers would sometimes fire at one another, but there were few gains for either side, causing a **STALEMATE**.

> **STALEMATE**
> a situation in which nothing can be done or won by either side; also called an impasse

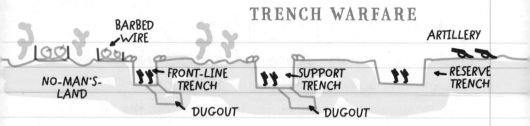

TRENCH WARFARE

In 1916, Allied and Central powers tried to end the impasse on the WESTERN FRONT. In February, the Germans incited the Battle of Verdun. In July, the Allies instigated the Battle of the Somme. The battles caused high casualties.

MORE NEW WAYS of FIGHTING

Modern weapons caused far more casualties at a faster rate than ever before. The slaughter on the battlefields led to despair and the destruction of an entire generation of men.

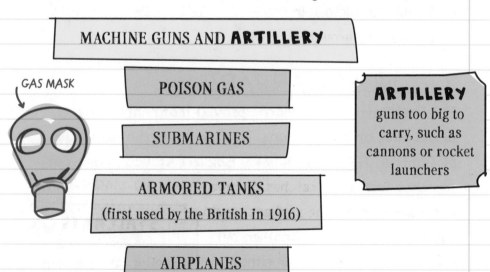

MACHINE GUNS AND **ARTILLERY**

GAS MASK

POISON GAS

SUBMARINES

ARMORED TANKS
(first used by the British in 1916)

AIRPLANES

ARTILLERY
guns too big to carry, such as cannons or rocket launchers

Pilots who shot down lots of enemy planes were called **ACES**. The most famous German ace was Manfred von Richthofen, also called the Red Baron. The most famous American ace was Eddie Rickenbacker.

The *LUSITANIA*

Naval warfare also changed. The Allies blocked off German ports. The Germans retaliated by targeting Allied ships with submarines called UNTERSEEBOOTS, or U-BOATS.

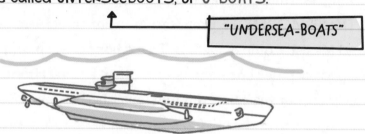

"UNDERSEA-BOATS"

On May 7, 1915, a U-boat sank the British ship *LUSITANIA*, killing 1,000 people, including over 100 Americans. There were ammunitions and unlawful goods in the cargo, but the *LUSITANIA* was a passenger ship, and the civilian deaths seemed inhumane. Still determined to remain neutral, Wilson convinced Germany to make the SUSSEX PLEDGE (named after another ship torpedoed by U-boats) and promise not to target ships that didn't carry weapons.

The war had cost the lives of millions of Europeans. Wilson was reelected president in 1916 on the slogan "HE KEPT US OUT OF WAR."

343

The next year, the Germans went back to attacking all Allied ships, using a policy of "unrestricted submarine warfare." They intended to cut off the British Isles from supplies, forcing an end to the war before American intervention. It almost worked.

The ZIMMERMANN NOTE

In early 1917, British intelligence intercepted a telegram from a German official named Arthur Zimmermann. The ZIMMERMANN NOTE proposed an alliance between Germany and Mexico against the U.S. In exchange, Germany would help Mexico get back Texas and other lost territories. Mexico declined, but the telegram was published by American newspapers, and anti-German sentiment boiled over. On April 2, 1917, Wilson asked Congress to declare war. After three days of debate, the U.S. entered the Great War (they didn't know there'd be a World War II yet, so nobody called it World War I).

CONVOY

The U.S. helped the Allies by introducing the **CONVOY** system, sending cargo ships across the Atlantic accompanied by warships to protect them from U-boat attacks.

> **CONVOY**
> a group traveling together, often for safety

OVER THERE: The AMERICAN EXPEDITIONARY FORCES

When the American army, called
the AMERICAN EXPEDITIONARY
FORCES (AEF), led by
GENERAL JOHN PERSHING, arrived
in France, it provided an influx of
energy to the Allies. French and British
troops were exhausted and running out of supplies.

> Many believe that the
> AEF soldiers were called
> **DOUGHBOYS** because the
> buttons on their uniforms
> looked like dough.

READY to FIGHT

Even with a large number of volunteers—including women and
African Americans—the U.S. military wasn't ready to handle
such a big war. In May of 1917, the SELECTIVE SERVICE ACT
started a DRAFT for all men between the ages of 21 and 30.
Black draftees were segregated from whites in the American
forces, but some fought with the French army, which was
less discriminatory. Some were awarded the French Croix de
Guerre (Cross of War) medal for their bravery.

The government got supplies and funding by:

Selling Liberty **BONDS**, which basically means
individual citizens lending money to the government

Setting up the WAR INDUSTRIES BOARD to manage the
distribution and production of supplies, and the
NATIONAL WAR LABOR BOARD to settle conflicts
with unions without strikes

Urging people to save resources
(through the FUEL ADMINISTRATION) and food
(through the FOOD ADMINISTRATION)

Encouraging citizens to plant VICTORY GARDENS
so that a higher percentage of the food from
larger farms could go to soldiers

The U.S. had to work hard to produce enough supplies for its
own army *and* its allies.

The HOME FRONT

The U.S. government had to deal with:

A LABOR SHORTAGE: With young men away fighting, women, immigrants, and African Americans got access to jobs they couldn't get before.

PUBLIC OPINION: The COMMITTEE ON PUBLIC INFORMATION created propaganda about German atrocities to keep people riled up. It worked, but it encouraged anti-German-American discrimination.

LIMITING CRITICISM: President Wilson signed into law the **ESPIONAGE** Act (specific penalties for spies) and the SEDITION ACT (making it illegal to express negative thoughts about the government).

> **ESPIONAGE**
> spying

Many pacifists and Socialists were jailed, including Eugene V. Debs. In the 1919 Supreme Court case of *SCHENCK v. UNITED STATES*, the Court ruled that limitations on free speech were valid in a time of war.

> The **SEDITION ACT** was passed during World War I.
> The **ALIEN AND SEDITION ACTS** were passed in 1798.
> Both made **SEDITION**, or going against the government, illegal.

The FOURTEEN POINTS

On January 8, 1918, well before the war ended, President Wilson justified why the U.S. was going to war and gave a set of goals. He also informed Congress that this was "the war to end all wars" and he had made a plan to prevent another major war. The plan became known as the FOURTEEN POINTS, which stipulated:

1. No secret treaties/alliances

2. Freedom of navigation on the seas

3. Equality of trade

4. Smaller militaries

5. An adjustment of colonial claims

6. The evacuation and restoration of Russian territory

7. The evacuation and restoration of Belgian territory

8. The evacuation and restoration of French territory

9. A readjustment of Italian borders

10. **AUTONOMY** for the people of the former Austro-Hungarian Empire

11. The evacuation and restoration of the Balkan Peninsula (Romania, Serbia, and Montenegro)

12. Autonomy for Ottoman territory

13. The establishment of an independent Poland

14. A LEAGUE OF NATIONS—an organization of countries working together to resolve disputes

> **AUTONOMY**
> self-government

The RUSSIAN REVOLUTION

The Russians had taken huge casualties and the country was struggling. In March 1917, the Russian Revolution began. CZAR NICHOLAS II was forced to step down. The interim democratic government that replaced him failed to help with food shortages and low morale. In November 1917, a group called the **BOLSHEVIKS**, led by Vladimir Ilich Lenin, seized power and set up a **COMMUNIST** government. He promised "Land, Peace, Bread," which was a powerful message to a war-weary people.

BOLSHEVIK
a member of the movement that led the Russian Revolution in November 1917 and later became the Communist Party of the Soviet Union

COMMUNISM
a political/social system whereby the state owns and controls everything

Russia was stretched too thin. It signed the TREATY OF BREST-LITOVSK with Germany in March 1918 to get out of the war. The treaty forced Russia to cede much of its territory to Germany. Germany was certain the war would end soon.

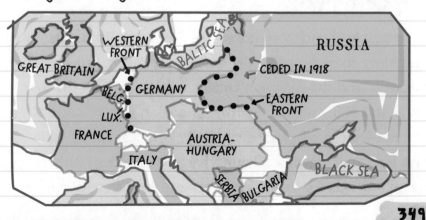

The SECOND BATTLE of the MARNE

On March 21 of 1918, in the SPRING OFFENSIVE, Germans marched nearly all the way to Paris hoping to end the war before the rest of the American forces arrived. In May and June, American forces stopped them at the battles of CHÂTEAU-THIERRY and BELLEAU WOOD. In July, the Spring Offensive ended with a turning-point battle: the SECOND BATTLE OF THE MARNE. The Germans lost the territory they had gained that spring, and the Allies went on the offensive.

BATTLE of the ARGONNE FOREST

That September, the Allies continued to push the Germans back toward Germany. The AEF defeated them at the battle of SAINT-MIHIEL and then joined Allied troops for the BATTLE OF THE ARGONNE FOREST (also known as the MEUSE-ARGONNE OFFENSIVE) on September 26, 1918. Both sides took massive losses.

ARMISTICE

Germany had underestimated the American forces. Its navy was close to mutiny. The Central Powers were falling apart. Bulgaria and the Ottoman Empire withdrew from the war in early fall 1918, and the Austro-Hungarian Empire soon after. Parts of these empires, such as Poland, Czechoslovakia, and Hungary, declared themselves independent nations. Germany was experiencing a severe food shortage.

On November 9, 1918, the German emperor, KAISER WILHELM II, stepped down. The new government of Germany agreed to President Wilson's terms for armistice. The cease fire became official at 11 a.m. on November 11, 1918: the eleventh hour of the eleventh day of the eleventh month.

The COST of WAR

The war had ravaged Europe and devastated an entire generation of European men. Historians' best guess is 37 million were killed or

> **PANDEMIC**
> an epidemic, or widespread disease, that affects an entire country or continent, or even the entire world

wounded in four years of fighting. With no working farms or factories, the European economy was devastated as well. And a flu **PANDEMIC** in 1918 killed more people than had died during the war. The world was ready for peace.

3%–5% OF THE ENTIRE WORLD'S POPULATION

The TREATY of VERSAILLES

In 1919, the BIG FOUR—President Wilson, Prime Minister David Lloyd George of England, Premier Georges Clemenceau of France, and Prime Minister Vittorio Orlando of Italy—met at Versailles, near Paris. (No Central Powers were invited.) Wilson wanted to end the war with minimal animosity.

The European nations wanted Germany to take full blame, lose its colonies, lose its military, and pay **REPARATIONS**.

> **REPARATIONS**
> financial compensation paid to someone who has been wronged

On June 28, 1919, exactly five years after the assassination of Archduke Franz Ferdinand and his wife, the Allies and Germany signed the TREATY OF VERSAILLES. It harshly punished Germany, split up the Austro-Hungarian and Ottoman Empires, and established the League of Nations. The treaty radically redrew the boundaries of Europe and the Middle East. The goal was to solve ethnic divisions, but the treaty led to more conflicts. (It is still a source of tension in the Middle East, where countries were literally created by drawing lines in the sand.)

The treaty did overlap with some of Wilson's Fourteen Points—but not all. Wilson returned to the U.S. and campaigned for the Treaty of Versailles, but Congress rejected it. They worried that the League of Nations would rob Congress of power by deciding when and where the American military would fight. Although Wilson had come up with the idea of the League of Nations, the U.S. never joined. Americans wanted to return to **ISOLATIONISM**.

> Wilson suffered a massive stroke while campaigning for support of the League of Nations.

> **ISOLATIONISM**
> the policy of isolating one's country from the affairs of other nations by declining to enter into alliances or other international agreements

CHECK YOUR KNOWLEDGE

1. Which country was the first to declare war in the conflict that would become World War I?

2. Why was the attack on the *LUSITANIA* significant?

3. Why were there far more casualties than in previous wars?

4. What was the motivation behind the Spring Offensive?

5. How was the Second Battle of the Marne a turning point in the Great War?

6. What was the point of the League of Nations?

7. Why did Congress reject the Treaty of Versailles?

ANSWERS

CHECK YOUR ANSWERS

1. Austria (against Serbia)

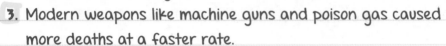

2. American civilians were killed, and anti-German feeling in the U.S. increased.

3. Modern weapons like machine guns and poison gas caused more deaths at a faster rate.

4. Germany wanted to end the war before the rest of the American forces arrived.

5. The Allies went on the offensive after the battle, rather than just defending their territory. The Germans also lost territory.

6. To use diplomacy to prevent another global war

7. They believed the League of Nations would take power away from them.

Chapter 33

The ROARING ✦✦✦✦✦✦✦✦✦✦✦ TWENTIES

BACK to NORMAL...OR NOT

World War I left a scar on American life.

1. THE ECONOMY:

When soldiers returned home, the government didn't need extra workers to make supplies for them anymore; this led to high unemployment.

2. LABOR:

Wages and prices had been kept down during the war; after the war, prices went up, but not wages, leading to strikes.

3. NATIVISM AND RACISM:

With a lack of jobs, racism and anti-immigrant feelings rose ("They're taking our jobs!").

The RED SCARE

Americans were afraid the Communist takeover in Russia would repeat itself in the U.S. and put an end to capitalism. This led to the RED SCARE, a fear of Communists, or REDS, and other "radicals." When bombings took place across the country, Reds were blamed, and ATTORNEY GENERAL A. MITCHELL PALMER led the PALMER RAIDS ← **BUT NO MAJOR DISCOVERIES WERE EVER MADE** on suspected Communists, **SOCIALISTS**, and anarchists, often without warrants. Labor unions were deemed Communist organizations, and when workers began to strike, violent government intervention was seen as justified.

SOCIALISM
a system in which property and the means of production are owned and controlled by the state

The trial and execution of NICOLA SACCO and BARTOLOMEO VANZETTI suggested that the Red Scare had a nativist foundation: The two Italian-born anarchists were sentenced to death for killing two men during a robbery. They probably didn't get a fair trial.

HARDING'S REPUBLICANISM

Americans wanted to return to the "normal" way of life before the war. During the 1920 presidential election, WARREN G. HARDING, a Republican senator from Ohio, made this idea his campaign promise. A strong believer in small government, as president he instituted income tax reductions, especially for the wealthy, and high tariffs.

TEAPOT DOME

Harding appointed his friends from Ohio, many of whom were unqualified and corrupt, to important positions. Secretary of the Interior Albert Fall was convicted of accepting bribes from oil executives for rights to drill on government land in Teapot Dome, Wyoming, which became known as the TEAPOT DOME SCANDAL. When Harding died of a heart attack on August 2, 1923, his vice president, CALVIN COOLIDGE, became president.

CALVIN COOLIDGE

Coolidge was seen as quiet and honest. He believed in laissez-faire economics and tried to keep the government out of the economy. He was reelected in 1924 on the strengths of his beliefs in minimal government, high tariffs, and low taxes. Coolidge is known for the KELLOGG-BRIAND PACT in 1928, which made war illegal. More than 60 nations signed the agreement (but think about it: How do you enforce something that says you can't fight?).

In 1924, the year Coolidge was reelected, **NELLIE T. ROSS** of Wyoming and **MIRIAM A. FERGUSON** of Texas were elected the nation's first female governors. In 1916, **JEANNETTE RANKIN** had become the first woman elected to the U.S. Congress.

AUTOMOBILES

By the 1920s, prosperity was on the rise again, which meant Americans wanted to own fancy new things—like Henry Ford's MODEL T automobile (the "Tin Lizzie"). Ford made the price of his car affordable using the assembly line system and let customers pay on an INSTALLMENT PLAN.

HOW AUTOMOBILES AFFECTED AMERICAN LIFE:

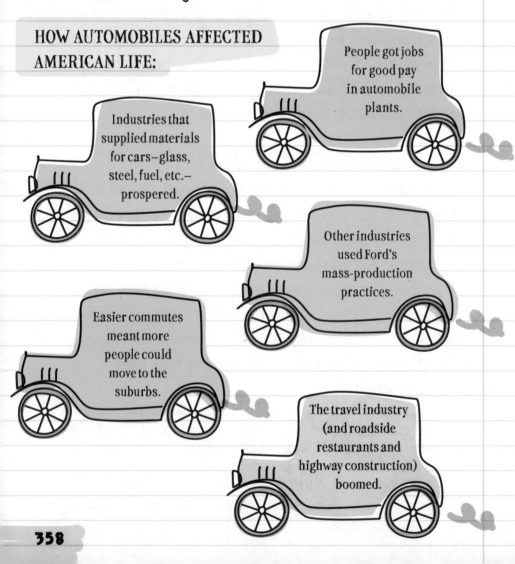

People got jobs for good pay in automobile plants.

Industries that supplied materials for cars—glass, steel, fuel, etc.—prospered.

Other industries used Ford's mass-production practices.

Easier commutes meant more people could move to the suburbs.

The travel industry (and roadside restaurants and highway construction) boomed.

ALL THAT JAZZ

People had shorter workdays, more leisure time, and a live-for-today attitude. Young people moved to the cities. The excitement and modernity of this time period gave it the nickname the ROARING TWENTIES.

RADIOS became a part of every home, and radio networks like NBC and CBS made sure that Americans from coast to coast listened to the same programs (and ads).

The FILM INDUSTRY grew. Hollywood became the center of a major industry. "Talkies"—as opposed to silent movies—were introduced.

Americans followed the lives of celebrities, from sports stars (like BABE RUTH) to pilots (like CHARLES LINDBERGH and AMELIA EARHART).

Women were voting, were better educated, and were working (still mostly as nurses, teachers, secretaries, and clerks). Women called FLAPPERS wore their hair and skirts short to rebel against traditional ideas of ladylike behavior.

Other new aspects of popular culture were ART DECO architecture, crossword puzzles, and dances like the Charleston.

MUSIC was a big part of pop culture, specifically JAZZ. Jazz originated in New Orleans. It was influenced by African American music and is a truly American art form. This decade is also called the JAZZ AGE.

The HARLEM RENAISSANCE

During World War I, many African Americans moved from the South to the North to work in factories in the GREAT MIGRATION.

African Americans brought jazz and the blues with them to the North. The Great Migration was met with resistance, especially by the KKK, which was no longer limited to the South. To fight back, organizations like the NAACP worked to secure civil rights. A reformer, MARCUS GARVEY, founded the UNIVERSAL NEGRO IMPROVEMENT ASSOCIATION (UNIA) and advocated for a large-scale return to Africa. The plans fell short, but he did encourage BLACK NATIONALISM, a sense of African American racial dignity.

DON'T CONFUSE WITH THE GREAT MIGRATION FROM ENGLAND TO THE PRESENT-DAY U.S. IN 1629 TO 1640.

The KKK was virtually wiped out after the Force Acts under the Grant administration. It returned after D. W. Griffith released his film *The Birth of a Nation*, which portrayed the KKK as heroic.

African American communities thrived in New York City's HARLEM, a neighborhood where overdevelopment had driven down the price of real estate. Harlem became home to many artists and gave rise

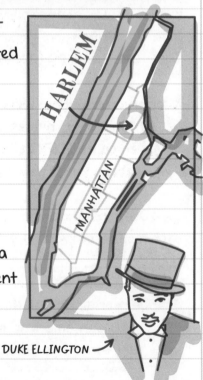

HARLEM

MANHATTAN

DUKE ELLINGTON

to the HARLEM RENAISSANCE—a movement of vibrant intellectual and artistic development. Prominent names of this movement include writers like LANGSTON HUGHES and ZORA NEALE HURSTON and jazz artists such as DUKE ELLINGTON.

African Americans weren't the only minority group fighting for their civil rights in the 1920s. The **LEAGUE OF UNITED LATIN AMERICAN CITIZENS** (LULAC) was founded, and the **INDIAN CITIZENSHIP ACT**, granting full citizenship to Native Americans, was passed.

BACKLASH

Rapid modernization also created a backlash, especially in rural areas:

More NATIVISM:

The EMERGENCY QUOTA ACT of 1921 and the NATIONAL ORIGINS ACT of 1924 set limits on the number of immigrants who could come to the U.S.

FUNDAMENTALISM:

This religious movement centered on the belief in a literal interpretation of the Bible, particularly regarding **CREATIONISM**.

CREATIONISM
the belief that man was created by God exactly as described in the Judeo-Christian Bible

In 1925, a teacher named JOHN SCOPES broke Tennessee law by teaching his students about evolution. During his trial (the "Scopes Monkey Trial"), WILLIAM JENNINGS BRYAN represented the prosecution and CLARENCE DARROW (and the American Civil Liberties Union) defended Scopes. Scopes was originally found guilty of violating the law, but the state supreme court overturned the ruling on a technicality. The law itself was eventually ruled unconstitutional. However, it was not repealed until 1967.

PROHIBITION:

Prohibition (a ban on alcohol) began in 1920.
It was hard to enforce because people could make their own alcohol or buy it in underground bars called SPEAKEASIES. Outlaws known as BOOTLEGGERS also smuggled alcohol. Some worked with gangsters like AL CAPONE. Prohibition made organized crime worse. It was repealed by the TWENTY-FIRST AMENDMENT in 1933.

The LOST GENERATION:

Many well-educated and creative people—including writers like ERNEST HEMINGWAY and F. SCOTT FITZGERALD— grew disenchanted with the violence of World War I, consumerism, and the U.S. in general. Many lived as EXPATRIATES.

> **EXPATRIATE**
> someone who chooses not to live in his home country

CHECK YOUR KNOWLEDGE

1. What caused unemployment after WWI?

2. What were the Palmer Raids meant to uncover?

3. Why were the twenties "roaring"?

4. What were the musical origins of jazz?

5. How did Harlem become a thriving neighborhood of African American artists?

6. What was the verdict in the Scopes Monkey Trial?

7. How did Prohibition support the spread of organized crime?

8. Which parts of American culture were members of the "Lost Generation" upset about?

ANSWERS

CHECK YOUR ANSWERS

1. Soldiers returning home meant an excess of labor.

2. They were meant to uncover Communists, Socialists, and anarchists, but no major discoveries were made.

3. The economy was doing better and American culture was experiencing a period of excitement and leisure.

4. Jazz originated with African American music in New Orleans.

5. Affordable real estate attracted many artists to settle in the area.

6. The state supreme court of Tennessee overruled the original guilty verdict on a technicality, but the law itself was eventually ruled unconstitutional.

7. With alcohol illegal, people who wanted to drink depended on bootleggers and mobsters to smuggle it in.

8. They were disillusioned by consumerism and war.

☆ Chapter 34 ☆

The GREAT
★★*★*★*★*★*★*★*★*
DEPRESSION

STOCK
MARKET
CRASH

During the boom of the 1920s, many
people hoped to grow their wealth by
speculating in the STOCK EXCHANGE, a
market for shares of companies. If a
company does well, the value of the stock
increases and the owner can then sell the
stock for a profit.

During the BULL MARKET of the 1920s,
people bought stocks eagerly, because their

values were increasing, even though the companies were not worth any more than they had been. Some people bought stocks using borrowed money, which they hoped to pay back with the profit from their stock. People were also "buying on margin," which meant they only paid 10 percent of the stock price initially. They hoped the price would rise quickly so they could resell for a profit.

In the middle of 1929, the value of stocks reached a high point, and some people decided to sell their shares. The more people sold, the fewer people wanted to buy, decreasing and decreasing the value of the stocks. On October 29, 1929, a day known as BLACK TUESDAY, the stock market CRASHED to almost zero value. Many people lost all their money in a single day.

 BUY!

During a **BULL MARKET**, stock prices rise or are expected to rise, so people tend to purchase stocks; during a **BEAR MARKET**, stock prices fall or are expected to fall, so people tend to sell stocks.

 SELL!

The GREAT DEPRESSION

Black Tuesday was the beginning of the GREAT DEPRESSION, the worst economic crisis in American history. Many people had bought stocks on the EASY CREDIT of the 1920s, but when they **DEFAULTED** on their loans, banks and stockbrokers lost

DEFAULT
to fail to pay a debt

money too. However, the stock market crash was only a small part of the cause of the Great Depression:

The illusion of wealth that swept the country in the previous decade had led to overproduction in factories and agriculture. In reality, few people could afford to purchase the goods produced. The surplus (an excess) caused prices to fall, which caused profits to fall, which led companies to lay off their workers. Due to high unemployment, even fewer people could afford the goods, causing the cycle to **SNOWBALL**.

SNOWBALL
to grow or become larger or more intense at an accelerating rate

Anyone who deposited money into a bank account lost it if the bank went out of business. When people with savings in banks saw that loans were being defaulted on, they panicked and withdrew as much money as possible, causing a run on the banks. This put more banks out of business, making it impossible for other businesses to take out loans; layoffs followed, and this process snowballed too.

Tough economic times in other countries reduced the market for exports.

HOOVER'S ECONOMICS

The president at the start of the Great Depression was HERBERT HOOVER. During the election of 1928, the Republican Party was credited with the perceived prosperity of the time, so when the Republican Party nominated Hoover, he was virtually assured a victory.

Hoover was a strong believer in laissez-faire economics and small government. Hoover's stance on the Depression was that it was not the job of the federal government to take care of people; instead, the crisis would take care of itself as part of what many thought was a normal cycle of the economy.

24 PERCENT OF AMERICANS (12 MILLION PEOPLE) WERE UNEMPLOYED.

High unemployment, hunger, and homelessness were on the rise across the country. Children left school to work or ran away because they felt they were a burden on their parents. Families fell apart. Even when the nation pleaded with the government to act, Hoover refused. The **SHANTYTOWNS** that sprang up to house people evicted from their homes became known as HOOVERVILLES.

> **SHANTYTOWN**
> a neighborhood of informal houses, usually made from discarded materials

Eventually, Hoover gave in.

In 1931, he authorized spending on public works (such as the Boulder Dam, now the HOOVER DAM) to create jobs, and in 1932, he agreed to the creation of the Reconstruction Finance Corporation, which made loans to banks and businesses.

The BONUS ARMY

Hoover's reputation was damaged even more when, in the summer of 1932, World War I veterans who were due to receive bonus pay in 1945 marched on Washington to demand early payment. When Hoover and the Congress refused, some of the protestors stayed in a D.C.-area Hooverville. Under Hoover's direction, GENERAL DOUGLAS MacARTHUR led the military to drive out the "BONUS ARMY" using tanks and tear gas. Several Great War veterans were killed, and the public was shocked.

FRANKLIN DELANO ROOSEVELT

Hoover ran for president again in 1932, even though he knew that his chances of winning were slim. His Democratic rival, FRANKLIN DELANO ROOSEVELT (FDR), was a distant cousin of Teddy Roosevelt, and he was paralyzed from the waist down from polio. Roosevelt had an excellent record of helping the people of New York, where he was governor, and a strong group of advisers known as the BRAIN TRUST helped him with policy. His campaign promised a "NEW DEAL" for Americans, and he won the election easily.

WHAT DO YOU THINK?

I TRUST YOU...WHAT DO YOU THINK?

The FIRST NEW DEAL

In his first inaugural address, FDR famously told the nation that "THE ONLY THING WE HAVE TO FEAR IS FEAR ITSELF," and he quickly set out to destroy that fear. Roosevelt became president on March 4, 1933, and he called a special session of Congress that is known as the HUNDRED DAYS. He instituted a BANK HOLIDAY, closing all banks in the nation for a few days while the EMERGENCY BANKING RELIEF ACT was passed, and only reopened the ones that were stable. He then gave the first of his many radio addresses to the nation—a FIRESIDE CHAT—in which he explained the new banking policy and eased fears. Beginning during the Hundred Days and continuing until 1935, President Roosevelt instituted the programs that comprised the FIRST NEW DEAL, which included the founding of these agencies:

← CALLED THE "ALPHABET AGENCIES" FOR ALL THE ACRONYMS

> FEDERAL EMERGENCY RELIEF ADMINISTRATION (FERA), which helped the unemployed

> AGRICULTURAL ADJUSTMENT ADMINISTRATION (AAA), which **SUBSIDIZED** farmers for occasionally destroying their crops. This kept food supplies low and prices high (this policy was controversial, as hunger remained a problem for many people and yet food was being thrown away).

SUBSIDY
money given by the government to help an industry or business to achieve a public goal

PUBLIC WORKS ADMINISTRATION (PWA), which sponsored public works and created jobs

PUBLIC WORKS work like building roads, schools, and infrastructure that is done by the government for the public

CIVILIAN CONSERVATION CORPS (CCC), which was similar to the PWA but focused on conservation projects

FEDERAL DEPOSIT INSURANCE CORPORATION (FDIC), which insured bank deposits so people would not lose their money if banks failed

TENNESSEE VALLEY AUTHORITY (TVA), which brought electricity to the Tennessee Valley through new dams and created jobs in the area

NATIONAL INDUSTRIAL RECOVERY ACT (NIRA), which set labor standards (such as minimum wage and a ban on child labor)

SECURITIES AND EXCHANGE COMMISSION (SEC), which regulated the stock market

The SECOND NEW DEAL

In the 1934 midterm elections, and then during the 1936 presidential election, the nation showed strong support for the Democratic Party and Roosevelt, who won in a landslide victory. Although some conservatives thought the New Deal was a Socialist abuse of presidential power, and some liberals (notably Senator Huey Long of Louisiana) thought it didn't go far enough toward redistribution of wealth, most people needed more assistance. The Depression was still in full force.

So when the New Deal began to expire, Roosevelt instituted a SECOND NEW DEAL. More than the first set of programs, these initiatives attempted to instigate true social change rather than simply help people get by. The new WORKS PROGRESS ADMINISTRATION (WPA) was much like the PWA but went further to employ artists and young people. The REVENUE ACT OF 1935 raised taxes on the rich, and the WAGNER ACT made sure that labor unions had the right to fair negotiations. Perhaps most importantly, the SOCIAL SECURITY ACT (August 1935) gave birth to the modern system of **WELFARE** in America: People pay Social Security taxes throughout their working lives and, in return, receive payment back when they retire or if they are unable to work.

> **WELFARE**
> assistance from the government, usually in the form of money

The DUST BOWL

In addition to the Depression, Americans were hit with another misfortune during the 1930s: In 1931, a severe drought struck the Great Plains, which turned the area into a DUST BOWL that lasted more than a decade. For years before, farmers had cleared land in such a way that the natural grass lost the roots that would connect it to topsoil. When winds came through, the dry dirt, unanchored by grass, was swept into dust storms. Farmers from Oklahoma in particular left the area to become MIGRANT WORKERS in California. The poverty-stricken Oklahoma natives were known as OKIES.

John Steinbeck's Great Depression-era novel *THE GRAPES OF WRATH* is about this experience.

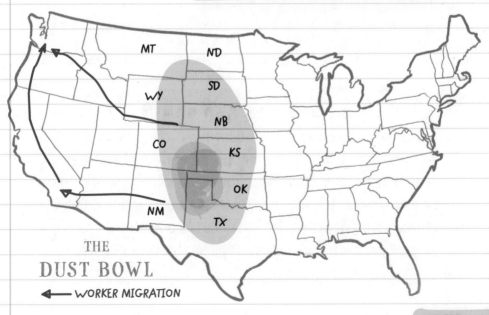

THE
DUST BOWL

◄— WORKER MIGRATION

LABOR STRENGTH

The Supreme Court struck down the NIRA as an unconstitutional restriction of commerce. Congress responded by passing the NATIONAL LABOR RELATIONS ACT, also known as the WAGNER ACT, in 1935, guaranteeing certain rights to unions. The AFL remained strong, and the newly founded CONGRESS OF INDUSTRIAL ORGANIZATIONS (CIO) increased its membership by welcoming women, minorities, and unskilled laborers. Unions began using SIT-DOWN STRIKES, which were strikes that took place within the factories. Remarkably, unions and labor organizations grew at a time when America had a surplus of labor.

The Supreme Court struck down key pieces of FDR's New Deal legislation. In response, in February 1937, Roosevelt proposed adding more justices, which would ensure a liberal majority in the court. However, Democrats and Republicans in Congress opposed the so-called court-packing scheme.

UNIONS' UPS AND DOWNS

When people are worried about their jobs (low demand for labor), they are more motivated to protect themselves with unions but also don't want to make waves. On the other hand, when more workers are needed (high demand for labor), people have less of a need for unions, but the unions feel more free to make demands.

DISCRIMINATION

Another aspect of Roosevelt's presidency was his stance on civil rights. Especially during the 1936 presidential elections, many African Americans switched over to the Democratic Party thanks to FDR's policies. It was the first time, as a demographic group, that they stepped away from the "Party of Lincoln" (from which the current Republican Party developed). Roosevelt relied on his wife, ELEANOR ROOSEVELT, and a "BLACK CABINET" to advise him on matters affecting the black population.

At the same time, Eleanor Roosevelt rose to prominence in national life and became a sign of the advancement of women's rights. FDR appointed the first female cabinet member, FRANCES PERKINS, as secretary of labor.

Eleanor Roosevelt was a controversial first lady and an American politician, diplomat, and activist in her own right. She was outspoken and active in fighting for the rights of women, African and Asian Americans, and war refugees. She famously arranged a concert by the black singer Marian Anderson at the Lincoln Memorial after the Daughters of the American Revolution banned her from singing at Constitution Hall.

ESCAPISM

Although some art that emerged during the Great Depression took a serious look at American life (like *THE GRAPES OF WRATH* and Woody Guthrie's folk music), the 1930s were also the height of **ESCAPISM**. People watched movies

and listened to music and radio
to get away from daily life. Soap
operas, radio dramas, big band and
swing music, and movies such as
THE WIZARD OF OZ, KING KONG,
and *GONE WITH THE WIND*
helped many Americans
make it through the decade.

ESCAPISM
escaping from daily life, usually
through entertainment

The END of the DEPRESSION

In 1937, it seemed as though the New Deal was working.
Roosevelt decided that it was time to cut the **DEFICIT**,
which had grown during the Depression. However, to do so,
he needed to decrease spending on
recovery programs—and when he did
this, he miscalculated the stability of
the economy.

DEFICIT
the amount by which
more money is spent
than is coming in

Roosevelt's decision to decrease spending, combined with the
tight credit, led to another dip in the nation's economy, known
as the ROOSEVELT RECESSION. Full recovery did not occur
until World War II began. Most of the New Deal programs
expired or were canceled as the economy improved, but some
of them—such as Social Security, the FDIC, and the SEC—
remain central aspects of the relationship between American
citizens and the federal government.

CHECK YOUR KNOWLEDGE

1. Why was there a large surplus in manufactured goods at the start of the Depression?

2. What caused the runs on the banks at the start of the Depression?

3. How did Hoover think the Depression would end?

4. How did President Roosevelt's approach to the economy differ from Hoover's?

5. How did public works projects help the economy?

6. How does Social Security work?

7. Why did movies like *THE WIZARD OF OZ* appeal to audiences in the 1930s?

ANSWERS

CHECK YOUR ANSWERS

1. Most people were not actually rich in the 1920s, despite the economic boom. However, the commonly held belief that the whole country was wealthy led to overproduction of goods.
2. Defaults caused banks to go out of business.
3. He thought it would be resolved as part of the cyclical nature of the economy.
4. FDR actively intervened to end the Depression.
5. They created jobs.
6. People pay a tax on their salaries when they are working, and receive a share back when they retire or become otherwise unable to work.
7. People were looking for an escape from their daily lives.

Unit 8

World War II
1930s–1945

Once again, the world would split into two warring sides:

The AXIS POWERS
Germany
Italy
Japan

The ALLIED POWERS
Great Britain
France ← UNTIL GERMANY INVADED
The Soviet Union ← AFTER 1941
The U.S. ←
China
(and many more countries)

Like any war, World War II had its causes and effects, its heroes and victims, and it led to destruction. Only, in this war, the destruction was more extreme.

Chapter 35

WORLD WAR II BEGINS

TOTALITARIANISM

After World War I, poverty, instability, and dissatisfaction in Europe led to the rise of **TOTALITARIAN** dictators, who promised they could create change if only they had complete control of EVERYTHING.

Totalitarian leaders did bring stability to their countries—at the cost of individual liberty.

> **TOTALITARIANISM**
> a system in which the government acts as absolute ruler with complete control over every element of life

Italy had been one of the Big Four nations to negotiate the Treaty of Versailles, but economic failure led to chaos. In 1922, BENITO MUSSOLINI, the leader of a **FASCIST** totalitarian movement, forced the king of Italy to grant him power. He named himself dictator under the title *IL DUCE* (the leader).

> **FASCISM**
> a form of totalitarianism practiced by Mussolini, emphasizing nationalism and conformity

The USSR formed in 1922 when the Russian Socialist Federative Soviet Republic (RSFSR) united with three smaller Soviet republics.

"USSR" OR "SOVIET UNION"

In the UNION OF SOVIET SOCIALIST REPUBLICS, after the death of Lenin in 1924, JOSEPH STALIN took control. He began to **EXTERMINATE** any Soviet citizen he thought was an enemy.

EXTERMINATE
put to death

In Germany, the debt from reparation payments for World War I and from having to shut down its military had pretty much brought about an economic collapse and destroyed the nation. ADOLF HITLER and the NATIONAL SOCIALIST GERMAN WORKERS' PARTY—the NAZIS (from the German word NATIONALSOZIALISTISCHE)—won the 1932 German elections, and Hitler was appointed CHANCELLOR. He promoted the idea of **ARYAN** superiority and gave Germans someone to blame for their problems: the Jewish population. Hitler named himself **FÜHRER** and took control.

ARYAN
of Northern European heritage; non-Jewish

FÜHRER
German for "leader"

TOTALITARIAN EXPANSIONISM

Each totalitarian leader believed that his country was superior to all others and had the right to conquer. JAPAN NEEDED COLONIES WITH THEIR NATURAL RESOURCES TO EXPAND.

In 1931, Japan invaded Manchuria; in 1937, Japan invaded China, where it perpetrated the NANJING MASSACRE, which was a violent attack on the city of Nanjing and its people.

In 1935, Italy conquered Ethiopia and left the League of Nations. In 1939, Italy conquered Albania.

In 1936, Germany annexed the RHINELAND, a coal-rich area that the Treaty of Versailles had declared a neutral **BUFFER ZONE**. In 1938, Germany conquered Austria.

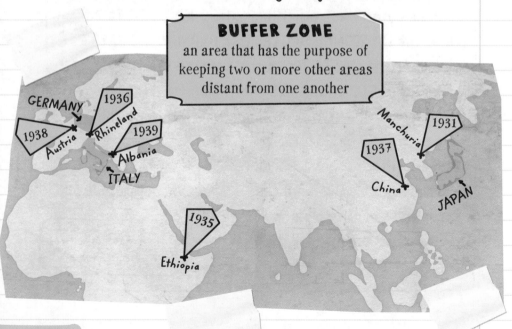

BUFFER ZONE
an area that has the purpose of keeping two or more other areas distant from one another

GERMANY
1936
1938
Austria
Rhineland
1939
Albania
ITALY
Manchuria
1931
1937
China
JAPAN
1935
Ethiopia

APPEASEMENT at MUNICH

APPEASEMENT
compromise; giving something
up in order to maintain peace

Hitler's next target was the
SUDETENLAND, an area of Czechoslovakia with a large
German population. Czechoslovakia turned to France and
England for help. In September 1938, British Prime Minister
NEVILLE CHAMBERLAIN proposed that Hitler could have the
Sudetenland if he promised not to invade anywhere else.
This **APPEASEMENT** was supposed to prevent another
war. In March of 1939, Hitler went ahead and conquered
Czechoslovakia. England and France warned that they'd
defend Poland, which seemed to be Hitler's next target.

The AXIS

With their similar philosophies, these dictators formed alliances.
In 1936, Hitler and Mussolini formed the Rome-Berlin Axis, aka
THE AXIS. Japan joined the pact in 1940. Stalin didn't join the
Axis, but signed a NON-AGGRESSION PACT with Germany. The
two countries agreed not to attack each other and secretly
agreed to grab Poland and divide it between them.

WORLD WAR...AGAIN

On September 1, 1939, Germany invaded Poland. On
September 3, Britain and France declared war on Germany,
as promised. World War II had begun. Hitler used a
BLITZKRIEG ("lightning war")—a tactic that combined
speed and surprise—to conquer Poland in only a few weeks.

The USSR also attacked Poland and then moved on to the Baltic Peninsula and Finland. Hitler moved north, conquering Denmark and Norway in April 1940, then Belgium, the Netherlands, and Luxembourg.

WAR in WESTERN EUROPE

France was the next target. Allied troops had set up along the MAGINOT LINE at the German border, but they were forced to retreat to DUNKIRK, a French town on the English Channel, where they were trapped as the Germans invaded from the north and Italy attacked from the south. On June 14, 1940, the

Germans seized Paris, and France surrendered on June 22. Thousands of French and British soldiers at Dunkirk escaped on fishing boats and went to England, where they joined the Free French Forces led by GENERAL CHARLES DE GAULLE.

It was far easier to replace military equipment than men, so it was important that they live to fight another day.

FUTURE PRESIDENT OF FRANCE

The BATTLE of BRITAIN

MEANS "AIR WEAPONS"

In the summer of 1940, Hitler began his air attack on England. During the BATTLE OF BRITAIN, the *LUFTWAFFE* (Germany's air force) heavily bombed London and other parts of England. Britain, led by PRIME MINISTER WINSTON CHURCHILL, refused to surrender. The ROYAL AIR FORCE (RAF) attacked the *LUFTWAFFE* until they retreated.

Hitler decided to change directions. Needing the resources and manpower of the Soviet Union, but worried about competition from Stalin, he decided to attack Russia in June 1941, breaking the pact the two countries had formed. The Soviets were forced to retreat, losing thousands of troops who were captured or killed. Stalin changed course as well: Stalin joined the Allies and ordered his people to destroy their own resources and burn their own cities before the Germans could get them. This is the SCORCHED EARTH tactic.

> A lot of children were evacuated from London during the bombings. This event even appears in the Chronicles of Narnia books: The main characters are sent away to live in the English countryside.

ISOLATIONISM v. REALITY

The U.S. tried to stay neutral. Between 1935 and 1937, Congress passed the NEUTRALITY ACTS, making it illegal for Americans to sell weapons or loan money to foreign nations. When FDR was elected for a third term (the first time any president had served more than twice) in 1940, he knew the nation was on the brink of war.

Congress had expanded the American military at FDR's request, and in 1940, it passed the SELECTIVE TRAINING AND SERVICE ACT, the first PEACETIME DRAFT in American history. In March 1941, the LEND-LEASE ACT made it legal to sell or lend weapons and supplies to the Allies. That August, after German attacks on American destroyers, FDR and Churchill issued the ATLANTIC CHARTER. It stated that neither country had any territorial ambitions in the war and that all people had the right to determine and live under a government of their own choosing.

PEARL HARBOR

Meanwhile, in Japan, HIDEKI TŌJŌ, a military leader, was elected prime minister in 1941. Tōjō became a dictator and soon had more influence than the emperor of Japan. After

386

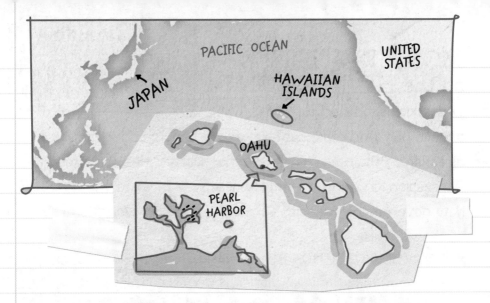

successful invasions in mainland Asia, Tōjō set his sights on islands like the Philippines (then controlled by the U.S.).

To destroy the American navy, on DECEMBER 7, 1941—the day President Roosevelt called "A DATE WHICH WILL LIVE IN INFAMY"—Japan launched a surprise attack on the naval base at PEARL HARBOR, Hawaii. It was a devastating attack that sunk or heavily damaged eight U.S. battleships along with three cruisers and several other ships. A total of 2,403 American civilians and servicemen were killed, and 1,178 were wounded. The only thing that spared even more U.S. lives was the fact that the U.S. carrier fleet was not in port and thus undamaged.

The next day, FDR asked Congress to declare war on Japan. Three days later, Germany and Italy declared war on the U.S., so Congress declared war back.

MOBILIZATION
on the HOMEFRONT

Industries produced tanks,
ammunition, and other war-related products under the
direction of the government. All that work ended the Great
Depression, creating an employment rate of almost 100 percent.
New government agencies formed, just like in World War I:

The **WAR PRODUCTION BOARD** decided which goods factories
would produce. Americans were encouraged to
RATION food and grow victory gardens.

The **OFFICE OF PRICE ADMINISTRATION** controlled inflation.

The **NATIONAL WAR LABOR BOARD** resolved labor conflicts.

The **REVENUE ACT OF 1942** raised taxes; the government
also raised money by selling **WAR BONDS**.

OPPORTUNITIES
and DISCRIMINATION

World War II provided opportunities
for women and minorities:

Posters of **ROSIE THE RIVETER** were
used to encourage women to work in
factories and the defense industry.

Women enlisted in high numbers as WACs (Women's Army Corps), WAVES (Women Appointed for Volunteer Emergency Service) in the navy, or WASPs (Women's Airforce Service Pilots), but as noncombatants.

Threats by black labor leader A. PHILIP RANDOLPH to protest in Washington, D.C., led Roosevelt to sign EXECUTIVE ORDER 8802 (the FAIR EMPLOYMENT ACT), prohibiting discrimination in factories supplying the war effort.

African Americans worked in defense factories in the North.

Army units were segregated at the beginning of the war, but there was integration over the course of the fighting. Famous black units included the TUSKEGEE AIRMEN.

Native Americans fought, and they also created unbreakable secret codes based on the Navajo language.

The government recruited Mexican American laborers called *BRACEROS* to work in agriculture.

ON THE FLIP SIDE:

Women were still paid much less than men.

Greater African American and Mexican American presence in cities led to tension and riots, including the 1943 "ZOOT SUIT RIOTS" in LA, so called after the clothing style worn by many young Latino men at the time.

Minorities were paid less than white workers.

JAPANESE INTERNMENT

Japanese immigrants (*ISSEI* in Japanese) and Americans of Japanese descent (*NISEI*) faced discrimination. Even people born in the U.S. were suspected of being spies. In February 1942, Roosevelt issued EXECUTIVE ORDER 9066, forcing Japanese Americans to leave their homes and move to INTERNMENT CAMPS. In 1944, in the case of *KOREMATSU V. UNITED STATES*, the Supreme Court upheld this as necessary.

> In 1942, the 442 Regimental Combat Team was created and composed of Japanese Americans. They served heroically during the war in Europe but were not allowed to fight in the Pacific.

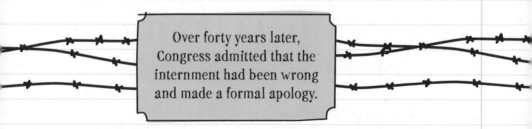

> Over forty years later, Congress admitted that the internment had been wrong and made a formal apology.

CHECK YOUR KNOWLEDGE

1. Which conditions in Europe contributed to the rise of totalitarianism?

2. What is fascism?

3. Why did Neville Chamberlain agree to give Hitler the Sudetenland?

4. What did Stalin instruct his people to do when Germany invaded Russia?

5. How did America help the Allies before Pearl Harbor?

6. How did World War II contribute to the end of the Great Depression?

7. What were Japanese Americans suspected of that led to Executive Order 9066?

ANSWERS

CHECK YOUR ANSWERS

1. Instability, low morale, and economic trouble
2. Fascism is nationalistic totalitarianism that was practiced by Mussolini.
3. He thought that appeasement would prevent further German invasions.
4. He told them to destroy their resources so the Germans couldn't get them.
5. The Lend-Lease Act allowed weapons and supplies to be leased to the Allies.
6. The economy was improved by the high demand for war supplies and labor.
7. Espionage

☆ Chapter **36** ☆

AMERICA ENTERS
the
WAR in EUROPE

ALLIED STRATEGY

With a draft and volunteers, the American military was ready to fight with the Allies. But where? The U.S. had to fight in the Atlantic and Pacific. Stalin wanted continental Europe to be the first target. Churchill thought the inexperienced American troops would be easily defeated and stretched too thin. He suggested that Americans head to German-occupied North Africa. In December of 1941, FDR agreed to Churchill's plan, leaving Stalin to handle Europe.

FIRST, NORTH AFRICA

The fighting in North Africa stretched throughout several countries. In June 1942, the German AFRIKA KORPS, led by the "DESERT FOX," GENERAL ERWIN ROMMEL, pushed into Egypt. In the BATTLE OF EL ALAMEIN, the British stopped the German advance, preventing them from capturing the

strategically located SUEZ CANAL, the British-controlled
water route between the Mediterranean and Red Seas.
Later that year, GENERAL DWIGHT D. EISENHOWER set up
headquarters in Gibraltar, and in 1943, the Allies helped
drive the Afrika Korps out of North Africa.

THEN, ITALY

The Allies reentered Europe from the south. In July 1943,
they landed on Sicily, an Italian island. Led by GENERAL
GEORGE S. PATTON, they moved on to mainland Italy. By
then, after losses in Africa and shortages in Italy, Italian
leaders had overthrown Mussolini, and the new government
surrendered to the Allies. Hitler didn't accept defeat. He
sent more Axis troops. In January 1944, the Allies surprised
German troops at Anzio, a city on the western coast of
Italy, and, after several months, defeated them. By June
1944, Rome was liberated.

MEANWHILE, in RUSSIA

After their invasion of Russia in September 1942, German troops advanced to the industrial city of STALINGRAD. But when winter came, the cold was so severe that much of the German army starved or froze to death. Still, Hitler refused to withdraw. In January of 1943, German commander General von Paulus defied the Führer's wishes and retreated. The Soviets suffered massive losses, but their victory was a turning point in the war because it showed Hitler's totalitarianism was weakening. The Germans tried to seize Leningrad (modern-day St. Petersburg), but the Russians pushed them west.

> Just as harsh weather conditions in Russia stymied the German army, weather was a factor in the defeat of Napoleon's army in 1812. Russia has been a challenging country to conquer because of its natural safeguards.

D-DAY

After freeing Italy, the Allied forces were finally ready to enter German-occupied France. In June 1944, General Eisenhower, who was then the Supreme Allied Commander in Europe, started OPERATION OVERLORD. Hitler expected any invasion to be near the town of Calais.

Early on June 6, 1944—which came to be known as D-DAY—
Allied forces landed, but not at Calais. PARATROOPERS (who
arrived by parachutes) and AMPHIBIOUS troops (trained
to operate on both land and sea) arrived in NORMANDY in
France. There were thousands of casualties, but the invasion
was successful.
American General
Omar Bradley led
the troops inland.
On August 25, Paris
was liberated.
Other Western
European nations
soon followed.

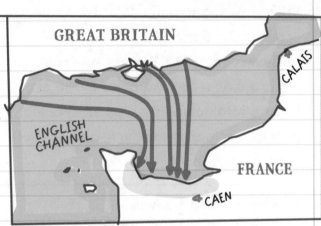

BATTLE of the BULGE

Hitler made a final attempt to turn the tide. On December 16,
1944, he attacked the Belgian
region of ARDENNES. The
attack forced Allied lines
to move back in one spot,
turning their line into a bubble
shape (a bulge, which is how
this attack came to be known
as the BATTLE OF THE BULGE).
By January, the Allies stopped
the German advance.

The HOLOCAUST

Hitler rose to power by convincing his people that Jews were to blame for Germany's hardships.

In September 1935, Germany passed the NUREMBERG LAWS, stripping Jews of citizenship. On November 9, 1938—KRISTALLNACHT (the "night of the broken glass")—Jewish businesses, synagogues, and other property were

> ### GHETTO
> a section of a city that is occupied by only one group of people, usually because they cannot live elsewhere as a result of economic hardships

destroyed in riots. The HOLOCAUST (literally, "destruction") had begun. Jews were moved into **GHETTOS** and forced to wear identifying yellow labels in the shape of the Star of David, a Jewish symbol. **ANTI-SEMITISM** became the law in Germany.

In January of 1942, Hitler and the Nazis came up with a plan they called the FINAL SOLUTION: They planned to kill every Jew in a **GENOCIDE** in concentration camps. The young and healthy were forced to work in camps until they died; others were killed immediately in

> ### GENOCIDE
> a killing of a race, ethnicity, or religious group of people

gas chambers. Six million Jewish people were killed, along with about five million others who didn't fit in with Hitler's idea of a perfect Aryan society—homosexuals, Gypsies (Roma), people with disabilities, and anyone who opposed the Nazis.

Although Allied leaders heard rumors of these horrors, they didn't make the rumors public. When they freed camp prisoners later, Allied soldiers were shocked to see the hugeness of Nazi brutality.

PRESIDENT TRUMAN

In the election of 1944, Roosevelt became the only person to be elected president for the fourth time in a row. But his health was fading. On April 12, 1945, FDR died, and Vice President HARRY S. TRUMAN took charge.

> The "S" wasn't short for a middle name. It stood for his two grandfathers, who both had S names. Apparently that wasn't such an odd thing to do with a middle initial in some places. And Harry was his full first name.

VICTORY in EUROPE

After other air raids on German cities, the Allied forces launched a major attack on Dresden in February 1945. As Soviet troops entered Berlin, Hitler went into hiding. On April 30, 1945—two days after Mussolini was killed by Italian partisans—Hitler committed suicide so he wouldn't have to face Germany's defeat. On May 7, after the Soviet army captured Berlin, the Germans surrendered to the Allied forces. May 8 was declared V-E DAY in honor of the victory in Europe. But World War II wasn't over yet.

CHECK YOUR KNOWLEDGE

1. Why did Churchill think the Allies ought to focus on North Africa before Europe?

2. How did Hitler react to the surrender of Italy?

3. How was the siege of Stalingrad a turning point in the war?

4. Whom did Hitler blame for Germany's problems in the 1930s?

5. Which groups other than Jews were to be exterminated as part of the Final Solution?

6. Did the Allies know about the Holocaust during the war?

7. Where did Allied forces land to commence Operation Overlord?

8. How did the Battle of the Bulge get its name?

ANSWERS
399

CHECK YOUR ANSWERS

1. He thought the troops were not ready for Europe yet and would be stretched too thin.

2. He did not accept it and sent his soldiers to fight for Italy. (They lost.)

3. Hitler's officers disobeyed his command not to retreat, showing that totalitarianism was weakening.

4. Jews

5. People with disabilities, homosexuals, Gypsies (Roma), and anyone who opposed the Nazis

6. The leaders had heard about it, but many people did not know.

7. Normandy

8. It is named after the bulge shape created in the Allied line when the Axis attacked at one point.

☆ Chapter 37 ☆

☆ WAR in the PACIFIC

The OTHER FRONT

It was time for the U.S. to defeat Japan and end the war.

ASIA
JAPAN
PACIFIC OCEAN

SEA OF JAPAN
PACIFIC OCEAN

HIROSHIMA

NAGASAKI

TOKYO

EAST CHINA SEA

JAPAN

JAPANESE VICTORIES

On the same day the Japanese bombed Pearl Harbor, they also attacked American bases in Guam, Wake Island, and the Philippines. They invaded Thailand, Hong Kong, Malaya, and Burma. Japan took over   NOW PART OF MALAYSIA ↗   ↖ "MYANMAR" TODAY

Manila, the capital of the Philippines.

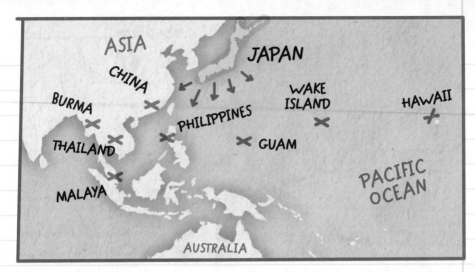

After months of conflict, American General Douglas MacArthur, his family, and some key aides were ordered to leave the Philippines to defend Australia. The Philippines surrendered to Japan. The troops still in the Bataan province of the Philippines were captured and forced on a brutal walk of over 60 miles to the Bataan Peninsula prison camps, where hundreds of Americans and thousands of Filipinos were killed; the event came to be known as the BATAAN DEATH MARCH.

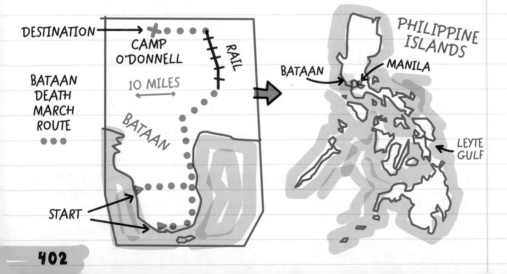

TURNING the TIDE

In April 1942, Americans launched air raids on Tokyo, which wasn't militarily significant but did boost American morale. In the BATTLE OF THE CORAL SEA, they blocked Japan from reaching Australia, helped by ADMIRAL CHESTER NIMITZ of the U.S. Pacific Fleet intercepting Japanese communications. Code-cracking also helped the Allies prepare for the BATTLE OF MIDWAY on June 4, 1942. In a major American victory and turning point, the American navy destroyed four Japanese aircraft carriers.

> The U.S. used Navajo **CODE TALKERS**—Navajo soldiers who communicated in codes based on their tribal language. It was impossible for the Japanese or other outsiders to figure out the codes and was an invaluable contribution to the war.

MacArthur and Nimitz adopted a strategy called ISLAND HOPPING to secure air bases in order to launch larger attacks on Japan: capture small islands, use each as a base to capture other islands, hop closer to the Philippines and Japan. It was time-consuming but effective. From August 1942 to February 1943, the marines fought to capture the island of GUADALCANAL. In the October 1944 BATTLE OF LEYTE GULF, the Allies destroyed almost the entire Japanese navy. Allied forces liberated Manila in March 1945 and headed for Japan.

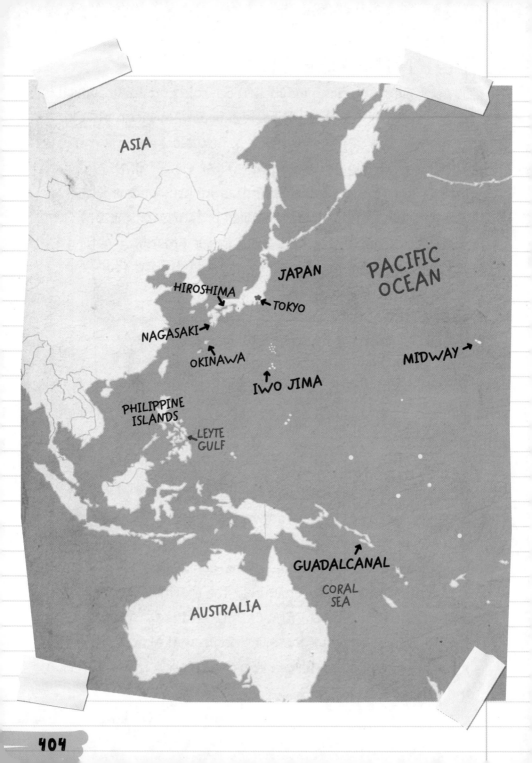

REACHING JAPAN

The Allied forces targeted two Japanese islands:
IWO JIMA in February 1945 and OKINAWA in April.
In a desperate attempt to gain the upper hand, the
Japanese used KAMIKAZES—suicide pilots—to attack
Allied ships, but the Allied forces still advanced.

The A-BOMB

Japan was unwilling to surrender, and the Allies considered
a full-scale invasion. However, the Allies had also conducted
the first successful test of an ATOMIC BOMB on July 16, 1945,
after three years of work on the "MANHATTAN PROJECT,"
led by scientist J. ROBERT OPPENHEIMER. (FDR founded the
Manhattan Project after Albert Einstein and other scientists
had warned him that an atomic weapon was being developed
by Germany.) Even though he knew that a single atomic bomb
could cost thousands of civilian lives, President Truman saw
it as a justifiable way to end the war and to save countless
Americans. Truman issued the POTSDAM DECLARATION: If
Japan did not surrender, the U.S. would inflict "prompt and
utter destruction."

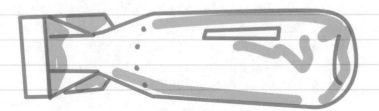

This seemed like just another threat, so Japan did not surrender. On August 6, 1945, the airplane *ENOLA GAY* dropped an atomic bomb on the city of HIROSHIMA. At least 75,000 people were killed in a single instant. Japan remained firm.

On August 9, the U.S. dropped another atomic bomb on the city of NAGASAKI, killing over 20,000 civilians. Many of those who survived the bombings later died from radiation and horrific burns or lived with severe health problems and disabilities.

PEACE

On August 15, 1945, Japan surrendered. August 15 was Victory over Japan Day, or V-J DAY. (Some consider August 14 to be V-J Day because of time differences between the U.S. and Asia.) On September 2, Japan signed the surrender documents. World War II was finally over.

 WHAT MAKES A NUCLEAR WEAPON NUCLEAR?

The power comes from reactions in the NUCLEI of atoms of RADIOACTIVE elements, which emit energy. When the particles collide, the result is so strong that a tiny amount of material can create a huge explosion. Atomic bombs, or "A-bombs," get their power by splitting the nucleus. Even more powerful hydrogen bombs, or "H-bombs," invented in the 1950s, fuse multiple nuclei together.

CHECK YOUR KNOWLEDGE

1. What happened to the Allied troops who stayed in the Philippines when MacArthur left?

2. What was a major communications advantage the Allies had over the Japanese?

3. What is "island hopping" and how does it work?

4. What were the first two Allied targets within Japan?

5. What inspired FDR to found the Manhattan Project?

6. What did President Truman think about the morality of using an atomic weapon?

7. What was the name of the plane that dropped the bomb on Hiroshima?

8. What happened to many people in Hiroshima and Nagasaki who survived the initial blast of the atomic weapons?

ANSWERS

CHECK YOUR ANSWERS

1. They were forced to make the Bataan Death March.

2. Japanese codes had been broken, but the Navajo-based American codes had not.

3. "Island hopping" is the strategy of taking one island at a time and using it as a base to attack the next.

4. Iwo Jima and Okinawa

5. Einstein alerted him to the possibility that the Germans could develop the technology first.

6. He thought it was okay if it would save American lives.

7. ENOLA GAY

8. Many later died from burns and radiation or lived with severe disabilities.

Unit 9

Post-World War II Era
1945-1980

The post-World War II era was full of exciting change. Television became the main form of entertainment. Rock and roll swept the nation. African Americans and women fought for equal rights. Also significant: America entered the Korean and Vietnam Wars; the Cold War began; and everyone was afraid of Communism and nukes.

☆ Chapter 38 ☆

AMERICA
AFTER the WAR

The WORLD AFTER the WAR

The only major world power to have had minimal fighting
on the home front, the U.S. came out of the war better off
than its allies and enemies in almost every way. (The only
fighting that took place on U.S. soil was the attack on
Pearl Harbor.) The economy had been helped by the war
and continued to grow.

YALTA and POTSDAM

When it was clear that the Allies would win, the Allied
leaders discussed ways to prevent another world war.
In February 1945, the BIG THREE—Churchill, FDR, and
Stalin—met at the YALTA CONFERENCE and decided they
needed a better peacekeeping group than the League of
Nations to prevent war. Even Stalin agreed that nations

The BIG THREE

CHURCHILL   FDR   STALIN

should have the right to autonomy and democracy (though he later forced nations into Communism, so there's that). Stalin also agreed to fight against Japan after Germany was defeated. The leaders decided to divide Germany into four parts. The city of Berlin would also be divided in four. The U.S., the U.K., France, and the Soviet Union would each control a quarter.

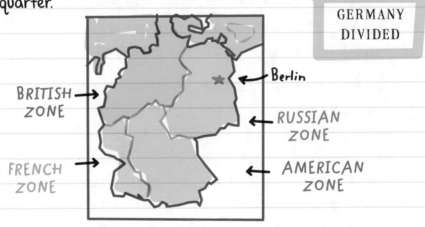

GERMANY DIVIDED

BRITISH ZONE

Berlin

RUSSIAN ZONE

FRENCH ZONE

AMERICAN ZONE

In July, President Truman also met with Churchill, Clement Attlee (also from Great Britain), and Stalin at the POTSDAM CONFERENCE. There they focused on the prosecution of Japan and confirmed Soviet involvement in the war in the Pacific.

The UNITED NATIONS

The UNITED NATIONS (or UN) formed on June 26, 1945, when fifty countries signed its charter in San Francisco. The UN's goal is to preserve world peace through diplomacy.

One of the UN's first tasks was to create Arab and Jewish states from a British-controlled area in the Middle East called Palestine. After the Holocaust, many Jews sought a homeland to call their own. In 1948, by UN mandate, the state of ISRAEL was officially formed. The region that was formerly called Palestine had a mainly Muslim Arab population that was not happy with a new Jewish state taking control.

Neighboring Arab countries attacked the newly formed Israel in 1948, but Israel fought back hard. Thousands of Palestinian Arabs fled the area and sought refuge in the West Bank and the Gaza Strip, two Arab-controlled lands. Arab forces attacked again in 1967, and this time Israel gained control of the West Bank, the Gaza Strip, and parts of Syria and Egypt.

The conflict between Palestine and Israel continues to this day.

The NUREMBERG TRIALS

In November 1945, in Nuremberg, Germany, the NUREMBERG TRIALS began, trying Nazis for CRIMES AGAINST HUMANITY and war

crimes. In the first round of trials, nineteen Nazis were found guilty and twelve were sentenced to death. Over a hundred more were found guilty before the process ended. A similar **TRIBUNAL** (the International Military Tribunal for the Far East) was held in Tokyo, where Hideki Tōjō and five other Japanese leaders were convicted and executed.

The IRON CURTAIN

Even though the U.S. and the Soviet Union fought on the same side during World War II, their political differences were clear. Without a common enemy, they became enemies of each other. Although Stalin had promised free, democratic elections in the Eastern European nations, he set up Communist **SATELLITE** governments there under his control.

Each side thought the other was trying to take over the world.

SATELLITE describes something that is subordinate to another authority

The tension between Communist (USSR and Eastern Europe) and capitalist (U.S. and Western Europe) governments became known as the COLD WAR, which consisted of threats and intimidation, as opposed to a "hot" war with actual fighting. In a speech in 1946, Winston Churchill stated that an IRON CURTAIN had descended on Eastern Europe, separating it from the rest of the world.

The TRUMAN DOCTRINE

President Truman decided that the U.S. would fight the Cold War through CONTAINMENT. Truman convinced Congress to allocate money to help defeat Communist rebels in Greece and Turkey and prevent the spread of Communism to two more countries. Holding back Communism through containment and giving assistance to groups committed to fighting Communism was the TRUMAN DOCTRINE.

The MARSHALL PLAN

In June of 1947, Secretary of State GEORGE MARSHALL came up with his MARSHALL PLAN to rebuild Europe. The U.S. hoped to contain Communism, boost European economies, and continue U.S. trade with Europe. The U.S. gave about $13 billion in aid to Western European nations between 1948 and 1951. Economic aid was supposed to protect countries that were unstable and poor and prevent radicals from taking over. The U.S. also provided economic assistance to Asian countries, including Japan, which it continued to occupy.

The BERLIN AIRLIFT

The U.S., the U.K., and France announced that they would combine their shares of Germany and Berlin into a single democratic nation. Truman believed that a unified Germany was the key to Europe's recovery. Stalin saw this as a threat, not only to the Soviet-controlled part of Germany, but also to Europe in general if the Germans regained power.

Stalin began the **BERLIN BLOCKADE**—a strategy to cut off the city's access to the West. Truman organized the BERLIN AIRLIFT: U.S. and British planes brought food and supplies to West Berlin until Stalin ended the blockade. Still, Berlin remained divided into East and West Berlin.

> **BLOCKADE**
> the blocking of something (can also be used as a verb)

BERLIN DIVIDED

WEST BERLIN

FRENCH

EAST BERLIN (SOVIET)

BRITISH

AMERICAN

SPREE RIVER

Berlin

GERMANY

By the end of 1949, Germany was also divided into two nations: The Federal Republic of Germany (democratic, West Germany) and the German Democratic Republic (Communist, East Germany).

NATO and the WARSAW PACT

In 1949, the U.S. and Canada joined with Western Europe to form an alliance, the NORTH ATLANTIC TREATY ORGANIZATION (NATO). It was a defensive alliance meant to prevent a Soviet assault on Western Europe. In 1955, the Communists established their own alliance, the WARSAW PACT.

FIRST PEACETIME
MILITARY ALLIANCE

In spite of NATO, the U.S. decided it shouldn't rely on other countries to protect the world against Communism. America would lead the world.

The FAIR DEAL

Truman began preparing a slate of domestic reforms in 1945. This extension of the New Deal was called the FAIR DEAL and promised:

a higher minimum wage

better Social Security

job creation

better public housing

national health insurance

WHAT'S THE DEAL?

Remember: The **SQUARE DEAL** was Teddy Roosevelt's domestic program that focused on conservation, control of corporations, and consumer protection.

The **NEW DEAL** was a series of economic programs enacted by FDR during his first term in office.

The **FAIR DEAL** was a series of domestic reforms proposed by Harry Truman.

Truman established a Committee on Civil Rights in 1946. When his Fair Deal bills didn't pass in Congress, Truman took other steps. For example, he issued an executive order that desegregated the army.

The ELECTION of 1948

The Republican Party was sure they'd win. Truman hadn't succeeded with the Fair Deal, and the Democratic Party was divided: Some Southern Democrats, angry about Truman's support of civil rights, formed a new party, called the States' Rights Democratic Party, or the DIXIECRATS. Other Democrats formed a new PROGRESSIVE PARTY to try to reconcile with the Soviets.

The Republican candidate, THOMAS DEWEY, was so far ahead in the polls that the *CHICAGO DAILY TRIBUNE* newspaper released a special edition with a huge "DEWEY DEFEATS TRUMAN" on the front page before the votes were tallied. But Truman had gone on a **WHISTLE-STOP TOUR**, convincing Americans that the failure of the Fair Deal was the fault of the Republican Congress. Truman won a second term.

> **WHISTLE-STOP TOUR**
> a campaign trip from town to town, referring to the train stations where candidates would make a quick stop before continuing on

CHECK YOUR KNOWLEDGE

1. Why was the U.S. in a better position after World War II than its allies were?

2. What did the Allies decide when they met at the Yalta Conference?

3. What is the goal of the United Nations?

4. The defendants at the Nuremberg Trials were accused of what?

5. What made the Cold War "cold"?

6. What was the thinking behind the policy of containment?

7. Why did Stalin think a unified Germany was a threat? And to whom?

8. What were the components of Truman's Fair Deal?

9. What inspired the Dixiecrats to break away from the Democrats?

ANSWERS 419

CHECK YOUR ANSWERS

1. There had been no fighting on U.S. soil, other than Pearl Harbor, and the U.S. economy was thriving.

2. They decided they needed a better peacekeeping group, they would fight against Japan, and they would divide Germany into occupied zones.

3. To preserve peace through diplomacy

4. Crimes against humanity and war crimes

5. There were no active armed conflicts between the U.S. and the USSR.

6. Truman believed that it was best to prevent Communism from spreading.

7. He thought a unified Germany would become powerful and pose a threat to Eastern Germany and the rest of Europe.

8. The Fair Deal promised a higher minimum wage, job creation, health insurance, Social Security, and better housing.

9. They were opposed to Truman's civil rights programs.

Chapter 39

The KOREAN WAR

COMMUNISM in ASIA

In China, in 1949, MAO ZEDONG led the
Communist Party to drive CHIANG KAI-SHEK's
NATIONALISTS out of power. The Nationalists
fled to TAIWAN, where they set up a government that
the West recognized as the legitimate Chinese ruling body.
On the mainland, the PEOPLE'S REPUBLIC OF CHINA was
established on October 1, 1949. Many Americans felt that their
government should have done more to
stop a Communist nation and ally of
the USSR from forming.

MAO!

In 1949, the Soviets
detonated an atomic
bomb, which meant that
the U.S. no longer had a
nuclear monopoly.

The 38th PARALLEL

After World War II, a lot of colonized nations gained
independence. In some cases, the imperial nations had to be
forced to grant independence and the process turned violent.

KOREA had been an occupied Japanese colony. The U.S. proposed dividing Korea on the 38th PARALLEL. The Soviets helped Communists take power in North Korea, and the U.S. supported the democratic government in SOUTH KOREA.

On June 25, 1950, North Korean troops crossed the border to try to take over South Korea and unite Korea under one Communist government. Figuring that the Soviet Union was involved, Truman sent military assistance to South Korea and asked for assistance from the United Nations. He didn't declare a Korean war.

The KOREAN WAR

The United Nations put together soldiers from 16 different nations, but the majority were American. The forces were led by U.S. General Douglas MacArthur. MacArthur forced the North Korean troops to retreat, and the UN forces pushed them back toward China. MacArthur assumed that China and the USSR wouldn't intervene, so he got permission from Truman to invade North Korea. But on November 25, 1950, the Chinese army entered North Korea.

By 1951, the two sides reached a stalemate at the 38th parallel. General MacArthur wanted to go nuclear against China, but Truman refused. MacArthur publicly criticized Truman, and Truman fired him. Peace talks began in July 1951, but progress was slow.

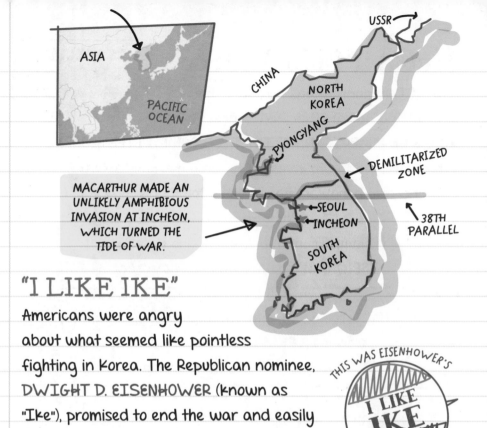

ASIA

PACIFIC OCEAN

USSR

CHINA

NORTH KOREA

PYONGYANG

DEMILITARIZED ZONE

SEOUL

INCHEON

38TH PARALLEL

SOUTH KOREA

MACARTHUR MADE AN UNLIKELY AMPHIBIOUS INVASION AT INCHEON, WHICH TURNED THE TIDE OF WAR.

"I LIKE IKE"

Americans were angry about what seemed like pointless fighting in Korea. The Republican nominee, DWIGHT D. EISENHOWER (known as "Ike"), promised to end the war and easily defeated Democrat ADLAI STEVENSON. He was the first Republican to defeat a Democrat in a presidential election since 1928.

THIS WAS EISENHOWER'S I LIKE **IKE** MAIN POLITICAL SLOGAN

It took more than a year, but a cease-fire finally ended fighting on July 27, 1953. A

DE FACTO in effect

DEMILITARIZED ZONE (DMZ) was established not far from the 38th parallel as a no-man's-land and **DE FACTO** border. There was still a North Korea. Thirty-three thousand Americans and nearly 2 million Koreans and Chinese died to show that neither side was afraid to use force. Still, it is often referred to as the "Forgotten War."

WE STILL DON'T HAVE A PEACE TREATY WITH NORTH KOREA.

423

McCARTHYISM

Fear of Communism was strong in the U.S., setting off another Red Scare. The HOUSE UN-AMERICAN ACTIVITIES COMMITTEE (HUAC) was established in 1938 to investigate "un-American activity"— meaning any behavior that seemed Communist-like.

President Truman investigated accusations of **ESPIONAGE** among government workers.

The HUAC targeted the movie industry; people who were charged were **BLACKLISTED** by movie studios if they refused to reveal information.

Communist groups were required to register with the government.

In 1951, a State Department employee named **ALGER HISS** was jailed for perjury in connection with giving information to the Soviets.

JULIUS and **ETHEL ROSENBERG** were executed in 1953 for selling atomic secrets to the Soviet Union.

In 1950, JOSEPH McCARTHY, a Republican senator, took charge of the hunt for Communists. He made reckless accusations (mostly against leftists) and claimed to have a list of

424

Communists working for the State Department, even though he never showed it. McCARTHYISM now refers to the practice of making unfounded accusations of treason and the use of accusations to prevent criticism. During televised hearings in 1954, McCarthy couldn't back up his accusations and lost all his credibility. As a result, he was censured by the Senate for distorting facts and violating senatorial ethics.

YOU CAN WATCH THESE ONLINE NOW.

There were some Soviet spies living among Americans, but McCarthy lumped everyone together: spies, Communists, people who believed in the theories of Communism but didn't act on them, people who had nothing to do with anything. Other than the spies, a lot of these people were patriotic Americans.

ARMS RACE

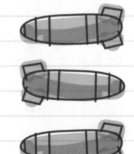

Using stolen technology, the Soviet Union built an atomic bomb in 1949. In 1950, the U.S. began working on a HYDROGEN BOMB, which was many times more powerful. The H-Bomb was tested successfully in 1952; by 1955, the Soviets had developed their own H-bomb. Both sides raced to stockpile the most weapons—way more nuclear weapons than needed to annihilate both sides.

The U.S. and USSR were developing missile technology and became locked in a SPACE RACE, starting when the Soviet Union launched the first artificial satellite, SPUTNIK, in 1957.

The next year, the U.S. launched
a satellite and founded the National
Aeronautics and Space Administration (NASA).
The technological advances were meant to be used for
both war and peace, and the Space Race led to a focus on
math and science in American schools.

BRINKMANSHIP

Eisenhower was a moderate Republican who balanced the
budget and supported the 1956 FEDERAL HIGHWAY ACT,
which created the first interstate highways. He believed that
containment wasn't strong enough for the Cold War. His
secretary of state, JOHN FOSTER DULLES, coined a new term
for their strategy: "BRINKMANSHIP," meaning that the U.S.
would issue warnings with increasing pressure (to go to the
BRINK of a crisis). The greatest way to prevent nuclear war
was knowing that there would be no winner; both sides would
be destroyed. The MUTUAL ASSURED DESTRUCTION (MAD)
doctrine under brinkmanship was a cornerstone of U.S. and
Soviet foreign policy during the Cold War.

Soviet leader NIKITA KHRUSHCHEV and Eisenhower
considered peace talks until Eisenhower sent a U-2 spy plane
over Russia, denied its purpose, and then refused to apologize
even when the pilot was captured. Relations between the U.S.
and the USSR deteriorated.

CHECK YOUR KNOWLEDGE

1. Which of the two Chinas did the U.S. officially recognize?

2. Why did North Korean troops cross the 38th parallel?

3. When did Congress declare war on North Korea?

4. Where was the DMZ established in Korea?

5. What was an "un-American activity"?

6. How did McCarthy lose his credibility?

7. How much of Russia could the U.S. have destroyed with its Cold War nuclear arsenal?

ANSWERS ➤

CHECK YOUR ANSWERS

1. Taiwan

2. They wanted to unite Korea under one Communist government.

3. Trick question! Never.

4. Along the 38th parallel, where the line had been at the beginning of the conflict

5. Anything suspected of Communist leanings

6. He couldn't back up his accusations.

7. All of it and more

☆ Chapter 40 ☆

AMERICAN AFFLUENCE
☆ ☆ ☆ and the ☆ ☆ ☆
BABY BOOM

AMERICAN AFFLUENCE

America prospered under Eisenhower. Although he wanted to decrease the size of government, he decided not to reverse the social reforms that Truman had put in place. He even expanded Social Security, increased the minimum wage, and established the Department of Health, Education, and Welfare.

The economy boomed. Americans bought home appliances, cars, clothes, and televisions. They watched programs like *I LOVE LUCY* and *THE LONE RANGER*, where they saw advertisements for more products to buy. The "AMERICAN DREAM" was linked to owning the same things as the families on television.

The G.I. BILL and the BABY BOOM

> **G.I.**
> an American soldier, from the acronym for "Government Issue" that appeared on their uniforms

One reason people could afford to buy so much was the **G.I. BILL** (or the G.I. BILL OF RIGHTS or the SERVICEMEN'S READJUSTMENT ACT), which President Roosevelt had signed into law in 1944. The G.I. Bill provided veterans with loans to get an education and buy homes. Home sales helped the economy. Many veterans were also ready to start families, leading to a sudden spike in the national birthrate. The BABY BOOM was a prosperous time. However, women often stopped working when the boomer babies were born. (Women were also asked to leave the workplace after World War II ended because returning veterans needed jobs.)

WHITE FLIGHT

The Highway Act created new highways, enabling more people to travel and commute. Families moved to the SUBURBS. Builders were eager to keep up with demand and keep homes affordable, so they began creating complexes where every house looked exactly the same. Built in 1951, LEVITTOWN, on Long Island, New York, became the first mass-produced suburb. Families moved from the cities to the suburbs, and also from the North and East to the South and West, to the region called the SUNBELT because of its warm climate and cheap land. People who couldn't afford to move

The Latin word root "urbs" means city. Something "urban" is a city, and "suburb" is "sub-" (under, or outside of) a city.

had to stay in the cities. Because of WHITE FLIGHT—the process of affluent, mostly white families moving out of the cities—many INNER CITY areas became ghettos. Taxes went to suburban infrastructures, causing a decline in the quality of public services in areas where only the poor remained. Conditions deteriorated so much that the federal government had to create URBAN RENEWAL initiatives. It wasn't just city people who missed out on the prosperity. Small farmers were hurt by the growth of **AGRIBUSINESS**.

> **AGRIBUSINESS**
> large-scale corporate farming

POP CULTURE and the GENERATION GAP

In the 1950s, a new kind of American music emerged when African American rhythm and blues (R&B) was picked up by white teenagers. The result was ROCK AND ROLL music. In 1956, teenagers fell in love with ELVIS PRESLEY and his music. Rock influenced culture, style, and what it meant to be a young American. For the first time, young people were being targeted as a generation with advertisements and fads. No surprise, many adults didn't understand the attraction.

BACKLASH and BEATNIKS

While teens rebelled with something wild like, say, staying out late at a drive-in movie, other Americans rebelled against consumerism and CONFORMITY by spending their time in coffeehouses and at poetry readings. They were called BEATNIKS, because they were followers of the BEAT literature movement led by writers like Allen Ginsberg and Jack Kerouac.

ROCK-AND-ROLL
FASHION

BEATNIKS

"VERY COOL."

CHECK YOUR KNOWLEDGE

1. How did Eisenhower's social beliefs differ from Truman's? How did that translate into his domestic policies?

2. How did television influence consumerism?

3. What did the G.I. Bill provide for veterans?

4. How did the baby boom help the American economy?

5. Why were homes mass-produced for some suburbs? Which suburb was most famous for this?

6. Why did many people move to the Sun Belt during the 1950s?

7. What were the effects of white flight on urban areas in the 1950s?

8. How did changes in technology affect farmers?

9. What were the roots of rock and roll music?

10. What were the beatniks rebelling against?

ANSWERS

CHECK YOUR ANSWERS

1. Eisenhower believed in smaller government, but he didn't actually reverse Truman's policies. He even expanded some welfare programs.
2. Television presented a vision of an ideal American life, and many people wanted to buy things to match it.
3. Home loans and subsidized education
4. As many people began families, they also spent a lot of money on family-related products and houses.
5. They were produced, notably in Levittown, to meet demand.
6. For the climate and cheap land
7. Inner city areas lost valuable tax dollars and became ghettos.
8. Technology allowed for large-scale corporate farming, which hurt small farmers' businesses.
9. R&B
10. Conformity and consumerism

Chapter 41

The CIVIL RIGHTS MOVEMENT

The MOVEMENT BEGINS

The CIVIL RIGHTS MOVEMENT was a period of **GRASSROOTS** efforts to put an end to racial discrimination, especially in the 1950s and '60s. Protests against segregation had begun decades earlier, but World War II helped raise more awareness—particularly among African American veterans—of the hypocrisy in fighting for freedom abroad while inequality persisted at home.

> **GRASSROOTS**
> from the people, as opposed to the government

GRASS HAS ROOTS THAT GO WIDE AND DEEP, EVEN THOUGH GRASS ISN'T VERY TALL. →

BROWN v. BOARD of EDUCATION

One of the first targets was segregation. The NAACP challenged this law in the early 1950s, on the basis that many "separate but equal" public schools for black kids were inferior to all-white schools in the same district. That was a violation of the Fourteenth Amendment, which states that all U.S. citizens are entitled to the EQUAL PROTECTION OF THE LAW.

The parents of a girl named Linda Brown sued her school district when she wasn't allowed to attend the (all-white) school near her house in Topeka, Kansas. The Supreme Court heard the arguments in the case of BROWN v. BOARD OF EDUCATION OF TOPEKA, KANSAS in 1952.

THURGOOD MARSHALL, a lawyer for the NAACP, presented arguments for the Brown family. He convinced

THURGOOD MARSHALL became the first African American Supreme Court justice.

IT WAS A UNANIMOUS 9-0 DECISION.

the court to make a landmark ruling on May 17, 1954, that placing African Americans in "separate but equal" schools was unconstitutional because things that are separate are never actually equal. In a case the next year (Brown II), the Supreme Court required that all segregated public schools integrate "WITH ALL DELIBERATE SPEED." The court did not give a deadline, so some schools delayed integration for years.

The LITTLE ROCK NINE

In September of 1957, an Arkansas high school was ordered by a judge to admit nine black students. Arkansas Governor ORVAL FAUBUS was a segregationist, and he sent the Arkansas National Guard to stop the students from going in. One of the LITTLE ROCK NINE, ELIZABETH ECKFORD, was threatened with lynching. For three weeks, the students were kept out. President Eisenhower ordered Faubus to allow the students in, and when Faubus continued to ignore these orders, Eisenhower sent paratroopers to escort the students and enforce the law.

ROSA PARKS and the MONTGOMERY BUS BOYCOTT

City buses were segregated too. Black riders were required to give up their seats if white riders wanted them. On December 1, 1955, in Montgomery, Alabama, a woman named ROSA PARKS refused. She was arrested and fined. In response, African Americans organized the MONTGOMERY BUS BOYCOTT, which lasted for more than a year.

Most people who rode the buses were black, so the boycott cost the city a lot of money, and also cost it its reputation when the national media picked up the story. Boycotters organized carpools or walked, even when faced with violent segregationists and the KKK. On November 13, 1956, the

During the Civil Rights era, Southern states resisted the Supreme Court decisions and vowed not to enforce them, in a strategy called MASSIVE RESISTANCE. Furthermore, various governors proposed to interject the state government between the federal government and its citizens in a tactic called STATE INTERPOSITION. Eisenhower, however, stood fast and used federal troops to enforce the law.

Supreme Court ruled that the bus segregation law had been unconstitutional in the first place. The boycott had worked.

MARTIN LUTHER KING JR.

A young reverend named DR. MARTIN LUTHER KING JR.
(MLK Jr.) rose to prominence during the Montgomery Bus
Boycott. His talent for speechmaking made him popular.
In 1957, he helped found the SOUTHERN CHRISTIAN
LEADERSHIP CONFERENCE (SCLC), a key organization
in the civil rights movement. MLK Jr. was influenced by
A. PHILIP RANDOLPH and by MOHANDAS GANDHI, who
had led protests in India
against British foreign rule
using nonviolent tactics of
civil disobedience.

> MOHANDAS GANDHI
> was also known as Mahatma, or
> "Great Soul." He used nonviolent
> protest to advocate for self-rule in
> India against British colonizers.

SIT-INS

One of the most efficient forms of nonviolent protest was
the SIT-IN—sitting in protest. On February 1, 1960, four black
students sat at a whites-only lunch counter in Greensboro,
North Carolina. Although the lunch counter staff refused
to serve them, the students returned each day with more
and more people. Eventually, store owners desegregated to
prevent further disruption of their business.

An organization called the STUDENT NONVIOLENT
COORDINATING COMMITTEE (SNCC) formed to help people
launch sit-ins across the South. The grassroots civil rights
movement—which consisted of large numbers of young
people—was growing and making its mark.

JOHN F. KENNEDY

In the election of 1960, JOHN F. KENNEDY (JFK), a young Democratic senator from Massachusetts, challenged incumbent Republican vice president RICHARD NIXON. JFK came from a prominent political family and was a WWII navy war hero. The Kennedy-Nixon debates were the first televised presidential debates. Americans saw that Kennedy was more youthful than Nixon. Although some people thought a Catholic like Kennedy would be more loyal to the pope than to the American people, Kennedy reassured them, and he promised supporters a "NEW FRONTIER" on domestic reforms, a call for public service, vigorous federal government, and strong anti-Communist foreign policy.

The election was close, but Kennedy won. He and his wife, JACQUELINE, were exciting, stylish, and popular.

JFK and Jackie O. were style icons, and you can be too!

NO HAT →

SKINNY TIE →

← PILLBOX HAT

← SUNGLASSES

→ PEARLS

← SUIT

Kennedy didn't immediately pursue the reforms he had promised, in order to avoid upsetting Southern Democrats. Civil rights leaders criticized him for not bringing about change fast enough.

FREEDOM RIDERS

In May 1961, the CONGRESS OF RACIAL EQUALITY
(CORE) sent blacks and whites to ride together as
FREEDOM RIDERS on interstate buses to segregated
stations in the South. They planned to refuse to obey racial
restrictions. The Freedom Riders faced some violent attacks,
but they continued riding. That autumn, the Interstate
Commerce Commission began enforcing desegregation in bus
depots. Another nonviolent protest had worked.

OUTRAGE in BIRMINGHAM

In spring 1963, the SCLC staged a major nonviolent protest
in Birmingham, Alabama. Its members urged business
leaders to end segregation in restaurants, stores, and
facilities. Birmingham police attacked nonviolent protestors,
including children, with high-pressure water jets and police
dogs. When the national news media captured images of
the violence, the public (outside of the South) was outraged.

During these protests, in April 1963, MLK Jr. was arrested
and spent over a week in jail. He wrote his famous
"LETTER FROM BIRMINGHAM JAIL," in which he eloquently
laid out the causes for protest and the philosophy of
nonviolence. He wrote, "Injustice anywhere is a threat to
justice everywhere."

The MARCH on WASHINGTON

JFK spoke on national television about the need for civil rights and introduced a bill on the issue. In support of this bill, MLK Jr. led a quarter of a million people in the MARCH ON WASHINGTON on August 28, 1963. The march was the scene of his "I HAVE A DREAM" speech.

The KENNEDY ASSASSINATION and the CIVIL RIGHTS ACT of 1964

On November 22, 1963, while campaigning in Dallas, President Kennedy was shot and killed. His assassin, LEE HARVEY OSWALD, was killed by nightclub owner Jack Ruby shortly after. A commission later confirmed that Oswald acted alone. ← A COMMUNIST SYMPATHIZER

Kennedy's vice president, LYNDON B. JOHNSON, was sworn in as president, and he prioritized the civil rights bill in order to honor the late president's memory. The CIVIL RIGHTS ACT OF 1964 passed quickly. It:

outlawed discriminatory voter registration practices

ended segregation in establishments that affected interstate commerce, which was broadly defined as "any place of public accommodation" ← *SUCH AS HOTELS, RESTAURANTS, GAS STATIONS, ETC.*

ended segregation in public places and public schools

established the EQUAL EMPLOYMENT OPPORTUNITY COMMISSION

allowed the government to enforce the law

FREEDOM SUMMER

Once desegregation became law, the civil rights movement tackled voting rights. In the summer of 1964, after the Twenty-Fourth Amendment (which banned poll taxes) was ratified, the SNCC organized FREEDOM SUMMER, during which students from the North came to the South to conduct VOTER REGISTRATION drives. Three volunteers were murdered by the KKK.

In early 1965, the SCLC and MLK Jr. led a protest in SELMA, ALABAMA, including a march to Montgomery, during which protestors were attacked by state troopers. Americans watched the event in horror on national television. President Johnson signed the VOTING RIGHTS ACT OF 1965, allowing the federal government to protect all people's right to vote. It significantly increased the number of registered African American voters.

The GREAT SOCIETY

President Johnson proposed a sweeping plan to address economic inequality, called the GREAT SOCIETY, because that was the goal. Great Society programs, many of which still exist, included:

The "WAR ON POVERTY"

The establishment of **MEDICARE** and **MEDICAID**

Funding for public schools

Funding for environmental protection

The establishment of the
DEPARTMENT OF HOUSING AND URBAN DEVELOPMENT
and the DEPARTMENT OF TRANSPORTATION

MEDICARE
government-run and government-subsidized health insurance for the elderly

MEDICAID
government health insurance for the needy

ALTERNATIVE CIVIL RIGHTS TACTICS

Some leaders—such as MALCOLM X, a member of the black Muslim group NATION OF ISLAM—blamed the slow pace of reform on nonviolence. He proposed that blacks should embrace violence for self-defense and separate to form their own society. (He later changed his mind, instead advocating for a peaceful coexistence.)

Malcolm X was assassinated in 1965, but he inspired the **BLACK POWER** movement,

> **BLACK POWER**
> a movement led by some African Americans for political and economic power, as well as cultural pride, to promote racial equality and justice

which SNCC leader STOKELY CARMICHAEL popularized. HUEY NEWTON and BOBBY SEALE founded the radical BLACK PANTHER PARTY, which carried arms and demanded equality in housing, education, and employment.

The MLK ASSASSINATION

> "Long hot summer" refers to the summer of 1967, when there were many race riots.

As protests against discrimination continued and frustration about the slow pace of change mounted, race riots increased. They took place in major urban areas like Watts (in Los Angeles), Harlem, and Detroit every summer from 1965 to 1967. By the spring of 1968, however, the riots had another cause when Dr. Reverend Martin Luther King Jr. was assassinated on April 4, 1968, in Memphis, Tennessee.

CHECK YOUR KNOWLEDGE

1. How did World War II help raise awareness about civil rights issues among African American veterans?

2. Why were "separate but equal schools" a violation of the Fourteenth Amendment?

3. Under what circumstances were the Little Rock Nine finally able to attend school?

4. How did Mohandas Gandhi influence MLK Jr.?

5. How did television help Kennedy get elected?

6. What were the Freedom Riders riding?

7. What were Northern volunteers doing in the South during Freedom Summer?

8. Name the programs of the Great Society.

ANSWERS

CHECK YOUR ANSWERS

1. World War II raised more awareness of the hypocrisy in fighting for freedom abroad while inequality persisted at home.

2. The schools for African American children were far inferior to those for white children.

3. The president sent paratroopers to escort them.

4. Gandhi used nonviolent tactics to advocate for self-rule in India.

5. In the first televised presidential debates, Kennedy appeared youthful compared to Nixon.

6. They were riding interstate public buses to protest illegally segregated bus depots in the South.

7. They were registering voters.

8. The War on Poverty, Medicare, Medicaid, education funding, environmentalism, the Department of Transportation, and the Department of Housing and Urban Development

Chapter 42

CIVIL RIGHTS GROWS

The CIVIL RIGHTS MOVEMENT GROWS

As African Americans made civil rights gains, other minority groups and people who suffered from injustices began to work harder than ever for similar strides.

CIVIL RIGHTS for HISPANIC AMERICANS

The **HISPANIC** population in the U.S. had grown during the first part of the twentieth century. The largest group of Hispanic immigrants was from Mexico, but the Spanish-speaking population of the U.S. also included immigrants from Puerto Rico, Cuba, and elsewhere. Many immigrants worked as MIGRANT or SEASONAL farmworkers, particularly in California.

> **HISPANIC**
> of or relating to the heritage, people, culture, and language of Spain, Portugal, and Latin America

The UNITED FARM WORKERS union (UFW), founded in 1962 by CESAR CHAVEZ and DOLORES HUERTA, used nonviolent strategies to get rights for migrant workers. The best-known example was the GRAPE BOYCOTT of 1965–1970. The UFW convinced consumers to stop buying California grapes until the farms recognized the union.

Students in Los Angeles led a strike in 1968 for education reform, resulting in more bilingual education programs in public schools. In 1970, the organization LA RAZA UNIDA was founded to find better housing and job opportunities for Mexican Americans and help them get elected to public office.

CIVIL RIGHTS for NATIVE AMERICANS

During the 1950s, the federal government still operated on the policy that it was best to assimilate Native Americans into mainstream culture. The Bureau of Indian Affairs worked to remove Native Americans from their reservations so they could give that land to the states. Native Americans were one of the most poverty-stricken populations in the country.

The mid-twentieth century was a turning point for Native American rights. In 1944, the NATIONAL CONGRESS OF AMERICAN INDIANS (NCAI) was founded to advocate for national autonomy, preservation of languages and cultures, control of ancestral lands, and other civil and legal rights. The INDIAN CIVIL RIGHTS ACT OF 1968 ensured Native Americans of the rights shared by all American citizens, as well as tribal autonomy.

Some Native Americans wanted greater change. In 1968, they founded the AMERICAN INDIAN MOVEMENT (AIM). In 1972, AIM physically seized the Bureau of Indian Affairs, and in 1973, 300 Native Americans staged a violent occupation of the town of Wounded Knee, South Dakota. They were surrounded by U.S. Marshals and the National Guard. Both sides fired on one another and the standoff lasted 71 days. Native Americans convinced the government to discuss their demands and drew focus on the terrible conditions in which so many of them lived.

CIVIL RIGHTS for AMERICAN WOMEN

Women were in a similar position to African American veterans after World War II: When the war ended, they were expected to return to their roles in the home. Many realized they wanted more—they were unhappy only fulfilling traditional roles as wives and mothers. This was expressed in BETTY FRIEDAN's 1963 book *THE FEMININE MYSTIQUE*, one of the most significant books of the **FEMINIST** movement.

> **FEMINISM**
> the belief that men and women should have equal rights and opportunities

The 1963 EQUAL PAY ACT was a victory for equal rights in employment, and the Civil Rights Act of 1964 addressed some gender discrimination.

In 1966, feminists founded the NATIONAL ORGANIZATION FOR WOMEN (NOW) and campaigned for a complete ban on discrimination on the grounds of sex and gender. NOW's demands would have gone into effect if its 1972 campaign for an EQUAL RIGHTS AMENDMENT (ERA) had been ratified by the states.

THE ERA DATES BACK TO 1923 AND THE PROGRESSIVES.

WOMEN
DEMAND
EQUALITY

Opponents, led by PHYLLIS SCHLAFLY, convinced people that an equal rights amendment would disrupt the structure of American families. The amendment was passed by Congress but was never ratified by enough states for it to become a part of the Constitution.

Feminism made some advances: THE HIGHER EDUCATION ACT of 1972, also called TITLE IX, made it illegal to deny anyone the right to participate in federally funded educational programs or activities on the basis of sex or gender, creating funding for girls' and women's athletic programs in public schools and colleges.

CIVIL RIGHTS for EVERYONE

The '70s saw the establishment of legal defense funds and cultural foundations for all kinds of ethnic heritages in the U.S. population. Before, in the 1950s and 1960s, the first lesbian and gay rights organizations were established. The STONEWALL INN RIOTS of 1969 in New York City's Greenwich Village ignited the LESBIAN, GAY, BISEXUAL, AND TRANSGENDER (LGBT) rights movement. In 1979, an estimated 75,000 people marched on Washington to demand equal civil rights for LGBT individuals.

DISABLED IN ACTION was founded in 1970 to raise awareness about the issues faced by Americans with disabilities. It wasn't until 1990, with the passage of the AMERICANS WITH DISABILITIES ACT, that it became illegal to practice discrimination against people with disabilities.

WHEELCHAIR
WARRIOR

EQUAL RIGHTS
FOR ALL

EQUAL WORK
EQUAL PAY

CHECK YOUR KNOWLEDGE

1. In the middle of the twentieth century, where did most Hispanic Americans come from?

2. At that time, what was the most common job for immigrants from Latin America?

3. Why was there a grape boycott in the late '60s?

4. What did the Bureau of Indian Affairs want to do with the reservations in the 1950s?

5. What was the difference between the NCAI and AIM?

6. To which movement was the book THE FEMININE MYSTIQUE connected?

7. How did Title IX help female athletes?

8. What event ignited the LGBT movement?

ANSWERS ➤ 453

CHECK YOUR ANSWERS

1. Mexico
2. Migrant farmworkers
3. The grape farms would not recognize the United Farm Workers union.
4. They wanted to give the land to the states.
5. NCAI advocated for change, while AIM forced change with a violent occupation.
6. Feminism
7. Title IX required schools to fund women's and men's athletics equally.
8. The Stonewall Inn riots

☆ Chapter 43 ☆

The VIETNAM WAR

COLD WAR CRISES

Like Eisenhower, Kennedy invested money to help fight Communism abroad. This caused "cold" conflicts—threats and competitions, not all-out war.

The Bay of Pigs Invasion: In 1959, after Communist dictator Fidel Castro's rise to power, Eisenhower developed a plan to train Cuban **DISSIDENTS** to overthrow him. Kennedy launched the invasion on April 17, 1961, but it failed.

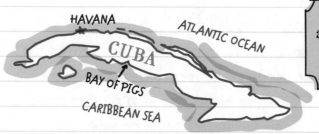

HAVANA

ATLANTIC OCEAN

CUBA

BAY OF PIGS

CARIBBEAN SEA

> **DISSIDENT**
> a person who disagrees or dissents from the belief in question

The Berlin Wall: In August of 1961, East Germany built a wall across the center of Berlin to close the border. The Berlin Wall symbolized the "Iron Curtain" between Western Europe and Communist Europe.

The Cuban Missile Crisis: In October of 1962, an American U-2 SPY PLANE saw potential Soviet nuclear missile sites in Cuba. JFK ordered a naval blockade to prevent Soviet ships from reaching the island. Nuclear war was avoided when the USSR agreed to remove the missiles and the U.S. agreed not to invade Cuba.

The Space Race: YURI GAGARIN of the USSR became the first person to orbit the earth in April of 1961. JFK set a goal of placing a man on the moon by the end of the decade. It took three sets of missions—Mercury, Gemini, and Apollo— but, on July 20, 1969, the U.S.'s NEIL ARMSTRONG and EDWIN "BUZZ" ALDRIN were the first people to walk on the moon. ← THE APOLLO PROJECT

On the OTHER HAND...

To try to promote world peace, in 1961, Kennedy created the PEACE CORPS, which sends volunteers to developing countries around the world. In 1963, he helped set up a direct hotline between D.C. and Moscow so leaders could communicate quickly in a crisis. Also in 1963, the U.S., the USSR, and the

U.K. signed the LIMITED NUCLEAR TEST BAN TREATY, which banned nuclear tests except underground.

CONFLICT in VIETNAM: A COLD WAR CRISIS

Vietnam was part of FRENCH INDOCHINA (the present-day nations of Cambodia, Laos, and Vietnam). Leader HO CHI MINH and his INDOCHINESE COMMUNIST PARTY (ICF) joined other nationalists to create the VIET MINH, a federation to take military action for independence.

Geneva Accords: In May 1954, the French suffered a major defeat at the BATTLE OF DIEN BIEN PHU. Afterward, the French and the Vietnamese met in Geneva, where it was decided that Vietnam would temporarily be divided along the 17th parallel (a similar tactic to what had been tried in Korea); the 1956 elections would decide who would run the whole country. In the meantime, Ho Chi Minh would control the Communist north and NGO DINH DIEM would control the anti-Communist south.

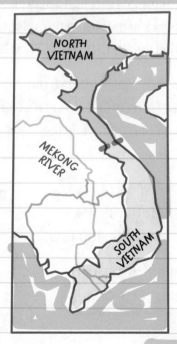

VIETNAM DIVIDED

Eisenhower sent a ton of money and weapons to support Diem's army.

Diem thought he'd lose the national elections, so he refused to participate.

Communists in the south formed the **NATIONAL LIBERATION FRONT**, a group also known as the **VIET CONG**.

The Viet Cong waged guerrilla war in South Vietnam and got assistance from northern Communists through a secret network of paths and tunnels called the **HO CHI MINH TRAIL**.

Kennedy sent soldiers from the **SPECIAL FORCES** (known as Green Berets) to help the south.

In November of 1963, Diem's army staged a coup and killed him.

South Vietnam was losing control ...

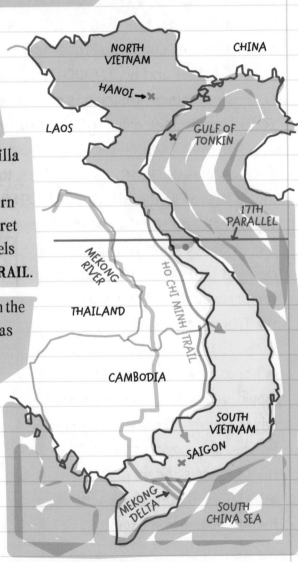

NORTH VIETNAM

CHINA

HANOI →

LAOS

GULF OF TONKIN

17TH PARALLEL

MEKONG RIVER

HO CHI MINH TRAIL

THAILAND

CAMBODIA

SOUTH VIETNAM

SAIGON

MEKONG DELTA

SOUTH CHINA SEA

Eisenhower and the U.S. government believed in the **DOMINO THEORY** about the spread of Communism: If one country "fell," then its neighbors would fall too.

The GULF of TONKIN RESOLUTION

When Lyndon Johnson became president, Secretary of Defense ROBERT McNAMARA told him that he needed to either send more troops to Vietnam or give up the war. In 1964, North Vietnamese patrol boats attacked two U.S. destroyers in international waters. This led Congress to issue the GULF OF TONKIN RESOLUTION, giving the president the power to take military action without declaring war. In March 1965, the U.S. committed combat forces to South Vietnam. U.S. offensive operations in Vietnam ESCALATED, led on the ground by WILLIAM WESTMORELAND.

The USSR was involved in the Vietnam War, but indirectly. The Soviets fought a **PROXY WAR**—they contributed supplies and used a **PROXY**, or stand-in, to do the fighting. The proxies were North Vietnamese Communists. Direct conflict between the U.S. and the USSR would have been too dangerous.

ESCALATION

The U.S. used SEARCH-AND-DESTROY missions to find Viet Cong bases. There was a high rate of civilian casualties because soldiers took refuge in villages.

The U.S. launched a bombing campaign called OPERATION ROLLING THUNDER—which lasted three years and involved dropping hundreds of thousands of bombs.

The fast-burning chemical NAPALM was used to wipe out forests and villages that lined the Ho Chi Minh Trail.

The herbicide AGENT ORANGE was used to kill the jungle where Vietnamese guerillas took cover. Agent Orange was later shown to cause serious illnesses, including cancer.

Most U.S. soldiers were inexperienced draftees unprepared to fight guerrillas in an unfamiliar tropical climate. The Viet Cong seemed to have an endless reserve of highly motivated soldiers, who infiltrated the south by going through Laos and Cambodia.

The TET OFFENSIVE

On January 31, 1968, during a cease-fire in honor of the Vietnamese New Year celebration of *TET*, the Viet Cong and North Vietnam forces ambushed American bases and South Vietnamese villages in attacks called the TET OFFENSIVE. They didn't make any gains, but the Vietnam War was getting costly.

THESE ATTACKS RAN ALL ALONG THE HO CHI MINH TRAIL.

The COUNTERCULTURE

Many people thought the U.S. didn't belong in another country's civil war. The DRAFT was controversial: Wealthy individuals and college students could **DEFER**, so poor or undereducated minorities were drafted at a larger proportion. Young people turned to the **COUNTERCULTURE**: movements led by HIPPIES and dedicated to peace.

> **DEFER**
> to put off

The MY LAI MASSACRE of March 16, 1968—during which American soldiers murdered hundreds of Vietnamese civilians—drove more people to the antiwar movement.

> **COUNTERCULTURE**
> a culture that is in opposition to (counter to) the mainstream culture

> **CONSCIENTIOUS OBJECTOR**
> someone excluded from military service on the grounds of a moral opposition to war

Some young men declared themselves **CONSCIENTIOUS OBJECTORS**; others burned their DRAFT CARDS or went to Canada to avoid fighting. STUDENTS FOR A DEMOCRATIC SOCIETY led protests on college campuses. They were all accused of being unpatriotic.

> Half a million people attended a counterculture event called the Woodstock Music and Arts Fair, better known as the **WOODSTOCK FESTIVAL**. The August 1969 concert was advertised as "3 Days of Peace & Music."

The ELECTION of 1968

President Johnson announced he wouldn't run for president again because of the stalemate in Vietnam. Three people were in the running for the Democratic nomination: incumbent vice president HUBERT HUMPHREY; antiwar Minnesota senator EUGENE McCARTHY; and JFK's brother ROBERT F. KENNEDY, a senator from New York. RFK made a strong start, but on June 6, 1968, he was assassinated by a Palestinian, Sirhan Sirhan, because of his support for Israel. Hubert Humphrey won the nomination.

The Republican nominee, RICHARD M. NIXON, won the presidency by appealing to a "SILENT MAJORITY" of patriotic Americans who wanted the war to end but didn't like the counterculture. Nixon promised he'd lead the country out of Vietnam without a shameful retreat. Nixon pledged "Peace with Honor."

Alabama governor **GEORGE C. WALLACE** ran on a segregationist third-party platform and won over 13 percent of the popular vote. In 1963, Wallace had tried to block desegregation at the University of Alabama. (In his old age, he apologized for his former beliefs.)

NIXON'S VIETNAM

On the advice of National Security Adviser HENRY KISSINGER, Nixon began to withdraw soldiers from Asia and promised to end the draft. Gradually turning over the fighting to the

ARMY OF THE REPUBLIC OF VIETNAM (ARVN) was called the "VIETNAMIZATION" of the war. But at the same time, Nixon secretly bombed Cambodia and sent troops there to cut off the Ho Chi Minh Trail. When Americans found out, there were protests, most of them peaceful. But at KENT STATE UNIVERSITY in Ohio, four students were killed by the National Guard; another protest turned violent at Jackson State University.

NOW CALLED THE "KENT STATE SHOOTINGS" OR THE "KENT STATE MASSACRE"

In 1971, secret documents known as the PENTAGON PAPERS were leaked to the NEW YORK TIMES. They revealed what people suspected: The country had been lied to about how much the U.S. was involved in the war. They also revealed that the U.S. had no idea how to bring about victory in Vietnam.

In the presidential election of 1972, Democrat GEORGE McGOVERN ran on an antiwar platform. But Nixon still won in a landslide of 49 out of 50 states. Nixon had withdrawn almost all American combat troops and drastically reduced American casualties—progress at that point was based on "body counts" and not military objectives.

THE TWENTY-SIXTH AMENDMENT (1971)

Why was the voting age lowered to 18? Because a guy could be drafted at 18. The slogan was, "Old enough to fight, old enough to vote."

OUT of VIETNAM

In the PARIS PEACE ACCORDS of January 27, 1973, the U.S. agreed to withdraw from Vietnam, and North Vietnam agreed to return American prisoners of war. But fighting continued between the North and South Vietnamese. In January 1975, the North launched a full-scale invasion of the South under the belief that the U.S. would not return. Hundreds of thousands of South Vietnamese fled the country; these refugees were called "THE BOAT PEOPLE" because many escaped by boat. The war finally ended on April 30, 1975, when the Communists captured Saigon, the capital of South Vietnam, and renamed it HO CHI MINH CITY. The nation was united as the SOCIALIST REPUBLIC OF VIETNAM.

VIETNAM AFTERSHOCKS

The war cost 58,000 American lives. Hundreds of thousands were wounded, and others were classified as MIA (missing in action) and were never found. Some soldiers suffered from POST-TRAUMATIC STRESS DISORDER (PTSD). Civilian confidence in the government was low.

Dissatisfaction influenced Congress to pass the WAR POWERS ACT in 1973, limiting how the president could use military force without a declaration of war by Congress.

CHECK YOUR KNOWLEDGE

1. How was the Cuban Missile Crisis resolved?

2. What is the domino theory?

3. What were the terms of the Geneva Accords?

4. What were President Johnson's two choices for how to proceed in Vietnam?

5. Why was the Tet Offensive such a surprise?

6. Why was the draft a subject of protests against the Vietnam War?

7. Under what name was Vietnam reunited?

ANSWERS

1. Kennedy instituted a blockade, the USSR agreed to remove the missiles, and the U.S. agreed not to invade Cuba.

2. The theory that if one nation becomes Communist, its neighbors will quickly fall

3. Vietnam would be divided along the 17th parallel until the 1956 elections.

4. He could either pull out or invest fully—he could not continue on a middle path.

5. It came during a cease-fire in honor of the holiday of Tet.

6. Deferments meant that most people who were drafted were poor or minorities.

7. Socialist Republic of Vietnam

☆ Chapter 44 ☆

☆ NIXON'S POLITICS ☆

INFLATION

Nixon was elected in 1968 as a socially conservative candidate who promised to end the protest culture of the 1960s. He appointed conservative Supreme Court justices and believed in NEW FEDERALISM, or transferring power from the federal government to the states. *AND MONEY!*
He also didn't want to increase taxes.

"DEFICIT SPENDING"

Because of the Vietnam War and the Great Society, the U.S. was spending more money than it brought in. Nixon's solution was to end inflation by keeping interest rates high (to discourage borrowing) and freezing wages and prices. None of his policies fixed the problem.

The OPEC EMBARGO

The economy was also crippled by the price of oil. The price was so high that some businesses could scarcely function.

In 1973, during the Jewish holiday of Yom Kippur, Egypt and Syria instigated hostilities against Israel in the YOM KIPPUR WAR. The U.S. sent weapons to help Israel. In response, the ORGANIZATION OF PETROLEUM EXPORTING COUNTRIES (OPEC)—a **SYNDICATE** of the Middle Eastern nations that provide most of the world's oil—refused to sell to the U.S. This led to soaring gas prices and massive shortages throughout the U.S. The embargo didn't end until March of 1974, when Kissinger helped negotiate a cease-fire between Israel and Egypt.

> **SYNDICATE**
> a group of people or organizations that come together to carry out a specific project, duty, or business

REALPOLITIK

Nixon and Kissinger were believers in REALPOLITIK, the theory that a country should pursue policies that are in its best interest regardless of political or moral ideals. For example:

In China: Nixon decided that a policy of not recognizing the Communist government just kept the U.S. from doing business with an important world player. In the early 1970s, when he saw tensions rising between China and the Soviet Union, he used the opportunity to communicate with China.

China invited the U.S. Ping-Pong team to visit in April 1971. That "PING-PONG DIPLOMACY" led to stronger ties between Nixon and Chinese Premier ZHOU ENLAI. In February 1972, Nixon became the first president to make a state visit to China. Nixon's support of China went against the U.S.'s longstanding policy of containment.

In Chile: When **MARXIST** Salvador Allende was elected president in 1970, Nixon feared that Chile would become "another

> **MARXISM**
> the economic theory of Karl Marx, who originated the ideas of modern Socialism and Communism

Cuba" and ended economic aid. He helped Allende's political enemies instead. In 1973, when Allende was overthrown by GENERAL AUGUSTO PINOCHET, the U.S. supported Pinochet even though he was a **DESPOT**.

> **DESPOT**
> a dictator

DÉTENTE

Nixon went to Moscow to meet with Soviet ruler LEONID BREZHNEV. The Soviets were eager to reduce hostilities and keep the U.S. from becoming too close an ally of China. The two nations signed the STRATEGIC ARMS LIMITATION TREATY OF 1972 (SALT I), which called for a reduction of nuclear arsenals and intended to reduce the fear of nuclear disaster. This led to a DÉTENTE, or a relaxation of international hostilities.

SOCIAL ISSUES

Many major upheavals took place during the Nixon presidency; for example:

In 1973, the Supreme Court ruled in *ROE V. WADE* that, on the issue of abortion, women have the right to choose.

The first EARTH DAY was celebrated on April 22, 1970, and the ENVIRONMENTAL PROTECTION AGENCY (EPA) was formed amid rising concerns over pollution and environmental conservation.

Initially mentioned in executive orders issued by President Kennedy and President Johnson, **AFFIRMATIVE ACTION** policies were promoted by the Nixon administration in an effort to create opportunities for minorities.

AFFIRMATIVE ACTION
policies that take factors such as race, religion, sex, and national origin into consideration to create equality

WATERGATE

Although Nixon won the 1972 presidential election in a landslide, he hadn't expected an easy victory. After all, he hadn't managed to end the Vietnam War, and the U.S. economy was in poor shape. He asked some of his aides (notably JOHN EHRLICHMAN, H. R. HALDEMAN, and JOHN MITCHELL) to help him. His first goal was to make a list of enemies (anybody who didn't support him) and get the FBI and IRS to investigate the people on it.

On June 17, 1972, five people working for the COMMITTEE TO REELECT THE PRESIDENT broke into a Democratic National Committee office in a Washington, D.C., office-apartment-hotel complex called the WATERGATE to steal campaign secrets; they were caught. Nixon denied any involvement and used his presidential powers to prevent investigations of the burglary.

BOB WOODWARD and CARL BERNSTEIN, two reporters for the *Washington Post*, investigated the break-in with the help of a secret inside source called "Deep Throat."

FORMER FBI OFFICIAL MARK FELT FINALLY REVEALED HIMSELF AS DEEP THROAT IN 2005.

In February of 1973, a Senate investigation began. JOHN DEAN, one of the president's lawyers, testified that Nixon was involved in a cover-up. The Senate committee found out that Nixon had secretly recorded his conversations with members of the White House staff. Impeachment proceedings began in the House. Knowing the tapes would prove he had committed a criminal abuse of power, on August 9, 1974, Richard Nixon became the first president in history to resign.

> Americans lost confidence in the honesty of the government.

BUT

> The fact that Nixon was caught and charged showed that the government's system of checks and balances worked.

In a later interview, Nixon defended some of his actions by claiming, "When the president does it, that means that it is not illegal."

CHECK YOUR KNOWLEDGE

1. What are the tenets of "New Federalism"?

2. Why did OPEC stop selling oil to the U.S. in 1973?

3. Which sports team visited China as a sign of goodwill between the U.S. and China?

4. What is the theory of realpolitik and how did it influence Nixon's decisions about Chile?

5. What major treaty did Nixon and Brezhnev sign in 1972, and what did it do?

6. What is détente?

7. What was the Watergate?

ANSWERS ➤ 473

CHECK YOUR ANSWERS

1. States would get more power and money, thus reducing the size of the federal government.
2. To protest U.S. support for Israel during the Yom Kippur War
3. The Ping-Pong team
4. Realpolitik is a theory that a country should pursue policies that are in its best interest regardless of political or moral ideals. Nixon supported the dictator Pinochet in his revolt against the Marxist president.
5. SALT I shrank nuclear arsenals and led to détente.
6. A relaxing of tensions
7. An office-apartment-hotel complex in Washington where the Democratic National Convention had an office

☆ Chapter 45 ☆
CARTER
☆ in the 1970s ☆

GERALD FORD and the NIXON PARDON

Nixon's original VP, SPIRO AGNEW, had resigned in 1973 because of a bribery and tax scandal. GERALD FORD was the first—and ONLY—VP to be appointed with the consent of Congress. When Nixon resigned, Ford became president. Ford's early decisions made him seem a little suspicious as well:

Ford **PARDONED** Nixon for any crimes he may have committed during his presidency. Ford reasoned that it would help the country move on, but Americans couldn't understand why Nixon shouldn't be punished.

> **PARDON**
> release from liability of an offense

Ford stirred up more controversy by offering **AMNESTY** to people who dodged the draft during Vietnam.

> **AMNESTY**
> an official pardon for an offense or group of offenders

Ford was unsuccessful at fixing the poor economy he inherited, even after he froze prices, called on Americans to save money, and cut taxes.

On the plus side, Ford signed the **HELSINKI ACCORDS**, a step toward détente in the Cold War.

A LIST OF RULES TO FOLLOW TO HELP COMMUNICATION BETWEEN THE COMMUNIST BLOC AND THE WEST

ELECTION of 1976

The Democratic Party nominated JIMMY CARTER, former governor of Georgia. He had an appealing image as an ordinary and honest man. These qualities helped him win but also made it difficult for him to put his plans into action once he arrived in Washington. For example:

Carter announced a NATIONAL ENERGY PLAN in 1977 to help solve the energy crisis, but maybe he wasn't tough enough to get the support of Congress.

Carter cut and later raised taxes, coming across as indecisive.

Carter's economy suffered from STAGFLATION— high inflation, interest rates, and unemployment— which led to little to no economic growth.

Carter supported **ALTERNATIVE ENERGY SOURCES** but was politically hurt by an incident at the THREE MILE ISLAND nuclear power plant in March 1979, when an overheated reactor released radiation into the environment. Amid protests, the president continued to support nuclear power to reduce the U.S.'s reliance on oil.

ALTERNATIVE ENERGY
any energy source that is not a fossil fuel

JIMMY CARTER and HUMAN RIGHTS

President Carter achieved success in his foreign policy. He rejected realpolitik, saying that he couldn't compromise his ideals regarding equality and human rights.

Carter curtailed U.S. relations with South Africa to protest their **APARTHEID** regime.

APARTHEID
the rigid policy of segregation in South Africa from 1948 to 1994

He signed a treaty with Panama in 1977 to allow the country to gain control of the Panama Canal by the end of 1999 as long as it remained a neutral waterway.

He condemned the Soviet Union's violations of human rights, damaging the Cold War détente.

On the plus side, Brezhnev and Carter signed the SALT II treaty in June 1979 (but it was never formally ratified by the U.S.).

In December 1979, the USSR invaded Afghanistan. In protest, Carter made the controversial decision not to send teams to the 1980 Olympic Games in Moscow.

The CAMP DAVID ACCORDS

Carter's greatest achievement was in 1978, when he invited Muhammad Anwar el-Sadat, the president of Egypt, and Menachem Begin, the prime minister of Israel, to CAMP DAVID, the president's retreat in Maryland. They agreed on the CAMP DAVID ACCORDS, which led to a peace treaty between the two nations—the first-ever Israeli-Arab treaty.

IRAN HOSTAGE CRISIS

A revolution was brewing in IRAN, the U.S.'s other major Middle Eastern ally. The ruler of Iran was SHAH MOHAMMAD REZA PAHLAVI, a pro-American leader who was thought to be corrupt. In early 1979, supporters of AYATOLLAH KHOMEINI, a religious leader, overthrew the shah and instituted fundamentalist religious rules. In November, with the new government's support, students in TEHRAN took over the city's U.S. embassy. Embassy workers were held hostage for more than a year. Carter's inability to resolve the crisis gave him a reputation as an ineffective leader.

CHECK YOUR KNOWLEDGE

1. Why did Ford pardon Nixon?

2. What did American voters find appealing about Jimmy Carter's image?

3. What incident hurt the U.S.'s chances of relying on nuclear power for alternative energy?

4. What is "apartheid"?

5. What was the effect of Carter's stance on human rights issues on the Cold War?

6. Which two nations were signers of the Camp David Accords and why was the treaty significant?

7. How did the Iran Hostage Crisis affect Carter's image?

ANSWERS ➤ 479

CHECK YOUR ANSWERS

1. He thought it would help the country move on.
2. Americans thought he was an ordinary and honest guy.
3. The Three Mile Island incident
4. The policy of segregation in South Africa from 1948 to 1994
5. He called attention to Soviet human rights violations, which hurt relations between the two powers.
6. Egypt and Israel. It was significant because it was the first Israeli-Arab treaty ever.
7. He seemed ineffectual because he could not get the hostages freed.

Unit 10

American History...
and Current-ish Events!

It's history in the making, and the end is still being written....

Chapter 46

RONALD REAGAN

RONALD REAGAN

In the 1980 presidential elections, the Republicans nominated RONALD REAGAN, an actor and the former governor of California. Reagan was a hard-line conservative with beliefs in:

TAX CUTS   **SMALL GOVERNMENT**

DEREGULATION OF BUSINESS

He won by a landslide. Carter spent the remainder of his **LAME-DUCK** presidency trying to free the hostages in Iran, who were released on the day of Reagan's inauguration.

> **LAME DUCK**
> refers to a politician in between the time he has been voted out of office and the time he actually leaves office

In March 1981, Reagan was wounded in an assassination attempt by John Hinckley, but returned to the Oval Office within a month. He instituted conservative reforms. By dealing harshly with striking air traffic controllers, he established himself as a more decisive president than Carter.

REAGANOMICS

Reagan appointed the first female Supreme Court justice, Sandra Day O'Connor, in 1981.

Reagan's conservatism was clear in his economic agenda—dubbed REAGANOMICS. It was based on the idea of SUPPLY-SIDE ECONOMICS: Tax cuts and lenient business regulations would increase investments and business growth, which was supposed to TRICKLE DOWN by providing jobs and then come back to the government in tax revenue.

Reagan cut taxes and social service programs to spur growth in the private sector, but he also increased military spending. More military spending with lower tax revenues created a big deficit, and the country went into a recession in the early 1980s. In 1983, the economy turned back around as consumers began to spend more and unemployment started to decline.

The EVIL EMPIRE

Reagan's military spending was based on his belief that the Soviet Union was an "EVIL EMPIRE." He wanted to beat them by outspending them in the arms race. In March 1983, Reagan

created an antimissile defense
program called the STRATEGIC
DEFENSE INITIATIVE (SDI),

OOPS!

BZZP!

or by its nickname: "Star Wars."
It was supposed to shoot missiles
out of the sky. It seemed far-fetched, and scientists had
difficulty developing the technology.

The ELECTION of 1984

WON 49 OUT OF
50 STATES

As the economy remained strong and Reagan
continued to project an image of confidence and optimism,
Reagan and the Republicans easily won the election of 1984.
The Democratic ticket included WALTER MONDALE (who
was vice president under Carter) alongside vice presidential
candidate GERALDINE FERRARO, the first woman to be
included on a major-party ballot for national office.

The IRAN-CONTRA AFFAIR

Reagan supported revolutions against Communism in
Central and South America with money or supplies. When
a revolutionary Socialist group called the SANDINISTAS
came to power in NICARAGUA in 1979, Reagan supported
their opposition, called the CONTRAS (because they were
AGAINST the rulers). Congress worried that Reagan was
leading the country into another pointless foreign conflict.
In 1984, it passed a law banning the president from
assisting the Contras.

To get around the ban, members of the White House NATIONAL SECURITY COUNCIL (NSC), notably OLIVER NORTH, sold weapons to Iran in exchange for helping to free hostages in Lebanon and then gave those proceeds to the Contras. By creating alternative funding through arms sales, the NSC bypassed Congress's role in appropriating funds. The IRAN-CONTRA AFFAIR was exposed in 1986. Reagan said he wasn't aware of it, so he wasn't found to have broken any laws.

The COLD WAR THAWS

MIKHAIL GORBACHEV became the Soviet Communist Party's leader in 1985. Gorbachev instituted two policies:

perestroika ("reorganization," or economic reforms)

glasnost ("openness" to freedom of political opinion)

Reagan was encouraged by these moves, and in 1987, Reagan and Gorbachev negotiated and signed the INTERMEDIATE-RANGE NUCLEAR FORCES (INF) TREATY, reducing the size of their nuclear arsenals.

ELECTION of 1988

In 1988, on the strength of Reagan's popularity, his vice president, GEORGE H. W. BUSH, became president. (The Democratic candidate was MICHAEL DUKAKIS, the governor of Massachusetts.) In 1991, the U.S. and the USSR signed the

STRATEGIC ARMS REDUCTION TREATY (START), in which they agreed to destroy many of their nuclear weapons.

The COLD WAR ENDS

Gorbachev meant for his reforms to strengthen and modernize the Soviet Union. Letting people express their dissatisfaction but not fixing the economy led to something he didn't expect: The Soviet bloc began to advocate for independence. In October 1989, protests forced the leader of East Germany to resign, and the new government agreed to open the border with West Germany. At midnight on November 9, 1989, the gates were opened and people began to tear down the Berlin Wall, the symbol of the Cold War. Soon, Germany was reunited into a single, democratic nation.

On July 1, 1991, the Warsaw Pact was disbanded and the Czech Republic, Hungary, Poland, and more declared independence. Advocates of democracy led by BORIS YELTSIN, who had just been elected president of the Russian Federation, forced the defeat of the Communist Party in the Soviet Union. On December 1, 1991, Yeltsin, along with the presidents of Ukraine and Belarus, declared that the Soviet Union was finished. Gorbachev resigned on December 25. The USSR dissolved on December 26. The Cold War was over.

Communism was still going strong in China. In 1989, soldiers opened fire on pro-democracy protesters in **TIANANMEN SQUARE**, killing hundreds.

CHECK YOUR KNOWLEDGE

1. How did Reagan think that tax cuts would help the economy?

2. When were the hostages in Tehran released?

3. Who were the Sandinistas?

4. How did the National Security Council get money to help the Contras in Nicaragua?

5. What is the difference between *perestroika* and *glasnost*?

6. How did *perestroika* and *glasnost* influence U.S.–USSR relations?

7. How did *glasnost* hurt Gorbachev's power?

8. When did the Cold War end?

ANSWERS ➤ 487

CHECK YOUR ANSWERS

1. He believed the wealth would trickle down because it would give people jobs and more money to spend and spur the economy.

2. The day of Reagan's inauguration

3. A revolutionary Socialist group that came to power in Nicaragua. The U.S. supported their opposition.

4. They sold weapons to Iran.

5. *Perestroika* refers to economic reforms, and *glasnost* is a policy of openness.

6. Reagan was encouraged by Gorbachev's new policies and was willing to negotiate the INF treaty.

7. Once dissent was allowed, there were many protests and calls for democracy.

8. The Cold War ended when the USSR dissolved—on December 26, 1991.

Chapter 47

To the PRESENT DAY

The PERSIAN GULF WAR

After the Cold War ended, President Bush turned to the Middle East. In August of 1990, SADDAM HUSSEIN, the dictatorial leader of Iraq, invaded Iraq's oil-rich neighbor KUWAIT, and then ignored UN demands that he withdraw.

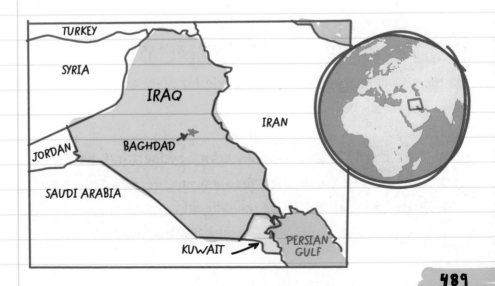

TURKEY

SYRIA

IRAQ

IRAN

JORDAN   BAGHDAD

SAUDI ARABIA

KUWAIT   PERSIAN GULF

Under GENERAL NORMAN SCHWARZKOPF JR. and GENERAL COLIN POWELL, the U.S. led a coalition force on a mission called OPERATION DESERT STORM. The PERSIAN GULF WAR began with troops on the ground on February 24, 1981, and, within days, halted with a cease-fire on February 28th. Casualty rates for American troops were very low.

The ELECTION of 1992

President Bush should have been in a strong position for the next presidential election. He had successfully implemented the CLEAN AIR ACT and the AMERICANS WITH DISABILITIES ACT, and he had begun the "WAR ON DRUGS." But the economy was weak. The Democratic nominee, Arkansas governor WILLIAM (BILL) CLINTON, defeated Bush and third-party candidate ROSS PEROT, an Independent.

CLINTON:
43 PERCENT OF VOTES

BUSH:
37 PERCENT OF VOTES

PEROT:
19 PERCENT OF VOTES
AND NO ELECTORAL
VOTES

ACHIEVEMENTS of CLINTON'S PRESIDENCY

Clinton's two-term presidency included a number of achievements:

He persuaded Congress to balance the budget, and the U.S. government had a surplus for the first time in 30 years. During the Clinton presidency, one of the biggest economic expansions in recent memory took place: the BOOM of the 1990s.

The NORTH AMERICAN FREE TRADE AGREEMENT (NAFTA) opened up trade with Canada and Mexico without tariffs.

He appointed MADELEINE ALBRIGHT as the first female secretary of state.

He nominated JANET RENO as the first female attorney general.

He convinced YITZHAK RABIN, prime minister of Israel, and YÁSIR ARAFÁT, head of the PALESTINE LIBERATION ORGANIZATION, to come to the White House in 1993 and agree to recognize each other's right to exist—a landmark moment in the Middle East.

He was part of the 1999 decision by NATO to intervene to end **ETHNIC CLEANSING** in KOSOVO, a region of the former YUGOSLAVIA where religious and territorial disputes had led to civil war.

ETHNIC CLEANSING
removal or killing of an ethnic group in a society

However, Clinton's two terms in office were marked by scandal:

the WHITEWATER controversy, in which the ethics of a real-estate deal he had been involved with in Arkansas came into question;

accusations of an inappropriate relationship with a White House intern, MONICA LEWINSKY, which he denied under oath; it later became clear that a relationship had existed.

In 1998, Clinton became the second president to be impeached, for **PERJURY** and OBSTRUCTION OF JUSTICE. The Senate, however, rejected the conviction on the grounds that lying about an affair was not a "high crime" (which would qualify for removal from office according to the Constitution).

PERJURY
lying under oath

Congressman **NEWT GINGRICH** led the Republican Party to regain control of Congress for the first time in forty years during the 1994 midterm elections. He did so by releasing their "Contract with America"— an outline of what they would do if they became the majority in the House of Representatives.

THE WORLD WIDE WEB

In 1989, a British software consultant named TIM BERNERS-LEE created an open computer network for research purposes, which would become the template for the WORLD WIDE WEB. Following this crucial step, Berners-Lee made key innovations that helped shape the web we know today:

HTTP (hypertext transfer protocol, which allows you to click on a link and be redirected to that page)

URLs (uniform resource locators, which are web addresses)

HTML (hypertext markup language, which allows you to put links in pages and documents so they connect)

Still, the larger public didn't begin using the internet until the mid-'90s, when companies like Netscape and AOL made browsers and mailed software to people so they could get on the web.

PERSONAL COMPUTERS (PCs) were first mass-marketed in the late 1970s. Prior to then, people assembled computers from parts themselves. STEVE JOBS and STEVE WOZNIAK sold the first fully assembled Apple computers (Macs) in 1976.

BUSH v. GORE

In 2000, Clinton's vice president, AL GORE, ran for president against Republican candidate GEORGE W. BUSH, the governor of Texas and the son of the first President Bush.

The election was a close one. In fact, it was so close that it had no result: Gore won the popular vote, but the electoral result was in question due to disputed vote

> **RALPH NADER** also ran for president in 2000 as a candidate of the Green Party, which advocates grassroots democracy, social justice, and environmentalism.

counts in Florida. Gore requested that a recount be done in two counties by hand. Bush sued to prevent a recount, and the case went to the Supreme Court.

On December 12, 2000, in the case of BUSH v. GORE, the Supreme Court ruled that hand recounts would not be

> A **CHAD** is the tiny portion of paper on a ballot that voters punch out to indicate their candidate. However, it is difficult to read them accurately.

BALLOT

I'M JUST HANGING...

> **PARTISAN**
> having to do with party politics

uniform and would thus be a denial of equal protection of the law. The court also ruled that an alternative recount method could not be established in the time remaining set by Florida law. The original vote count in Florida became official, and Bush became president. The close election led to **PARTISAN** bitterness, made worse by a 50–50 split in the Senate. STILL CONTINUES TODAY

494

The RISE of TERRORISM

President Bush followed through on a campaign promise to cut taxes. He also instituted a public education policy, called NO CHILD LEFT BEHIND, to create national testing standards, and he appointed a diverse cabinet. However, his presidency was eclipsed by the issue of TERRORISM—violent and intimidating actions that have a political or ideological purpose but are not backed by a state.

During Clinton's presidency, terrorism was on the rise:

> **the 1993 World Trade Center bombing**

> **the 1995 Oklahoma City bombing**

> **a series of embassy bombings in Africa in 1998**

> **the 2000 bombing of a U.S. Navy ship in Yemen**

The Oklahoma City bombing was perpetrated by an American named TIMOTHY McVEIGH, but the others were the work of **FUNDAMENTALIST** Islamic groups including AL-QAEDA, which had been founded to fight Soviets in Afghanistan and then expanded to oppose the policies of the Western world. Because terrorists lack traditional armies or diplomats, it proved difficult to fight them.

> **FUNDAMENTALIST**
> the strict adherence to a set of basic ideas or principles

9/11

On the morning of SEPTEMBER 11, 2001, terrorists hijacked four airplanes in the U.S. Two were flown into the WORLD TRADE CENTER in New York City, toppling the TWIN TOWERS, symbols of American economic world power. A third crashed into the PENTAGON, and a fourth that was headed toward Washington, D.C., was brought down by the passengers in a Pennsylvania field.

Thousands of people were killed. The nation experienced a surge of patriotism and was supported by allies all over the world.

> The **PENTAGON** is the headquarters of the Department of Defense and is located in Arlington, Virginia.

WAR on TERROR

The attacks had been orchestrated by al-Qaeda and its leader, OSAMA BIN LADEN. The terrorists were being protected by the TALIBAN, the fundamentalist party in power in Afghanistan. On October 7, 2001, the U.S. and its allies attacked, beginning the WAR IN AFGHANISTAN. The Taliban was quickly removed from power.

President Bush switched the focus to Iraq. He expressed concern that Saddam Hussein had chemical or nuclear WEAPONS OF MASS DESTRUCTION (WMD). Although many allies asked the U.S. to allow UN weapons inspectors more time to look for WMDs, the U.S. (with the help of Britain) began the WAR IN IRAQ in March 2003. Baghdad was occupied, and Saddam was ousted.   ← HE WAS TRIED AND EXECUTED.

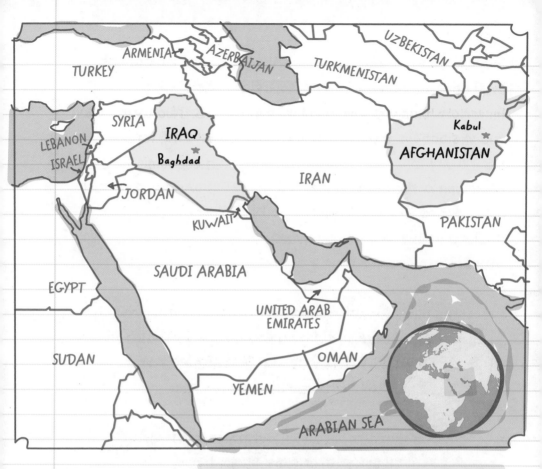

NO ONE KNOWS THE HISTORICAL SIGNIFICANCE
OF THIS—HISTORY IS STILL BEING WRITTEN.

Still, the U.S. continued to occupy both Iraq and Afghanistan.
Its process of NATION BUILDING involved maintaining a
presence until there was stability in each region—but stability
did not come. **INSURGENTS** continued to fight against the
U.S. military, and different Muslim sects
(notably the SUNNI and SHIA) fought
for power. In October 2001, Bush signed
the USA PATRIOT ACT, which broadened

> **INSURGENT**
> a rebel or a
> revolutionary

the discretion of law enforcement officials' investigations of people suspected of terrorism-related acts, which many Americans believed infringed on their civil liberties. With no end in sight for the wars, domestic dissatisfaction grew.

Bush won a second presidential term, but confidence in him declined as the wars in Iraq and Afghanistan continued:

During Bush's second term, **CONDOLEEZZA RICE** became the first female African American secretary of state.

The Bush administration was tried and convicted in several cases regarding its detainment and torture of **ENEMY COMBATANTS** at **GUANTÁNAMO BAY,** a U.S. military compound in Cuba.

It was revealed that the government was illegally tapping Americans' phone lines.

The government was criticized for failing to prepare for or respond promptly to the August 2005 devastation from **HURRICANE KATRINA,** which destroyed much of New Orleans.

In December 2005, Bush faced controversy over his decision to launch a program that allowed the National Security Council to monitor the phone calls and emails of Americans suspected of having links to al-Qaeda.

BONUS SECTION:
REALLY RECENT HISTORY

PROBABLY TOO BUSY TO STUDY OBJECTIVELY

In the 2006 midterm elections, Democrats took both houses of Congress, and NANCY PELOSI became the first female speaker of the house. Then, in the 2008 presidential race, the Democratic candidate—a young senator from Illinois, BARACK OBAMA—made an even more historic achievement when he defeated JOHN McCAIN and was elected the first African American president of the U.S.

President Obama ran on a platform of "hope" and "change," focusing on:

The ECONOMY: After the tech boom of the 1990s ended and a banking crisis in 2008 led to a major recession, Obama promised to boost the weak economy.

HEALTH CARE: Obama called for universal health care for all Americans, signing a bill into law in March 2010.

ENDING the WAR: Ending the war in Iraq was another priority of the Obama campaign.

The ENVIRONMENT: Problems like **CLIMATE CHANGE** (also called "global warming") have been acknowledged—but not fixed.

> ## CLIMATE CHANGE
> an increase in the overall average temperature of the earth's atmosphere, partially due to manmade causes

WHAT NEXT?

America has made big strides in recent history, from helping to sequence the human genome to innovating the World Wide Web. Recent major events include:

President Obama made history by nominating SONIA SOTOMAYOR to the Supreme Court. She is not only the first person of Hispanic heritage on the Supreme Court but also the third female.

After more than 50 years of no diplomatic relations, the U.S. and Cuba began restoring ties in 2015.

On June 26, 2015, the Supreme Court ruled in favor of MARRIAGE EQUALITY in *OBERGEFELL v. HODGES*, which challenged whether state gay marriage bans were constitutional. The ruling requires every state to allow same-sex couples to marry.

As America (and the rest of the world) moves further into the 21st century, it will continue to face issues that divide, enrich, and redefine the country.

CHECK YOUR KNOWLEDGE

1. What event sparked the Persian Gulf War?

2. What did Bill Clinton focus on during his first campaign for the presidency?

3. Why was Bill Clinton impeached?

4. What was the Supreme Court's reasoning in *BUSH v. GORE*?

5. What is terrorism?

6. Why was al-Qaeda originally established?

7. How did Hurricane Katrina hurt the reputation of the Bush administration?

8. What was the effect of the Supreme Court ruling in *OBERGEFELL v. HODGES*?

ANSWERS

CHECK YOUR ANSWERS

1. The Iraqi invasion of Kuwait
2. The economy
3. Perjury and obstruction of justice
4. Hand recounts could not be uniform and were thus a denial of equal protection.
5. Violent and intimidating actions that have a political or ideological purpose but are not backed by a state
6. To fight Soviets in Afghanistan
7. The Bush administration was criticized for lack of preparation and a slow response time.
8. Every state was mandated to allow same-sex couples to marry.